Carl Goerdeler and the Jewish Question, 1933–1942

In the 1930s, Carl Goerdeler, the mayor of Leipzig and, as prices commissioner, a cabinet-level official, engaged in active opposition against the persecution of the Jews in Germany and Eastern Europe. He did this openly until 1938 and then secretly in contact with the British Foreign Office. Having failed to change Hitler's policy against the Jews, Goerdeler joined forces with military and civil conspirators against the regime. He was hanged for 'treason' on 2 February 1945. This book describes the actions of Carl Goerdeler, the German Resistance leader, who consistently engaged in efforts to protect the Jews against persecution. Using new evidence and thus-far underresearched documents, including a memorandum written by Goerdeler at the end of 1941 with a proposal for the status of the Jews in the world, the book fundamentally changes our understanding of Goerdeler's plan and presents a new view of the German Resistance to Hitler.

Peter Hoffmann is William Kingsford Professor of History at McGill University, Montreal. He is the recipient of the Distinguished Service Medal of the state of Baden-Württemberg (Germany), the Officer's Cross of the Order of Merit (Germany), and the Konrad Adenauer Research Award. He is the author of books on the German Resistance including *The History of the German Resistance 1933–1945* (1977), *Hitler's Personal Security* (1979), *German Resistance to Hitler* (1988), and *Stauffenberg: A Family History, 1905–1944* (1995, 3rd ed. 2009).

Carl Goerdeler and the Jewish Question, 1933–1942

PETER HOFFMANN
McGill University

CAMBRIDGE
UNIVERSITY PRESS

CAMBRIDGE UNIVERSITY PRESS
Cambridge, New York, Melbourne, Madrid, Cape Town,
Singapore, São Paulo, Delhi, Tokyo, Mexico City

Cambridge University Press
32 Avenue of the Americas, New York, NY 10013-2473, USA

www.cambridge.org
Information on this title: www.cambridge.org/9781107007987

First published 2011
Reprinted 2011

A catalog record for this publication is available from the British Library.

Library of Congress Cataloging in Publication Data

Hoffmann, Peter, 1930–
Carl Goerdeler and the Jewish question, 1933–1942 / Peter Hoffmann.
p. cm.
Includes bibliographical references and index.
ISBN 978-1-107-00798-7 (hardback)
1. Germany – Politics and government – 1933–1945. 2. Germany – Ethnic relations – History – 20th century. 3. Jews – Government policy – Germany – History – 20th century. 4. Goerdeler, Carl, 1884–1945. 5. Antisemitism – Germany – History – 20th century. 6. Anti-Nazi movement. I. Title.
DD256.5.H64 2011
940.53′18092–dc22[B] 2010043685

ISBN 978-1-107-00798-7 Hardback

Contents

Prologue

The discrimination, persecution, and murder of Jews have a long history. Protection schemes in the Middle Ages and the Early Modern era tended to have economic and political motivations. Still, European and Near Eastern societies treated Jews as subjects with lesser rights, and most social and political classes were closed to them. The age of rationalism and enlightenment since the Reformation, and the principles of the French Revolution and Napoleon's wars, gave impulses to the gradual emancipation of the Jews. In Prussia, a royal decree in 1812 declared: 'The Jews and their families who are currently residents in Our States and are provided with general privileges, naturalisation patents, letters of protection and concessions are to be regarded as native residents and Prussian state-citizens'.[1]

Three main directions developed: acculturation, assimilation, and Zionism. Acculturation is defined as the Jews' attainment of legal equality, as 'integration into the economic, social and institutional life of their respective nations'. Acculturation was generally combined with the expectation of the retention of cultural and religious identities. Marion Kaplan put it pointedly: 'Jews flaunted their Germanness as they privatized their Jewishness'. Assimilation is understood as a stage beyond the development from emancipation to acculturation, to the extent of merging in a society and abandoning other cultural and religious

[1] 'Die in Unseren Staaten jetzt wohnhaften, mit General-Privilegien, Naturalisations-Patenten, Schutzbriefen und Konzessionen versehenen Juden und deren Familien sind für Einländer und Preussische Staatsbürger zu achten'. In 'Edikt betreffend die bürgerlichen Verhältnisse der Juden in dem Preussischen Staate', in Ernst Rudolf Huber, ed., *Dokumente zur deutschen Verfassungsgeschichte*, vol. 1, Stuttgart: W. Kohlhammer Verlag, 1961, p. 45.

identities than those dominant in a given society.[2] Zionism advocated the establishment of a Jewish homeland and state in 'Palestine', describing this as a 'return'.[3]

In Europe and elsewhere, hostilities against Jews soon accompanied evolving emancipation in the nineteenth century. Pogroms and riots occurred mainly in East European countries, including Russia, in the decades before and after the beginning of the twentieth century.[4] Jews were expelled from Moscow in 1891, the Kishinev massacre occurred in 1903, and pogroms followed the revolution of 1905. The Dreyfus affair was a symptom in France.[5] Religion-based anti-Jewish views intermingled with vulgar antisemitism in Germany. Both found literary expressions in the works of Paul de Lagarde, Karl Marx, Heinrich von Treitschke, Julius Langbehn, Benedikt Momme Nissen, and Friedrich Delitzsch.[6] Heinrich Class, president of the Pan-German League, in his *Wenn ich der Kaiser wär* (If I Were Emperor), first published in 1912, demanded

[2] Jonathan Frankel, 'Assimilation and the Jews in Nineteenth-Century Europe: Towards a New Historiography?' in Jonathan Frankel and Steven J. Zipperstein, eds., *Assimilation and Community: The Jews in Nineteenth-Century Europe*, Cambridge, New York, Port Chester, Melbourne, Sydney: Cambridge University Press, 1992, pp. 21–23; Marion A. Kaplan, 'Gender and Jewish History in Imperial Germany', in Frankel and Zipperstein, pp. 201, 205; Paula E. Hyman, 'The Social Contexts of Assimilation: Village Jews and City Jews in Alsace', in Frankel and Zipperstein, p. 110.

[3] 'Zionism', in *Encyclopaedia Judaica*, 2nd ed., vol. 21, Detroit: Thomson Gale, 2007, pp. 540–43.

[4] *Encyclopaedia Judaica*, 2nd ed., vol. 16, Detroit: Keter, 2007, pp. 279–82; Gershon David Hundert, ed., *The YIVO Encyclopedia of Jews in Eastern Europe*, vol. 2, New Haven, London: Yale University Press, 2008, pp. 1375–81.

[5] Cf. Phyllis Cohen Albert, 'Israelite and Jew: How Did Nineteenth-Century French Jews Understand Assimilation?' in Jonathan Frankel and Steven J. Zipperstein, eds., *Assimilation and Community: The Jews in Nineteenth-Century Europe*, Cambridge, New York, Port Chester, Melbourne, Sydney: Cambridge University Press, 1992, pp. 89, 95, 101.

[6] Cf. Paul de Lagarde, *Ueber die gegenwärtige lage des deutschen reichs, ein bericht, erstattet von Paul de Lagarde*, Göttingen: Dieterichsche Verlagsbuchhandlung, 1876; Paul de Lagarde, *Deutsche Schriften*, Göttingen: Dieterichsche Verlagsbuchhandlung, 1878; Paul de Lagarde, *Deutsche Schriften: Gesammtausgabe letzter Band*, Vierter Abdruck, Göttingen: Dieterichsche Verlagsbuchhandlung, 1892; Paul de Lagarde, *Das verborgene Deutschland*, Offenbach a.M.: [Privatdruck der Schriftgießerei] Gebr. Klingspor, 1920; Karl Marx, *Zur Judenfrage*, ed. Stefan Grossmann, Berlin: Ernst Rowohlt Verlag, 1919; Heinrich von Treitschke, 'Herr Graetz und sein Judentum', in *Aufsätze, Reden und Briefe*, Meersburg: F.W. Hendel Verlag, 1929, pp. 483–93; [Julius Langbehn; published anonymously], *Rembrandt als Erzieher: Von einem Deutschen*, Leipzig: Verlag von C.L. Hirschfeld, 1890; Benedikt Momme Nissen, *Der Rembrandtdeutsche Julius Langbehn*, Freiburg im Breisgau: Herder and Co.G.m.b.H. Verlagsbuchhandlung, 1927; Friedrich Delitzsch, *Babel und Bibel: Ein Vortrag*, Leipzig: J.C. Hinrichs'sche Buchhandlung, 1903; Friedrich Delitzsch, *Zweiter Vortrag über Babel und Bibel*, Stuttgart: Deutsche Verlags-Anstalt, 1903.

the exclusion and expulsion of the Jews.[7] Adolf Hitler, in a speech in Munich's Hofbräuhaus on 13 August 1920, threatened to kill the Jews, and he repeated his threat several times, and implicitly throughout his book *Mein Kampf* in 1925.[8] He reiterated it three years after he became chancellor, in his August 1936 Four-Year Plan memorandum, and again in his speech on 30 January 1939.[9] In September 1939 he initiated the largest campaign of genocide the world had ever witnessed.

In response to discrimination, mistreatment, and movements of persecution, there arose discussions, debates, and counter-efforts seeking solutions to what was known as the Jewish Question. British imperial geopolitical considerations led to the famous declaration of intent, the 'Balfour Declaration' of 2 November 1917.[10] In response to anti-Jewish pogroms particularly in Poland, East European Jewish groups petitioned the Paris Peace Conference in 1919 for 'the recognition of the national community of Judaism'.[11] When Adolf Hitler's appointment as *Reich* chancellor launched the acute phase of the persecution of Jews in Germany, politicians and others in the United Kingdom and America endeavoured to move their governments to counteract the mistreatment of the Jewish minority. President Franklin Delano Roosevelt, having been beseeched in vain for years, finally, responding to Hitler's annexation of

[7] Daniel Frymann [=Heinrich Class], *Wenn ich der Kaiser wär: Politische Wahrheiten und Notwendigkeiten*, Leipzig: Dieterich'sche Verlagsbuchhandlung, Theodor Weicher, 1912, pp. 74–78.

[8] Adolf Hitler, 'Warum sind wir Antisemiten?' in Eberhard Jäckel, ed., *Hitler: Sämtliche Aufzeichnungen 1905–1924*, Stuttgart: Deutsche Verlags-Anstalt, 1980, pp. 195–96; Adolf Hitler, *Mein Kampf*, 3rd ed., Munich: Verlag Franz Eher Nachfolger, 1930, pp. 70, 225, 382, 772.

[9] Wilhelm Treue, 'Hitlers Denkschrift zum Vierjahresplan 1936', *Vierteljahrshefte für Zeitgeschichte* 3 (1955): 184–210, here 210; *Documents on German Foreign Policy 1918–1945: Series C (1933–1937)*, vol. 5 (*DGFP C V*), London: HMSO, 1966, no. 490, pp. 853–62, here 861; *Völkischer Beobachter* 10 September 1936, pp. 1–2, and 1 February 1939, p. 9; Max Domarus, *Hitler: Reden und Proklamationen 1932–1945*, Neustadt a.d.Aisch: Verlagsdruckerei Schmidt, 1963, p. 1058; Max Domarus, *Hitler: Speeches and Proclamations 1932–1945: The Chronicle of a Dictatorship*, Wauconda: Bolchazy-Carducci Publishers, 1997, pp. 1448–49; cf. Norman H. Baynes, ed., *The Speeches of Adolf Hitler, April 1922–August 1939*, vol. 1, New York: Howard Fertig, 1969, pp. 736–41.

[10] *Documents on British Foreign Policy 1919–1931: First Series*, vol. 4, London: Her Majesty's Stationery Office, 1952, no. 242, pp. 340–49 ('Memorandum by Mr. Balfour (Paris), respecting Syria, Palestine, and Mesopotamia, August 11, 1919'); *Treaty of Peace with Turkey: Signed at Sèvres, August 10, 1920. [With Maps.] Presented to Parliament by Command of His Majesty. [Cmd. 964.]*. London: His Majesty's Stationery Office, 1920, section 7, articles 94–97.

[11] See Chapter 3 'Antecedents', herein.

Austria in March 1938, took an initiative that led to the international conference at Évian-les-bains on the French side of Lake Geneva. This failed to bring relief to German and Austrian Jews; it may even have spurred Hitler on.

The subject of the present study is the endeavour of Carl Goerdeler – the leading civilian personage in the German Resistance to Hitler and the candidate to succeed the dictator as chancellor – to find an alternative to the National Socialists' murder campaign against the Jews. One reading of what Isaiah 8.14 refers to as 'a stone of offense, and a rock of stumbling', which Paul quotes in his letter to the Romans 9.33 (λίθον προσκόμματος πέτραν), is the offence of the mass murder of the victims and of those who felt challenged to end it. The scandal of the greatest crime in the twentieth century is not controversial.

Carl Goerdeler's response to it is, however, controversial because it differentiates active opponents from those who stood by, those who assented, and those who were perpetrators. It embarrasses persons whose background does not include opposition to the regime, and those who prefer a form of collective guilt. In Hannah Arendt's words, 'where all are guilty, no one is'.[12] Goerdeler's views on 'the status of the Jews' in the world[13] (the issue he addressed in the central document of the present study, his memorandum 'The Aim' [*Das Ziel*] written in late 1941/early 1942) have to be examined with care and in their own context. This context is a global as well as a German one. Goerdeler's views and proposals are part of a wider consideration of the Jewish Question in the Western world.

The main sources for this study are Goerdeler's memoranda in the years from 1933 to 1944, communications with the British Foreign Office in 1938, and writings in prison in 1944 and 1945. They are in Goerdeler's papers in the German Federal Archives in Koblenz, in the Leipzig City Archive, and in the papers of Arthur Primrose Young, Modern Records Centre, University of Warwick Library. Most of Goerdeler's important memoranda appeared in a recent two-volume publication; Goerdeler's communications with the British Foreign Office have long been available.[14] Other sources in the international context were used where appropriate.

[12] Hannah Arendt, *Responsibility and Judgment*, New York: Schocken Books, 2003, p. 21.

[13] See Chapter 5.

[14] Sabine Gillmann and Hans Mommsen, *Politische Schriften und Briefe Carl Friedrich Goerdelers*, vol. 2 (continuous pagination through vols. 1 and 2), Munich: K.G. Saur, 2003; cf. Peter Hoffmann, ed., *Behind Valkyrie: German Resistance to Hitler: Documents*, Montreal: McGill-Queen's University Press, 2011, pp. 263–83.

The leading historians who have concerned themselves with Goerdeler have seen most of these documents, yet they virtually ignored all but one of them, and they never carefully analysed the one upon which they directed their attention, Goerdeler's ninety-nine-page memorandum 'The Aim' (*Das Ziel*) of late 1941/early 1942. On the basis of Goerdeler's concept of a global solution for the Jewish Question, they have classified him as a 'dissimilatory' antisemite.[15]

The historian has the task of discovering, understanding, and describing – to the extent that the sources and his or her analytic powers allow it – past events. Confronted with cases of unequivocal violations of natural justice and of universally accepted statutes (as against murder), or with fundamental ethical (non-ideological) imperatives, the historian may be compelled to take a position of disapproval or approval, as the case may be. Judging, however, with the benefit of hindsight what an agent in the past should have done – based on the historian's own contemporary social, ideological, and political persuasions such as a preference for or rejection of a socialist policy – is to act in an unprofessional manner, and it puts the historian in a false position.

When the leaders of the attempts to overthrow the German dictator first began to form a conspiracy with that goal in 1938, they sought to prevent a new war, to restore the rule of law, and to end discrimination; in 1938 they were spurred into action mainly by the present threat of war. They argued that a new war would end in Germany's destruction. As the Chief of the General Staff of the Army Lieutenant-General Ludwig Beck then predicted, Germany would face a coalition that would include the United States of America, and at the end of it the victors would insist on firmer guarantees for peace than in 1919. To many of Hitler's German opponents, including General Beck, a war of aggression was also morally wrong.

Hitler, from the summer of 1936, was setting dates for the war he intended to wage. In 1937 and 1938, using the mistreatment of the three million ethnic Germans in the Sudeten region of Czechoslovakia and their presumed wish to belong to Germany, he openly threatened war against that state. General Beck in 1937 and Carl Goerdeler in 1938 warned the French and British governments of Hitler's plans. Beck and Goerdeler

[15] Hans Mommsen, 'Gesellschaftsbild und Verfassungspläne des deutschen Widerstandes', in Walter Schmitthenner and Hans Buchheim, eds., *Der deutsche Widerstand gegen Hitler: Vier historisch-kritische Studien*, Cologne: Kiepenheuer and Witsch 1966, pp. 269–70n109; Hans Mommsen, *Alternative zu Hitler: Studien zur Geschichte des deutschen Widerstandes*, Munich: Verlag C.H. Beck, 2000, p. 389.

committed what German law at the time defined as treason against the country (*Landesverrat*, differentiated in German law from treason against the government, *Hochverrat*). Other prominent opponents of Hitler did the same.[16] At the time, however, in 1938, only Goerdeler made the persecution of the Jews a central concern in his contacts with the British government. Goerdeler was also the only one among the leading German opponents of Hitler who saw the situation of the Jews in global terms.

The Resistance leaders were motivated by all that was wrong with the regime and with the war – the general brutality, contempt for the rule of law, arbitrary arrests, secret police arbitrariness and violence, secret and 'special' courts, abolition of civil liberties, arbitrary imprisonment and murder of political dissidents and opponents on religious and ethical grounds and on grounds of their being 'social outcasts' or 'un-German' writers, mistreatment of civilians in occupied territories, and mass starvation of Soviet-Russian prisoners of war. Since the beginning of Hitler's wars on 1 September 1939 with the attack upon Poland and the beginning of killing operations against Polish intellectuals, professors, priests, and Jews; the systematic killing of hundreds of thousands of Jews in the Soviet Union from 22 June 1941; and the deliberate mass murder of the European Jews, the Resistance leaders saw the violence against the Jews as a crime of a different order. They did not know the numbers, but they knew they were in the hundreds of thousands. It is estimated that by the end of the war in 1945, the German murderers and assisting Ukrainian, Romanian, and other murderers had killed six million Jews. The SS' own statistic for Jews killed under German authority is 5.1 million.[17] A substantial number of the anti-Hitler conspirators are on record as having stated, when interrogated by the secret state police (*Geheime Staatspolizei, Gestapo*), that their ultimate motive, from the beginning of the war in 1939, was the violent persecution and mass murder of the European Jews.[18]

[16] Cf. Hoffmann, ed., *Behind Valkyrie*, pp. 231–37, 263–319; Peter Hoffmann, *The History of the German Resistance 1933–1945*, 3rd Eng. ed., Montreal: McGill-Queen's University Press, 1996, pp. 60–62.

[17] Raul Hilberg, *The Destruction of the European Jews*, New York, London: Holmes and Meier, 1985, pp. 1219–20.

[18] Peter Hoffmann, 'The German Resistance and the Holocaust', in John J. Michalczyk, ed., *Confront! Resistance in Nazi Germany*, New York: Peter Lang, 2004, p. 117; Peter Hoffmann, 'The German Resistance to Hitler and the Jews: The Case of Carl Goerdeler', in Dennis B. Klein, Richard Libowitz, Marcia Sachs Littell, and Sharon Steeley, eds., *The Genocidal Mind: Selected Papers from the 32nd Annual Scholars' Conference on the Holocaust and the Churches*, Saint Paul: Paragon House, 2005, p. 283.

At the same time, most of Hitler's German opponents had a clear sense of responsibility and guilt. Colonel Claus Schenk Graf von Stauffenberg, who placed a briefcase with explosives under Hitler's map table on 20 July 1944, expressed it thus: 'As General Staff officers we must all carry a share of the responsibility'.[19] His cousin, Peter Graf Yorck von Wartenburg, wrote two days before his execution for his part in the plot that he had been driven to act 'by the feeling of the guilt which lay so heavy on us all'.[20] In prison in January 1945, Carl Goerdeler wrote repeatedly of the hundreds of thousands of murdered Jews (he had no clear grasp of the true numbers, which the SS statisticians kept secret). Two days before he was hanged, he wrote that his motivation had been above all 'to bring to an end the horrible sacrifices for all nations, the senseless destruction in Europe', and that 'God would sit in judgement of the horrendous exterminations of the Jews'.[21] Many of the other resisters equally felt the burden of guilt.

The difficulties of writing the history of a recent past are well known. Historians are not free of contemporary influences. Prevailing political tendencies in any given period can have striking parallels in historiography. The historiography of the German Resistance is no exception to such influences and resulting difficulties. Five main post–Second World War historiographic phases may be distinguished. They ran nearly parallel to political and international developments.

The first and second phases partially ran simultaneously. The National Socialist minister for popular enlightenment and propaganda Joseph Goebbels had the advantage to be first to present his version of the failed uprising of 20 July 1944, with which he branded all resisters as traitors. It remained a dominant view among the general population in Germany for years after Germany's defeat in 1945.[22] In the second

[19] Nina Schenk Gräfin von Stauffenberg, from interview quoted in Joachim Kramarz, *Stauffenberg: The Architect of the Famous July 20th Conspiracy to Assassinate Hitler*, New York: The Macmillan Company, 1967, p. 122.

[20] Marion Gräfin Yorck zu Wartenburg, letter to the author 10 August 1972.

[21] Gillmann and Mommsen, *Politische Schriften*, pp. 1184, 1222, 1228, 1236, 1239–40, 1251–52.

[22] *Jahrbuch der öffentlichen Meinung 1947–1955*, ed. Elisabeth Noelle and Erich Peter Neumann, 3rd ed., Allensbach am Bodensee: Verlag für Demoskopie, 1956, p. 138; *Jahrbuch der öffentlichen Meinung 1957*, ed. Elisabeth Noelle und Erich Peter Neumann, Allensbach am Bodensee: Verlag für Demoskopie, 1957, pp. 144–45; *Jahrbuch der öffentlichen Meinung 1958–1964*, ed. Elisabeth Noelle und Erich Peter Neumann, Bonn: Verlag für Demoskopie, 1965, p. 235; Institut für Demoskopie Allensbach: Der 20 July 1944, Ergebnisse einer Bevölkerungs-Umfrage über das Attentat auf Hitler [Allensbach 1970]; Institut für Demoskopie Allensbach to the author, 20 November

phase, while Goebbels' line lingered, resisters not associated with the 20 July 1944 movement (and presumably not tainted by having initially approved of Hitler's government), Social Democrats, Communists, trades-union leaders, clergymen, and students were honoured by their political friends, although Social Democrats and Communists continued to be in discord and many nationalist pastors tended toward Goebbels' line. The actions of the plotters of the 20 July movement, of whom about two hundred were hanged, met with broad disapproval.[23] When surviving diaries, letters, and testimonies began to appear, and when memoirists and historians began publishing accounts, strong differences in the evaluation of the Resistance emerged between the versions prevalent in the zones of Germany occupied by Britain, the United States, and France, on the one side, and the Soviet-occupied zone, on the other.

In a third phase, in the German Democratic Republic (GDR), as the Soviet-occupied zone was constituted from 1949, Communists who had followed the approved Stalinist line were long regarded as the only legitimate resisters. GDR historiography divided the non-Communist Resistance into reactionary and progressive wings after 1965, that is, after a Soviet writer, Professor Daniil Mel'nikov, had included four leading non-Communist resisters (Colonel Claus Schenk Graf von Stauffenberg, Colonel Albrecht Ritter Mertz von Quirnheim, Carl Goerdeler, and Helmuth James von Moltke) among those leaning toward left-wing 'progressiveness'.[24] East German historiography did not stop short of forgery when it wished to claim that a resister was really or latently 'one of them', as in the case of Mertz von Quirnheim. Conservatives and military officers, however, received mostly negative assessments in the GDR.[25]

In the Federal Republic of Germany (FRG, also constituted in 1949 out of the three western zones of occupation) as well as in the GDR, all that suggested German 'greatness' was deprecated as nationalist, imperialist,

1978; Allensbacher Archiv, IfD-Umfrage 4056, April 1985; Claus Wiegrefe, 'Helden und Mörder', *Der Spiegel* 29 12 July 2004): 34–35, 44; Institut für Demoskopie Allensbach to the author 27 November 2003.

[23] Elisabeth Noelle and Erich Peter Neumann, eds., *Jahrbuch der öffentlichen Meinung 1947–1955*, Allensbach am Bodensee: Verlag für Demoskopie, 1956, p. 138.

[24] Daniil Mel'nikov, *Zagovor 20 ijulja 1944 goda v Germanii: Pričiny i sledstvija*, Moscow: Meždunarodnye otnošenija, 1965; Daniil Mel'nikow, *20. Juli 1944: Legende und Wirklichkeit*, Berlin: VEB Deutscher Verlag der Wissenschaften, 1964.

[25] Cf. Sigrid Wegner-Korfes, 'Der 20. Juli 1944 und das Nationalkomitee "Freies Deutschland"', *Zeitschrift für Geschichtswissenschaft* 27 (1979): 535–44.

aggressive, reactionary, and revengist. This dominant current has become subtly moderated since Germany's economic and political weight, not just in Europe, became undeniable.

The government of the German Federal Republic began in 1951, hesitantly, to honour the dead of the Resistance. The resistance of the few was, of course, an embarrassment to the many who had supported Hitler's regime or cooperated with it. Gradually, honouring the Resistance became an annual ritual although by no means a universally accepted one. Works of historiography contributed to this development.

In 1948, Hans Rothfels – a German Jew at the University of Chicago, a decorated veteran of the First World War, and moderate nationalist who had emigrated to England and later to America – published the first comprehensive historiographic assessment of the Resistance.[26] Eberhard Zeller in 1952 published a factual and enthusiastic history of the events culminating in the uprising of 20 July 1944, based on many interviews and the documentary sources then available.[27] Gerhard Ritter followed with a comprehensive and unsuperseded biography of Carl Goerdeler in 1954.[28] There were also collections of short biographic portraits of resisters, and other miscellaneous accounts.[29]

The fourth phase may be said to have begun after the Wall had gone up between East and West Germany on 13 August 1961, as national elections brought the conservative Christian Democratic Union/Christian Social Union (*Christlich Demokratische Union/Christlich-Soziale Union*, *CDU/CSU*) and the Free Democratic Party (*Freie Demokratische Partei*, *FDP*) into a Grand Coalition with the Social Democratic Party of Germany (*Sozialdemokratische Partei Deutschlands*, *SPD*) in 1966, and as the worldwide phenomenon of the Student Rebellion, opposition to the American war in Vietnam, and the 'extra-parliamentary opposition' (*Ausserparlamentarische Opposition*, *APO*) in Germany and the terror attacks and murders by the Baader-Meinhof Gang and the Red Army Faction (*Rote Armee Faktion*) emerged. A younger cohort of historians were concerned to analyse the 'social forces' – conservatism,

26 Hans Rothfels, *The German Opposition to Hitler*, Hinsdale IL: Henry Regnery, 1948.

27 Eberhard Zeller, *Geist der Freiheit: Der zwanzigste Juli*, Munich: Verlag Hermann Rinn, 1952.

28 Gerhard Ritter, *Carl Goerdeler und die deutsche Widerstandsbewegung*, Stuttgart: Deutsche Verlags-Anstalt, 1954.

29 Cf. Annedore Leber, *Das Gewissen steht auf. 64 Lebensbilder aus dem deutschen Widerstand 1933–1945*, Berlin: Annedore Leber, 1954; Hoffmann, *The History of the German Resistance*, bibliography.

antimodernism, capitalism, fascism, imperialism, 'social imperialism', Marxism – to which they attributed the policies of governments before, during, and after the First and the Second World Wars. Many historians were, and remain, confused by a perceived need to choose between fundamental ethical principles on the one hand, and an ideological belief system on the other. A benevolent view of the GDR became widely adopted – a benevolent view of an oppressive regime that trampled democracy and basic human rights, that held its citizens imprisoned behind a heavily armed and guarded wall and ordered the guards to shoot citizens who attempted to leave the First German Workers' and Farmers' State.

Since the 1960s, many historians looked for evidence that conservative resisters to National Socialism – the majority in the 20 July 1944 plot – did not follow the dictate of their consciences as they and their surviving relatives and friends claimed, and that they had not deliberately accepted that they would be tortured, prosecuted, and executed for their resistance. Historians tried to persuade their readers that all or most Germans, including those who gave their lives in the Resistance, really shared the National Socialists' and Hitler's aims, that the ideas of the Resistance were little better than those of the Nazis, that the resisters were 'not democrats' but authoritarians, and, the most damning judgement, that they had no fundamental objections to the regime's anti-Jewish policies, that in the German Resistance there had been a 'fundamental anti-Semitic sentiment' (*antisemitische Grundstimmung*); others parroted this line.[30] A few historians concentrated on indicting the leading resisters Carl Goerdeler, Henning von Tresckow, and Ludwig Beck. By discrediting the most prominent leaders, the entire Resistance would be implicated and discredited.[31] Many historians and other publicists regard Goerdeler as an

[30] Cf. Hans Mommsen, 'Der Widerstand gegen Hitler und die nationalsozialistische Judenverfolgung', in Mommsen, *Alternative zu Hitler*, pp. 386–91. Hans Mommsen, *Alternatives to Hitler: German Resistance under the Third Reich*, London, New York: I.B. Tauris, 2003, pp. 258–62, esp. 259 (the same collection of essays, with identical pagination, was republished by Tauris in 2009 under the title *Germans against Hitler: The Stauffenberg Plot and Resistance under the Third Reich*; these essays deal only marginally with 'the Stauffenberg plot').

[31] Mommsen, 'Gesellschaftsbild und Verfassungspläne', pp. 269–70n109; Mommsen, *Alternative zu Hitler*, pp. 386–91; Mommsen, *Alternatives to Hitler*, pp. 258–62; Christof Dipper, 'Der Deutsche Widerstand und die Juden', *Geschichte und Gesellschaft* 9 (1983): pp. 360–68; Christof Dipper, 'The German Resistance and the Jews', *Yad Vashem Studies* 16 (1984): 65–67, 70–75 (there are numerous misstatements, errors, and evidences of imprecise research in Dipper's work, too numerous to address each in turn; the object here is the correct reading of Goerdeler's concepts and proposals); Christian Gerlach, 'Männer des 20. Juli und der Krieg gegen die Sowjetunion', in Hannes

antisemite and 'dissimilationist' because he regarded the Jewish people as an ethnic entity, and they assert that he intended to deprive the majority of German Jews of their citizenship rights. The memorandum 'The Aim' that Goerdeler wrote in 1941 and 1942 proposing a secure status for the Jews in the world has held a central place in accusations of antisemitism against Goerdeler.[32] One historian in 2004 indicted Tresckow of opportunism, averring that Tresckow's conscience had been dormant while the campaign against the Soviet Union appeared to be succeeding, only to awaken when it turned out otherwise.[33] In the absence of conclusive evidence to convict individuals of such charges, historians used collective-biographic and social-history approaches, suppositions and assumptions, and unsubstantiated allegations.

This historiographic trend ran parallel with successive coalition governments led by the Social Democrats from 1969 to 1982; with social reform, renewed prosecution of Nazi criminals, a broad rejection of 'traditional' and 'conservative' values, and a struggle to come to terms with the National Socialist past, these topics expressed the Zeitgeist. The

Heer and Klaus Naumann, eds., *Vernichtungskrieg: Verbrechen der Wehrmacht 1941–1944*, Hamburg: Hamburger Edition, 1995, pp. 427–46; Christian Gerlach, *Kalkulierte Morde: Die deutsche Wirtschafts- und Vernichtungspolitik in Weißrussland 1941 bis 1944*, Hamburg: Hamburger Edition, 1998, pp. 1106, 1124–26; Johannes Hürter, 'Auf dem Weg zur Militäropposition. Tresckow, Gersdorff, der Vernichtungskrieg und der Judenmord: Neue Dokumente über das Verhältnis der Heeresgruppe Mitte zur Einsatzgruppe B im Jahr 1941', *Vierteljahrshefte für Zeitgeschichte* 52 (2004): 527–62; Theodore S. Hamerow, *On the Road to the Wolf's Lair: German Resistance to Hitler*, Cambridge, London: The Belknap Press of Harvard University Press, 1997, p. 296.

32 Dipper, 'Der Deutsche Widerstand', pp. 364–65; Dipper, 'German Resistance', p. 72; Dipper's treatise is marred by omissions, distortions, and incorrect statements; cf. Fritz Kieffer, 'Carl Friedrich Goerdelers Vorschlag zur Gründung eines jüdischen Staates', *Zeitschrift der Savigny-Stiftung für Rechtsgeschichte* 125 (2008): 474–500. Mommsen, 'Der Widerstand gegen Hitler', pp. 388–91; Mommsen (*Alternatives to Hitler*, pp. 258–62, esp. 259) wrote that Goerdeler 'wanted to treat all Jews living in Germany as registered aliens and to deprive them of citizenship, the right to vote and access to public office'. In an address upon the presentation of the publication of Goerdeler's main political writings and letters in Leipzig on 30 October 2003, Mommsen said that Goerdeler had demanded equal human rights for Jews and restitution of their assets, but added without citing evidence that Goerdeler had admitted that he was guilty of not having opposed the inhumanity of the persecution of the Jews; Hans Mommsen and Hinrich Lehmann-Grube, *Reden anlässlich der Präsentation der Edition 'Politische Schriften und Briefe von Carl Friedrich Goerdeler' in der Deutschen Bibliothek in Leipzig am 30. Oktober 2003*, Königswinter: Forschungsgemeinschaft 20 July, 2004, p. 3. Theodore Hamerow wrote that Goerdeler wanted to 'place most German Jews in the category of resident aliens'; Hamerow, *On the Road*, p. 296.

33 Johannes Hürter, 'Auf dem Weg zur Militäropposition', *Vierteljahrshefte für Zeitgeschichte* 52 (2004): 531.

SPD-led coalition governments hoped to change the Communist-Stalinist GDR regime through a policy of contacts and 'small steps', in tandem with the American-Russian policy of Detente. This period ended in the 1980s in an East–West confrontation about armaments – about the stationing of medium-range nuclear-armed Soviet (Sam-20) and American (Pershing II) missiles in Europe – and an unexpected resolution through historical personages and an episode of reason prevailing, an episode in which the American president Ronald Reagan and the Soviet-Russian secretary-general of the Communist Party of the Union of Soviet Socialist Republics Mikhail Gorbachev were the protagonists.

While the third and fourth phases of historiography on the Resistance continue unabated to the present, a fifth phase can be distinguished. The social-forces and social-structures school of historiography had its ambivalent, contradictory side in the attacks upon individuals (Goerdeler, Tresckow) with the aim of convicting a larger group (conservatives, patriots denounced as 'nationalists') collectively, without building cases against most of the individuals in the group. The Governing Board of the German Historical Association (*Verband der Historiker Deutschlands*) planned a section on biography for their 1984 annual conference in Berlin.[34] While a number of major biographies appeared – on Stauffenberg, Hermann Göring, William II, Hitler, Thomas Mann, Adolf Heusinger, Mildred Harnack, Friedrich Fromm, Beck, Heinrich Himmler, Adam von Trott zu Solz, Stefan George – the advocates of social-forces, structural, and collective historiography regrouped. In 1994, when the fiftieth year after Stauffenberg's assassination attack and coup was widely commemorated, leading critics of the Resistance repeated their assault upon the integrity of the resisters and simultaneously launched a comprehensive attack upon the German Armed Forces with a travelling exhibition of photographs, the *Wehrmachtausstellung*, which purported to show crimes committed by German soldiers. It included numerous false identifications and attributions – too numerous to be readily accepted as accidental, and in the eyes of many, it remains disgraced; modifications corrected false identifications, but not the general tendency of the exhibition.[35] All this fit into what Joachim Fest called

[34] Rudolf Vierhaus (secretary), minute 24 February 1983, Archiv des Verbandes der Historiker und Historikerinnen Deutschlands, Trier; the final programme did not include such a section; *Bericht über die 35. Versammlung deutscher Historiker in Berlin. 3. bis 7. Oktober 1984*, Stuttgart: Ernst Klett Verlag, 1985; cf. Jürgen Kocka, 'Bismarck-Biographien', *Geschichte und Gesellschaft* 7 (1981): 572–81.

[35] Hamburger Institut für Sozialforschung, ed., *Vernichtungskrieg: Verbrechen der Wehrmacht 1941 bis 1944: Ausstellungskatalog*, Hamburg: Hamburger Edition 1996, 3rd ed. 1997;

'the dominant denunciatory caprice toward the Resistance', the denial that they had honourable motives.[36]

This is the position. This study examines the evidence that tells a different story. The new examination and close reading of the evidence in the present work will reveal what Goerdeler in fact wrote and intended between 1933 and 1945. It will show also that Goerdeler was part of a global discussion on the Jewish Question.

I thank archivists, most of all Professor Dr Hartmut Weber, President of *Bundesarchiv*, and librarians in Europe and in Canada for their untiring assistance in my research. My special gratitude goes to Dr Fritz Kieffer, whose juristic examination of Goerdeler's 1941/1942 proposal has greatly advanced the understanding of this proposal and its implications, and who has since its publication corresponded with me about some hitherto unsolved questions. I thank Readers A and B, and Peter F. Hoffmann, for their careful reading of the typescript and their valuable suggestions, and Eliza R. Wood for her help in the preparation of the Index. I wish to express my appreciation to the *Landesstiftung Baden-Württemberg* for its support in defraying some of the costs of research.

Hannes Heer and Klaus Naumann, eds., *Vernichtungskrieg: Verbrechen der Wehrmacht 1941–1944*, Hamburg: Hamburger Edition, 1995; Bogdan Musial, '"Konterrevolutionäre Elemente sind zu erschiessen": Die Mordaktionen des sowjetischen NKWD nach dem Einmarsch der deutschen Truppen', *Frankfurter Allgemeine Zeitung* 30 October 1999, p. 11; Kriztián Ungváry, 'Echte Bilder – problematische Aussagen: Eine quantitative und qualitative Fotoanalyse der Ausstellung "Vernichtungskrieg – Verbrechen der Wehrmacht 1941 bis 1944"', *Geschichte in Wissenschaft und Unterricht* 50 (1999): 584–95; Dieter Schmidt-Neuhaus, 'Die Tarnopol-Stellwand der Wanderausstellung "Vernichtungskrieg – Verbrechen der Wehrmacht 1941 bis 1944": Eine Falluntersuchung zur Verwendung von Bildquellen', *Geschichte in Wissenschaft und Unterricht* 50 (1999): 596–603; Hamburg Institute for Social Research, ed., *The German Army and Genocide: Crimes Against War Prisoners, Jews, and Other Civilians in the East, 1939–1944*, New York: The New Press, 1999; Hamburger Institut für Sozialforschung, ed., *Vernichtungskrieg: Verbrechen der Wehrmacht 1941 bis 1944: Dimensionen des Vernichtungskrieges 1941–1941: Ausstellungskatalog*, Hamburg: Hamburger Edition, 2002.

[36] Joachim Fest, 'Das verschmähte Vermächtnis: Rede zur Verleihung des Eugen Bolz-Preises am 24.1.04', typescript, from J. Fest 18 June 2003.

1

Introduction

Carl Friedrich Goerdeler, born in 1884, witnessed the increasing turmoil that enveloped Jews in Eastern Europe during and after the First World War. He engaged in efforts to influence the fate of the Jews from the moment when Adolf Hitler was appointed chancellor in Germany in 1933. The events leading up to this sea change in German politics formed a part of Goerdeler's political and social consciousness.

When in October 1918 the German Empire could no longer withstand the overwhelming numbers of fresh American troops and their vastly superior quantities in weaponry and munitions, the imperial government addressed its request for an armistice to the American president Woodrow Wilson and invoked the Fourteen Points that he had declared as his basis for peace. The president replied that an armistice would be granted on condition that the monarchies were removed and a representative government put in place. Secretary of State Robert Lansing signed the final note of 23 October 1918 that contained this condition. On the following day, the leading German newspapers published the full text of Lansing's note on their front pages. Soldiers and socialists mounted demonstrations and other means of pressure, which by 9/10 November resulted in the departure of Emperor William II into exile in Holland, and in the abdications of his German brother monarchs. A temporary government, the Council of People's Commissars, presided over the withdrawal of the imperial armed forces from occupied territories, the evacuation of territories the enemies were going to annex, the military occupation of additional German territories, and the handing over of thousands of units of railway rolling stock including 5,000 locomotives, and most of Germany's artillery and other weapons, aeroplanes, submarines. On

19 January 1919, the Council of People's Commissars held elections for a national constituent assembly that met at Weimar to escape the revolutionary turmoil in Berlin; the Council of People's Commissars and, from 13 February 1919, the new government fought militant extremists of the right and the left. The Allied and Associated Powers excluded the German government from the negotiation of the 'treaty of peace'. Their 'treaty' declared Germany responsible and liable for having begun the war in 1914. They forced the German government, by continuing the food blockade against the German population and threatening military occupation of the entire country, to accept the Treaty of Versailles. The government had to agree to pay reparation sums in an amount of which it would be informed only in 1921. The government signed the treaty on 28 June 1919; the blockade was lifted on 12 July. The reparation payments were designed to weaken Germany in the long term and, when Germany predictably defaulted in reparation payments, to enable France to occupy more German territory than the Treaty of Versailles stipulated. The German government in April 1921 faced either foreign occupation of additional German territory, or acceptance of Allied reparation demands. The government hoped that in return for acceptance, the Allies would honour the results of the plebiscite in Upper Silesia that had decided against joining Poland by a margin of 228,028 votes in favour of Germany; 707,393 or 59.4 percent had opted for Germany, and 479,365 or 40.3 percent for Poland. At the same time, the German government had agreed, by signing the Treaty of Versailles, to pay whatever demands were made in 1921, and it adopted a 'fulfilment policy' of attempting to meet reparation demands in order to demonstrate that the demands were excessive. The long-term goal was to achieve a revision of reparation demands, or, by failing to meet demands, to sabotage the reparation policy. Chancellor Dr. Josef Wirth declared before the *Reichstag* on 1 June 1921 that loyal German efforts to meet the demands could save Germany from further enemy invasions and occupation, and that only a genuine effort could elicit the world's understanding for Germany's difficult situation.[1]

[1] *Rocznik staystyki. Rzeczypospolitej Polskiej. Rok wydania I 1920/22. Część II. Annuaire statistique de la République Polonaise. I-ère année 1920/22. Partie II.* Warszawa: Nakładem Glównego Urzędu Statystycznego, 1923, p. 358; *Encyclopedia Powstań Śląskich*, Opole: Instytut Śląski w Opolu, 1982, pp. 400, 677, et seq.; George J. Lerski, *Historical Dictionary of Poland, 966–1945*, Westport, Connecticut, London: Greenwood Press, 1996, pp. 545–46; Dr. Josef Wirth, *Reich* chancellor, 'Erklärung der Reichsregierung', in *Verhandlungen des Reichstags: I. Wahlperiode 1920*, vol. 349, Berlin: Norddeutsche Buchdruckerei und Verlags-Anstalt, 1921, pp. 3709–17; William Kleine-Ahlbrandt, *The Burden of Victory: France, Britain and the Enforcement of the Versailles Peace, 1919–1925*,

The implication was not hard to grasp of what would happen if the world's understanding did not come about. The Allies decided that Poland was to have Upper Silesia regardless. The German government and the nation felt duped, and the government did all it could to escape as many reparation demands as possible. Germany paid billions in gold marks and delivered millions and millions worth of goods, while asking for moratoria and allowing inflation to mount. In December 1922, the Allied Reparation Commission declared Germany in default for having failed to deliver 23,560 cubic meters of lumber out of 55,000, and 141,648 telephone poles out of 200,000.[2] On 11 January 1923, French and Belgian military forces occupied Germany's industrial heartland, the Ruhr region, and established a harsh regime with executions, mass expulsions, and economic restrictions making Germany even less able to meet her reparation obligations. The German currency collapsed in hyperinflation, and the government narrowly survived left-wing and right-wing

Lanham, New York, London: University Press of America, 1995, p. 109. Denise Artaud, *La Question des dettes interallies et la reconstruction de l'europe (1917–1929)*, Lille: Université de Lille, Atelier national de reproduction des theses, 1978, pp. 449, 457; see also J. Bariéty, *Les relations franco-allemandes après la première guerre mondiale*, Paris : Èditions Pedone, 1977; Derek Croxton, *Peacemaking in Early Modern Europe: Cardinal Mazarin and the Congress of Westphalia, 1643–1648*, London: Associated University Press, 1999; Conan Fischer, *The Ruhr Crisis, 1923–1924*, New York: Oxford University Press, 2003; Walter A. McDougall, *France's Rhineland Diplomacy, 1914–1924: The Last Bid for a Balance of Power in Europe*, Princeton: Princeton University Press, 1978; Allied Powers Reparation Commission, *Report on the Work of the Reparation Commission from 1920 to 1922*, vol. 5: *Reparation Papers of the Allied Powers Reparation Commission*, London: H.M. Stationery Office, 1928; Stephen A. Schuker argues that Minister-President (15 January 1922–26 March 1924) Raymond Poincaré was convinced that the German government deliberately ruined the German currency in order to create a false impression of bankruptcy and sabotage the reparation system, in *The End of French Predominance in Europe: The Financial Crisis of 1924 and the Adoption of the Dawes Plan*, Chapel Hill: University of North Carolina Press, 1976, pp. 22–24, 178–79; Schuker cites as 'documentary evidence' unspecified '*Reich* Chancellery, Foreign Ministry, and Finance Ministry files [that] confirm the contemporary impressions of Costantino Bresciani-Turroni', who then served as head of the export control section of the Committee of Guarantees of the Allied Reparation Commission; Sally Marks, 'The Myths of Reparations', *Central European History* 11 (1978): 238, cites specific British and French documents showing that British and French experts believed 'that Germany was deliberately ruining the mark, partly to avoid budgetary and currency reform, but primarily to escape reparations'; for German intentions, however, she cites Schuker, who fails to cite specific documents. See further Albert Schwarz, 'Die Weimarer Republik', in Leo Just, ed., *Handbuch der Deutschen Geschichte*, vol. 4, 1st part, 3rd section, pp. 78–79, 83; Klaus Hildebrand, *Das vergangene Reich: Deutsche Aussenpolitik von Bismarck bis Hitler 1871–1945*, Stuttgart: Deutsche Verlags-Anstalt, 1995, pp. 415–16.

2 *Reparation Commission*, vol. 5: *Report: On the Work of the Reparation Commission from 1920 to 1922*, London: His Majesty's Stationery Office, 1923, p. 141.

putsches, until America intervened and rescued Germany financially with the Dawes Plan of 1924. A period of relative recovery and prosperity followed. The Weimar Republic signed the Locarno Treaty with France that guaranteed the existing border between the two countries and provided France with a modicum of the security that she had sought in a treaty that Britain and the United States of America had not ratified. There was no guarantee of Germany's eastern border, and the German government did not conceal its wish to revise it. Germany also had tolerable relations with the Union of Soviet Socialist Republics (USSR). In October 1929 the New York stock market crashed, the Great Depression followed, banks failed, massive unemployment set in, political life in Germany became destabilised, and emergency governments under presidential authority tried to stem a virtual civil war.

By 1932, Adolf Hitler's National Socialist German Workers Party (*Nationalsozialistische Deutsche Arbeiterpartei, NSDAP*), running on a nationalist programme to exclude all foreign influences and especially Jews, attracted 37.4 percent of the vote in national elections. Hitler openly announced that he was using the liberties of the constitution in order to destroy the republic and its constitution, run the country on the *Führer* Principle, and have Marxists and Communists lined up against a wall and shot.[3] Political adventurers and intriguers in the entourage of the ageing president, Paul von Hindenburg, succeeded in having Hitler appointed chancellor on 30 January 1933.

The National Socialists soon called it the *Führer*'s Seizure of Power and everywhere began to act as their *Führer*'s agents and deputies. The party's *SA* Stormtroopers rounded up thousands of political opponents who disappeared in concentration camps, and political and personal enemies were targets, without judicial process or control. Hitler cited threats to public security and obtained presidential approval for an emergency decree of 4 February 1933 that allowed the government to suppress rival political activities.[4] On 17 February, Hermann Göring, as Prussian interior minister, ordered the Prussian police to use their firearms in encounters with 'Communist terrorist acts and attacks' and threatened disciplinary

[3] Cf. Hitler, *Mein Kampf*, pp. 588–89.

[4] Karl Dietrich Bracher, Wolfgang Sauer, and Gerhard Schulz, *Die nationalsozialistische Machtergreifung: Studien zur Errichtung des totalitären Herrschaftssystems in Deutschland 1933/34*, 2nd ed., Cologne-Opladen: Westdeutscher Verlag, 1962, pp. 31–168; Henry Ashby Turner Jr., *Hitler's Thirty Days to Power*, Reading: Addison-Wesley, 1996; 'Verordnung des Reichspräsidenten zum Schutze des Deutschen Volkes. Vom 4. Februar 1933', in *Reichsgesetzblatt. Teil I. Jahrgang 1933 (RGBl. [Reichsgesetzblatt] I 1933)*, Berlin: Reichsverlagsamt, 1933, pp. 35–40.

action against policemen 'who display weakness'. The decree was published verbatim on the front page of the *NSDAP*'s newspaper *Völkischer Beobachter* on 21 February 1933.[5] Thousands of citizens were detained and mistreated, and many were murdered, just as Hitler had promised he would do.[6] When a Dutch anarchist set fire to the Parliament (*Reichstag*) building on 27 February, a further emergency decree suspended all essential civil liberties.[7] More waves of arrests followed. According to a statistic prepared in the *Reich* Ministry of the Interior, 26,789 persons were held in 'protective custody' on 31 July 1933. This number included only detentions under judicial and police authority; additional thousands were detained in extralegal *SA* and *SS* prisons and camps. The average number of concentration-camp inmates from 1933 to 1 September 1939 was 25,000; in the aftermath of the November 1938 pogrom, when 35,000 Jews were put into concentration camps, it temporarily reached 60,000. During the war, the total number of concentration-camp inmates climbed to over 224,000 in August 1943, 524,286 in August 1944, and 714,211 by 15 January 1945.[8]

With new parliamentary elections scheduled for 5 March 1933, the National Socialists exploited all legal and illegal means at their disposal to bully and terrorise the voters into supporting the *NSDAP*, and they still received only 43.9 percent of the vote. The Communist Party received 12.3 percent; their elected deputies were not allowed to take their seats, but were imprisoned or driven into exile. A nationalist party in coalition with the *NSDAP*, the German National People's Party (*Deutschnationale Volkspartei, DNVP*) received 8.0 percent; this and the elimination of the Communists gave Hitler a comfortable majority, and promises and lies secured the support of two other parties to produce the necessary two-thirds majority to pass an Enabling Act that abrogated the constitution and gave the government dictatorial powers. The *Reichstag* became a rubberstamp for whatever the government decreed. The Jews in Germany were officially and aggressively discriminated against, persecuted, oppressed, and progressively robbed of their assets.

[5] *Völkischer Beobachter*, Munich ed., 21 February 1933, p. 1.

[6] Robert Gellately, *Backing Hitler: Consent and Coercion in Nazi Germany*, Oxford: Oxford University Press, 2001, pp. 58–59.

[7] 'Verordnung des Reichspräsidenten zum Schutz von Volk und Staat. Vom 28. Februar 1933', in *RGBl. 1933 I*, p. 83.

[8] Martin Broszat, 'Nationalsozialistische Konzentrationslager 1933–1945', in Hans Buchheim, Martin Broszat, Hans-Adolf Jacobsen, and Helmut Krausnick, eds., *Anatomie des SS-Staates*, vol. 2, Munich: Deutscher Taschenbuch Verlag, 1967, pp. 13–24, 80–81, 124–33.

Four days after his appointment as chancellor, on 3 February 1933, Hitler addressed the senior commanders of the armed forces (*Reichswehr*) to declare his intention to re-arm and to expand German 'living space' (*Lebensraum*) by force of arms, and to 'Germanise' the soil thus conquered, but not the population. If France has statesmen, he said, it will not allow Germany to re-arm.[9] Only extremely obtuse persons could have misunderstood Hitler. He was going to wage aggressive war, and he was going to cause large numbers of human beings to perish.

A reasonable balance of power on the continent, however, required a measure of German re-armament. The Treaty of Versailles limited the German Armed Forces to 100,000 men serving long terms, so that Germany had no qualified reservists. France had a peace-time standing army in 1933 of 600,000 and could mobilise 900,000 reservists; Poland had a 284,000-man standing army and could mobilise a total of 1.2 million; the Czechoslovak, Yugoslav, and Romanian armies were 110,000, around 100,000, and 562,000 strong, respectively, without reservists. France and Poland were allied from 1921, Czechoslovakia acceded in 1933, and France had alliances with Yugoslavia and Romania from 1933.[10]

There was talk about a Franco-Polish intervention against Germany.[11] In May 1933, the phrase 'the dismemberment of Germany' was heard in Paris and in Washington.[12] Józef Piłsudski, first marshal of Poland, who served as war minister in all Polish cabinets since May 1925, had long made preparations for a 'preventive war' against Germany; since 1930 he had been considering a 'police action' against Germany in conjunction with France and under the aegis of the League of Nations. In March 1933

[9] Thilo Vogelsang, 'Neue Dokumente zur Geschichte der Reichswehr 1930–1933', *Vierteljahrshefte für Zeitgeschichte* 2 (1954): 435; Andreas Wirsching, '"Man kann nur Boden germanisieren": Eine neue Quelle zu Hitlers Rede vor den Spitzen der Wehrmacht am 3. Februar 1933', *Vierteljahrshefte für Zeitgeschichte* 49 (2001): 547–48.

[10] *The Statesman's Year-Book: Statistical and Historical Annual of the States of the World for the Year 1934*, London: Macmillan 1934, pp. 796, 873–78, 950, 1217–18, 1247, 1260–61, 1377.

[11] The Chairman of the American Foreign Policy Association James G. McDonald, long active in League of Nations work, who became League of Nations high commissioner for refugees coming from Germany later in 1933, had known the German *Reichsbank* president Hjalmar Schacht for some years and also had other connections in Germany, one of them being Ernst Hanfstaengl, Hitler's foreign-press spokesman, whom McDonald saw almost daily in the spring of 1933. James G. McDonald, *Advocate for the Doomed: The Diaries and Papers of James G. McDonald 1932–1935*, ed. by Richard Breitman, Barbara McDonald Stewart, and Severin Hochberg, Bloomington and Indianapolis: Indiana University Press, 2007, p. 44.

[12] McDonald, *Advocate*, pp. 5–7, 68. Cf. Hans Roos, *A History of Modern Poland*, London: Eyre and Spottiswoode, 1966, pp. 129–30.

he intended to occupy Danzig, East Prussia, and German Upper Silesia as 'territorial pledges' in order to force Germany to obey the Versailles Treaty provisions concerning armament and frontiers. He would force Hitler to resign, whereupon he would evacuate all occupied territories except Danzig. France, however, wanted nothing to do with these Polish proposals in March and April 1933. When Piłsudski sent Hitler an ultimatum demanding a commitment, Hitler, informed of Polish plans for 'preventive war', promised to respect the German–Polish frontier. When the influential American journalist Walter Lippmann on 16 May asked James G. McDonald, chairman of the (American) Foreign Policy Association and a candidate for the post of American ambassador to Berlin, what would happen if France and Poland occupied Germany, McDonald said he guessed 'a wholesale slaughter of the Jews'.[13] McDonald understood better than most of his contemporaries what Hitler was about.

When rivalry between the party 'army' of more than four million Stormtroopers (*SA*) and the small professional army reached dangerous levels, Hitler decided against the militarily worthless *SA* and had their leaders murdered on 30 June and 1 July 1934. He secured 'revisions' of the Treaty of Versailles year after year, including a naval agreement with Britain in 1935, restoration of the universal draft in the same year, the unveiling of an air force, and the re-militarisation of the left bank of the Rhine in March 1936.

Persecution of the Jews was a constant in Nazi domestic policy, many Jews being insulted and assaulted in the streets of Berlin, Königsberg, Breslau, and Halle, with the regional and national press hurling threats and invectives against them. Hitler's anti-Jewish policies were not, to be sure, entirely innovative. The Prussian Interior Ministry had issued directives to curtail name changes by Jews with 'Jewish' names in November 1932, and there were restrictions upon immigration and naturalisation of Jews.[14] Facing anti-German boycott movements abroad as responses to antisemitism in Germany, Hitler used the opportunity on 28 March 1933 to call for a national counter-boycott against Jewish businesses.[15]

[13] McDonald, *Advocate*, p. 69.

[14] Uwe Dietrich Adam, *Judenpolitik im Dritten Reich*, Düsseldorf: Droste Verlag, 1972, pp. 43–46.

[15] Alfred Wiślicki, 'The Jewish Boycott Campaign against Nazi Germany and Its Culmination in the Halbersztadt Trial', in *Polin: Studies in Polish Jewry*, vol. 8, London, Washington: The Littman Library of Jewish Civilization, 1994, pp. 282–83; cf. *Encyclopaedia Judaica* 21, p. 219; McDonald, *Advocate*, pp. 27–29. For immigration and naturalisation restrictions, see below at pp. 38, 146, 154–58.

According to Hitler's foreign-press chief, Ernst Hanfstaengl, Hitler had been waiting for such an opportunity; when Hanfstaengl told him of the boycott agitation abroad, he said the Jews must be crushed, and now 'their fellows abroad have played into our hands'. And Hanfstaengl, in recounting this to McDonald, said the Nazis will handle 600,000 Jews easily, 'each Jew has his SA', and 'in a single night it could be finished'.[16]

The boycott day, 1 April 1933, was a Saturday when department stores were open while observant Jews kept their businesses closed, but there was violence, there were threats against Jews, and some were pilloried. The boycott ended after that first day.[17] It had only been a beginning. A far-from-complete list of other anti-Jewish measures includes the Law for the Restoration of the Professional Civil Service of 7 April 1933, which had been in preparation well before the boycott; it was a pervasive and enduring measure.[18] It resulted in distress for civil servants forced to retire; many physicians, notaries, lawyers, and other professionals were forced to cease practicing; Catholic priests and Lutheran ministers who were converts from Judaism lost their livings. Under this and other laws, ordinances, and decrees, and often by illegal actions and intimidation, many factory owners, businessmen, and bankers were expropriated, their property was 'Aryanised', and emigrants lost most of their assets. A law in July 1933 enabled the government to de-naturalise Jews of East European origin.[19] Jewish tax consultants had their licences withdrawn by decree on 6 April and by law on 6 May 1933.[20] Jews had to give up jury service and any honorary positions in organisations such as veterans' associations and social-insurance corporations. The Prussian Ministry for Science, Arts and Public Education (*Ministerium für Wissenschaft, Kunst und Volksbildung*) denied Jewish students and candidates for teaching posts admission to examinations and certification; Jewish soldiers and officers were to be dismissed, although the military authorities balked

[16] McDonald, *Advocate*, pp. 27, 31.

[17] Joseph Goebbels, *Die Tagebücher*, Teil I, Band 2/III, Munich: K.G. Saur, 2006, pp. 156–62.

[18] 'Gesetz zur Wiederherstellung des Berufsbeamtentums. Vom 7. April 1933', in *RGBl. I 1933*, pp. 175–77; 'Erste Verordnung zur Durchführung des Gesetzes zur Wiederherstellung des Berufsbeamtentums. Vom 11. April 1933', in *RGBl. I 1933*, p. 195.

[19] 'Gesetz über den Widerruf von Einbürgerungen und die Aberkennung der deutschen Staatsangehörigkeit. Vom 14. Juli 1933', and 'Verordnung zur Durchführung des Gesetzes über den Widerruf von Einbürgerungen und die Aberkennung der deutschen Staatsangehörigkeit. Vom 26. Juli 1933', in *RGBl. I 1933*, pp. 480, 538–39.

[20] Adam, *Judenpolitik im Dritten Reich*, p. 73; 'Gesetz über die Zulassung von Steuerberatern. Vom 6. Mai 1933', in *RGBl. 1933 I*, pp. 257–58.

at this. Jewish writers, journalists, and artists could no longer publish or publicly display their work, and academics were either dismissed under the 7 April 1933 law, or harassed into vacating their posts.[21]

Thousands of Jews emigrated. The depletion and contraction of many Jewish communities were reflected in synagogues and prayer rooms falling into disuse and being abandoned or sold. There were marked regional differences. In Baden and Württemberg, numerous synagogues and prayer rooms were either closed or sold long before 1933, a good number between 1933 and 1938.[22] Laws to regulate legitimate membership in the German *Reich* based on racial criteria were announced on 4 July 1933, but not promulgated until September 1935. On 18 August 1933, *Reichsbank* president Hjalmar Schacht described to McDonald the visit that the president of the Chase Bank, Winthrop Aldrich, had paid to Hitler. Before Aldrich could mention the Jews, Hitler told Aldrich that there had been no protest when some 20,000–30,000 black troops had occupied the German Rhineland, from 1919 to 1929. Moreover, if the other powers were so anxious to help the Jews, why did they not open their doors to them; Germany was only doing belatedly with the restrictions upon Eastern Jews and Jews of Eastern origin what the United States and other countries had long since done more effectively.[23] When the American secretary of state, Cordell Hull, in September 1933 wanted to know if the United States could issue a statement in favour of settling Jews in other parts of the world than Germany, the State Department chief of the Division of Western European Affairs, Jay Pierrepont Moffat, advised that this would be illogical when the United States limited admissions to a small number under the quota system while any German Jew who could prove that he would not become a public charge could enter the United States under the German quota (which was never exhausted).[24]

The question of assets that German authorities allowed Jewish emigrants to take with them remained one of the main obstacles to their emigration.[25] McDonald, from October 1933 League of Nations high commissioner for refugees coming from Germany, never tired of trying

[21] Adam, *Judenpolitik im Dritten Reich*, pp. 73–80; cf. Peter Hoffmann, *Stauffenberg: A Family History, 1905–1944*, 3rd ed., Montreal, Kingston, London, Ithaca: McGill-Queen's University Press, 2009, pp. 64–65.

[22] http://www.ashkenazhouse.org/memorialcoin.html.

[23] McDonald, *Advocate*, pp. 82–83.

[24] McDonald, *Advocate*, p. 101.

[25] Cf. McDonald, *Advocate*, pp. 141–42.

to find funding for German Jewish emigrants in 1933 and 1934, but the responses to his appeals from Jewish organisations as well as private persons who had the means were discouraging, to put it mildly.[26] On 5 May 1934, he wrote to Felix Warburg, Max Warburg's brother in America, one of the most important American Jewish leaders, that 'the more I hear of vague and always indefinite talks about possibilities of immigration to other parts of the world, the more I appreciate the value of Palestine. At any rate, there you have something more than beautiful sounding words which, when analyzed, so often mean nothing'.[27] When McDonald was preparing to leave his post as high commissioner, in July 1935, he reported that more than 80,000 Jewish persons had become 'refugees' (not counting tens of thousands of other Jews who had left Germany without becoming a factor in the statistic of refugees); 27,000 of them had settled in Palestine, 6,000 in the United States, 3,000 in South America, 800 in other countries, 18,000 had been repatriated to countries of Central and Eastern Europe, and 27,000 were still refugees in Europe. In the two years of McDonald's tenure, U.S. $10 million had been raised, of which $3 million were contributions from American Jews and 2.5 million from British Jews.[28] The German government rejected McDonald's efforts to obtain its agreement to a planned, orderly emigration of German Jews with the help of funds raised outside Germany, and Foreign Minister von Neurath in March 1934 refused to receive him a second time after he had made his proposal. On 12 March 1934, the American ambassador William E. Dodd informed Hitler that McDonald had some millions of dollars at his disposal to be spent mostly in Germany to assist Jews to emigrate, and that in this way the problem could be solved in about eight to ten years. Hitler replied that no matter how many millions of dollars were put into the project, nothing would come of it because the Jews in Germany and outside would only attack Germany and make endless trouble.[29] Attempts of American Jews and non-Jews to intervene on behalf of the German Jews only confirmed Hitler in his belief that the democracies as well as the Soviet Union were run by Jews.

Historians of Hitler's dictatorship have noted a pause in major anti-Jewish legislation during the months from July 1933 to September

[26] McDonald, *Advocate*, pp. 177–79, 342, 383.
[27] McDonald, *Advocate*, pp. 383, 387–88.
[28] McDonald, *Advocate*, p. 783; the editors cite the *New York Times* 18 July 1935, p. 1, for the full text of the report.
[29] McDonald, *Advocate*, pp. 317–18.

1935.[30] Uwe Adam conjectures economic and foreign-policy reasons.[31] Ian Kershaw states firmly: 'Chiefly on account of foreign-policy sensitivities and economic precariousness, the regime had during 1934 reined in the violence against Jews which had characterized the early months of Nazi rule'. But he continues to say that barbarity had far from totally subsided, that 'ferocious discrimination' continued 'unabated', and that 'intimidation was unrelenting'.[32] McDonald wrote to President Franklin D. Roosevelt under the date of 3 May 1935:

> It is frequently said these days in dispatches from Germany that the regime there is moderating its attitude towards the Jews and in other respects. I do not believe that there is any justification whatsoever for these reports. They seem to be designed to create a certain impression abroad, but to have [*sic*] no relationship whatsoever to the actualities of the situation within Germany. On the contrary, there are substantial indications that the notorious Aryan paragraph, hitherto applied chiefly to official and professional circles, may be extended not only as it has already in practice, but also in theory, to the economic field... I remain convinced that the regime, unless materially modified, is inconsistent with the peace of Europe.[33]

In fact, anti-Jewish policy and legislation continued 'unabated'. In Raul Hilberg's work, the numerous measures taken against Jews in the 1930s, including the years 1933–1935, appear under the headings of 'Dismissals', 'Aryanizations', 'Property Taxes', 'Blocked Money', 'Forced Labor and Wage Regulations', 'Special Income Taxes', and 'Starvation Measures'; 'Expropriation' and 'Forced Emigration' should be added.[34]

The pressure against Jewish businessmen and professionals continued. Physicians, lawyers, and bankers were being pushed out of their occupations. In May 1934, physicians with one or more Jewish grandparents and those married to a Jewish partner were excluded from approbation.[35] In July 1934 a law charged municipal health commissions with

[30] Adam, *Judenpolitik im Dritten Reich*, pp. 82–90; there are no entries for 'Jews' in the subject index of the German official law gazette (*Reichsgesetzblatt*) for the entire year 1934, and only a few for 1935.

[31] Adam, *Judenpolitik im Dritten Reich*, pp. 82–90.

[32] Ian Kershaw, *Hitler: 1889–1936: Hubris*, London: Allen Lane The Penguin Press, 1998, p. 559.

[33] McDonald, *Advocate*, pp. 383–84.

[34] Hilberg, *The Destruction of the European Jews*, New York, London: Holmes and Meier, 1985, pp. 81–154.

[35] 'Verordnung über die Zulassung von Ärzten zur Tätigkeit bei den Krankenkassen. Vom 17. Mai 1934', in *RGBl. I 1934*, Berlin: Reichsverlagsamt, 1934, pp. 399–410.

'heredity and race care' (*Erb- und Rassenpflege*).[36] Many Jews were pressed to sell their businesses, and the regime used every conceivable sham or quasi-legal means, such as an emigration tax called '*Reich* Flight Tax' (*Reichsfluchtsteuer*), to rob them.[37] This tax had been introduced during the Depression in December 1931 and had not been directed primarily against Jews. It was set at 25 percent of taxable property. After the pogrom in November 1938, all Jews had to pay a 20 percent tax, raised from November 1939 to 25 percent, on the value of their registered property. If Jews managed to emigrate at all, they therefore lost 50 percent of their property at the start, and of the rest they could take very little with them.[38] The fiscal authorities employed a variety of other methods, too, to rob the Jews. They used what they called 'intensified audits' (*verschärfte Betriebsprüfungen*), and prosecutions for infractions of foreign-currency regulations (*Devisenstrafverfahren*). A recent study found that the Bureaus of Currency and Customs Investigation of the Higher Fiscal Presidium in Hannover (*Devisen- und Zollfahndungstellen des Oberfinanzpräsidenten*) had become, by 1936, 'the most effective instrument in the expulsion [*Vertreibung*] and robbing of the German Jews', operating in the frontline of the battle against Jewry, as the *Deutsche Steuerzeitung* said three years later.[39] The 'Nuremberg Race Laws' were promulgated on 15 September 1935: the '*Reich* Citizen Law' (*Reichsbürgergesetz*) and the 'Law for the Protection of German Blood

[36] 'Gesetz zur Vereinheitlichung des Gesundheitswesens. Vom 3. Juli 1934', in *RGBl. I 1934*, pp. 531–32; 'Erste Durchführungsverordnung zum Gesetz über die Vereinheitlichung des Gesundheitswesens. Vom 6. Februar 1935', in *RGBl. I 1935*, pp. 177–80.

[37] '4. Verordnung des Reichspräsidenten zur Sicherung von Wirtschaft und Finanzen und zum Schutze des inneren Friedens. Vom 8. Dezember 1931', in *RGBl. I 1931*, Berlin: Reichsverlagsamt, 1931, pp. 699–745; *RGBl. I 1932* (ext. to 31 December 1934), p. 572; *RGBl. I 1934* (18 May 1934 lowered amounts subject to Reichsfluchtsteuer), pp. 392–93; *RGBl. I 1937* (ext. to 31 December 1938), p. 1385; J.F.H. Peters, *Die Reichsfluchtsteuer*, Cologne: Otto Schmidt, 1938; Kerstin Wolf and Frank Wolf, *Reichsfluchtsteuer und Steuersteckbriefe, 1932–1942*, Berlin: Biographische Forschungen und Sozialgeschichte, 1997; Dorothee Mussgnug, *Die Reichsfluchtsteuer 1931–1953*, Berlin: Duncker and Humblot, 1993.

[38] Hilberg, *Destruction*, vol. 1, pp. 136–38.

[39] Claus Füllberg-Stolberg, '"Wie mir bekannt geworden ist, beabsichtigen Sie auszuwandern...", Die Rolle der Oberfinanzdirektion Hannover bei der Vertreibung der Juden', in Carl-Hans Hauptmeyer, Dariusz Adamczyk, Beate Eschment, and Udo Obal, eds. *Die Welt querdenken*, Frankfurt: Peter Lang, 2003, pp. 219–34; Gerd Blumberg, 'Etappen der Verfolgung und Ausraubung und ihre bürokratische Apparatur', in Alfons Kenkmann and Bernd-A. Rusinek, eds., *Verfolgung und Verwaltung: Die wirtschaftliche Ausplünderung der Juden und die westfälischen Finanzbehörden*, Münster: Oberfinanzdirektion Münster, 1999.

and German Honour' (*Gesetz zum Schutze des deutschen Blutes und der deutschen Ehre*).[40] Nor was there an end of it. Implementation decrees were issued throughout the years until 1943.[41]

Persecutions and extralegal riots, assaults, robberies, and destruction of property, and general repression continued.[42] Incidents in 1935 produced mounting calls for both more radical persecution and moderation.

When the former economics minister and *Reichsbank* president Hjalmar Schacht was on trial in Nuremberg in 1945 and 1946, he explained that he had accepted the Economics Ministry in 1934 (3 August 1934–26 November 1937) in spite of the events of 30 June and 1 July because the only position from which one might attempt to influence policy and possibly to criticise and change it was a position inside the government itself.[43] Schacht was defending himself, of course, against the charge of conspiracy to wage a war of aggression, and he tried to explain his position and his role in Hitler's government. He could not deny that he had collaborated on the economic side in Germany's re-armament. Whether he then believed, as he suggested, that Hitler only wanted peace is open to doubt.[44] He explained plausibly enough, however, that he could raise any objections to Hitler's policy only on grounds relevant to his official function as economics minister and president of the *Reichsbank*, and that he had to cite the grave damage to his foreign-trade policy, which the hostility toward the churches, the unlawful treatment of the Jews, and the general arbitrariness of the *Gestapo* regime caused.[45] Schacht considered

[40] 'Reichsbürgergesetz. Vom 15. September 1935', in *Reichsgesetzblatt Teil I Jahrgang 1935*, Berlin: Reichsverlagsamt, 1935 (*RGBl. I 1935*), p. 1146; 'Gesetz zum Schutze des deutschen Blutes und der deutschen Ehre. Vom 15. September 1935', in *RGBl. I 1935*, pp. 1146–47; 'Erste Verordnung zum Reichsbürgergesetz. Vom 14. November 1935', in *RGBl. I 1935*, pp. 1333–34; 'Erste Verordnung zur Ausführung des Gesetzes zum Schutze des deutschen Blutes und der deutschen Ehre. Vom 14. November 1935', in *RGBl. I 1935*, pp. 1334–36; 'Zweite Verordnung zum Reichsbürgergesetz. Vom 21. Dezember 1935', in *RGBl. I 1935*, p. 1524–25. The terms of the 'Reichsbürgergesetz' have been widely misread; see Richard Breitman and Alan M. Kraut, *American Refugee Policy and European Jewry, 1933–1945*, Bloomington: Indiana University Press, 1987, p. 52.

[41] 'Verordnung zur Ausführung des Gesetzes zur Verhütung von Missbräuchen auf dem Gebiete der Rechtsberatung. Vom 13. Dezember 1935', in *RGBl. I 1935*, p. 1481–82; 'Dreizehnte Verordnung zum Reichsbürgergesetz. Vom 1. Juli 1943', in *RGBl. 1943 I*, p. 372.

[42] Kershaw, *Hitler: 1889–1936: Hubris*, p. 562.

[43] *Der Prozess gegen die Hauptkriegsverbrecher vor dem Internationalen Militärgerichtshof Nürnberg 14. November 1945–1. Oktober 1946*, vol. 12, Nuremberg: Sekretariat des Gerichtshofs, 1947, p. 503.

[44] *Prozess* 12: 505.

[45] *Prozess* 12: 560.

the regime's anti-Jewish policy 'a mistake'.[46] He handed Hitler a memorandum during a trial journey of the new capital ship *Scharnhorst* on 3 May 1935, written in terms ostensibly agreeing with the general line of an anti-Jewish policy, but sharply critical of 'the unbridled antagonism vented upon individual Jews, not merely illegally but against the explicit Government decree which guarantees to the Jew the opportunity of engaging in business', and of 'the agonizing persecution of Jewish individuals'. All this, he wrote, was causing 'an ever-repeated tightening of the Jewish boycott of German exports'. Hitler's vague reassurances to Schacht did not satisfy him. Schacht hoped, as he said later, to 'contain' the anti-Jewish agitation and persecution by confining anti-Jewish policy to the legal process.[47] He went further in criticising the anti-Jewish policies in his Königsberg speech on 18 August 1935, within the terms prevailing in the dictatorship and in the expectation that he would be able to publish his speech within these limits. He denounced Nazis who 'at night heroically smeared on windows and pilloried every German who shopped in a Jewish business as a national traitor', and who indiscriminately attacked the entire Catholic and Lutheran clergy. He pointed out that by law, and according to statements by Hitler's deputy as party leader, Rudolf Hess, and by Minister of the Interior Wilhelm Frick and Propaganda Minister Goebbels, and of course Economics Minister Schacht, Jewish businesses were allowed to operate. Schacht said,

> The Jews must realize that their influence is gone for all times. We desire to keep our people and our culture pure and distinctive, just as the Jews have always demanded this of themselves since the time of the prophet Ezra. But the solution of these problems must be brought about under state leadership, and cannot be left to unregulated individual actions, which mean a grave disturbance of the economy and which therefore again and again have been prohibited by state as well as Party agencies.

Confidence in Germany as a state with the rule of law, he continued, is indispensable for the conduct of our economic policy, and Jews, too, must

[46] Schacht to McDonald in New York, 13 May 1933; McDonald, *Advocate*, p. 68.

[47] Kershaw (*Hitler: 1889–1936: Hubris*, p. 563) cites Adam, *Judenpolitik im Dritten Reich*, p. 123, who cites Helmut Genschel, *Die Verdrängung der Juden aus der Wirtschaft im Dritten Reich*, Göttingen, Berlin, Frankfurt, Zurich: Musterschmidt Verlag, 1966, p. 111, who cites Schacht; see Hjalmar Schacht, *76 Jahre meines Lebens*, Bad Wörishofen: Kindler und Schiermeyer Verlag, 1953, pp. 437–39. See English Translation in Hjalmar Schacht, *My First Seventy-Six Years*, London: Allan Wingate, 1955, pp. 346–48; Schacht quotes verbatim from his memorandum, presumably from a copy then still in his possession.

not be subject to arbitrary despotism but to law.[48] National radio broadcast Schacht's speech, this alerted Goebbels, and he forbade its being printed in newspapers. Schacht, however, had 250,000 copies printed at the *Reichsbank* Printing Office and distributed them through the four hundred *Reichsbank* branches throughout the land. Goebbels called the speech 'impudent', a 'provocative speech à la Papen', in which Schacht 'had defended his semitism'.[49]

In the summer of 1935, Hitler saw that he had to make a decision, or lose control. The 'Nuremberg Race Laws' were promulgated on 15 September 1935: the '*Reich* Citizen Law' (*Reichsbürgergesetz*) and the 'Law for the Protection of German Blood and German Honour' (*Gesetz zum Schutze des deutschen Blutes und der deutschen Ehre*).

The '*Reich* Citizen Law' (*Reichsbürgergesetz*) used a legally meaningless term to distinguish between persons of 'German and ethnically-kindred[50] blood' and others, to separate 'Jews' from 'Germans'. *Reichsbürger*, literally '*Reich* citizen', or '*Reich* burgher', was explicitly not an equivalent of *Staatsangehöriger*, literally 'member of the state' or 'subject of the state'.[51] As far as German law was concerned, German persons defined

[48] Hjalmar Schacht, *Rede des Reichsbankpräsidenten und beauftragten Reichswirtschaftsministers Dr. Hjalmar Schacht auf der Deutschen Ostmesse. Königsberg, am 18. August 1935*, Berlin: Reichsbank, 1935, pp. 9–11; cf. *Prozess* 12: 561–62.

[49] Goebbels, *Tagebücher I, 3/I*, pp. 279–81 (21 August 1935). On 24 December 1935, Schacht wrote to the war minister, General (*Generaloberst*) Werner von Blomberg, that 'the economic-and legal-policy treatment of the Jews, the anti-church movement of certain Party organizations, and the judicial arbitrariness grouped about the *Gestapo* constituted an impairment of our armaments tasks'. *Prozess* 12: 562. Three years later, Göring as plenipotentiary for the Four-Year Plan found it necessary to inveigh against 'Aryanisation' of Jewish businesses and assets in the carryings-on of 'wild commissioners' as in Austria, where there were still 2 billion *Reich* Marks worth of Jewish assets. There had been 20,000 party commissioners operating in Austria, and in October 1938 there were still 3,500 of them, all of them worthless; the 'liquidation of the Jewish Question' must not be treated as a pension scheme for incompetent party members (*Prozess* 27 [1948]: 163).

[50] German: *artverwandt* can also be translated as congeneric.

[51] 'Reichsbürgergesetz', in *RGBl. I 1935*, p. 1146; 'Gesetz zum Schutze des deutschen Blutes', in *RGBl. I 1935*, pp. 1146–47; 'Erste Verordnung zum Reichsbürgergesetz[...]14. November 1935', in *RGBl. I 1935*, pp. 1333–34; 'Erste Verordnung zur Ausführung des Gesetzes zum Schutze des deutschen Blutes und der deutschen Ehre. Vom 14. November 1935', in *RGBl. I 1935*, pp. 1334–36; 'Zweite Verordnung zum Reichsbürgergesetz. Vom 21. Dezember 1935', in *RGBl. I 1935*, p. 1524–25; cf. Lothar Gruchmann, '"Blutschutzgesetz" und Justiz: Zur Entstehung und Auswirkung des Nürnberger Gesetzes vom 15. September 1935', *Vierteljahrshefte für Zeitgeschichte* 31 (1983): 418–42; Jeremy Noakes and Geoffrey Pridham, *Documents on Nazism, 1919–1945*, New York: The Viking Press, 1974, pp. 463–67. The terms of the 'Reichsbürgergesetz' are widely misread; see Breitman and Kraut, *American Refugee Policy*, p. 52.

as Jews did not lose their German state citizenship (*Staatsangehörigkeit*) through the 1935 Nuremberg Race Laws, or any other laws. In November 1941 a further change stipulated loss of citizenship for Jews who lived abroad or crossed the German border into another country.[52] The '*Reich* Citizen Law' states explicitly that German state citizenship, or being a German subject (*Staatsangehöriger*), 'is acquired according to the terms of the *Reich* Citizenship Law [*Reichs- und Staatsangehörigkeitsgesetz*]' of 1913, namely, by birth, legitimisation, marriage, acceptance, or naturalisation.[53] The '*Reich* Citizen Law' and its first implementation decree (*Erste Verordnung zum Reichsbürgergesetz*) marginalised Jews who were German state citizens (*Staatsangehörige*), by depriving them of the right to 'vote in political matters' and to hold public office, but it did not infringe upon their German state citizenship.

The 'Law for the Protection of German Blood and German Honour' (*Gesetz zum Schutze des deutschen Blutes und der deutschen Ehre*) prohibited marriages and any other intimate relations between non-Jews and Jews. It forbade Jews to employ female domestic servants of 'German and ethnically-kindred[54] blood' under the age of forty-five, and it forbade Jews from showing the German national flag.[55]

The promulgation of the Nuremberg Race Laws produced fresh concern and perturbation abroad. After 15 September 1935, Hitler warned party activists against taking direct economic actions against Jews. At the same time, however, and in the same context, he said that 'in case of war on all fronts, he would be ready for all the consequences'.[56] High Commissioner McDonald had an acute sense of direct danger to the Jews. On 10 October 1935, he told Felix Warburg, the leading American Zionist, that 'there can be no future for Jews in Germany'.[57]

52 'Elfte Verordnung zum Reichsbürgergesetz. Vom 25. November 1941', in *RGBl. 1941 I*, pp. 722–24.

53 'Reichsbürgergesetz', in *RGBl. I 1935*, p. 1146; 'Reichs- und Staatsangehörigkeitsgesetz. Vom 22 Juli 1913' (*RuStAG*), in *Reichs-Gesetzblatt: 1913*, Berlin: Herausgegeben im Reichsamte des Innern. Zu beziehen durch alle Postanstalten, n.d., §§ 3–16.

54 German: *artverwandt* can also be translated as congeneric.

55 'Gesetz zum Schutze des deutschen Blutes', in *RGBl. I 1935*, pp. 1146–47.

56 The editors of James G. McDonald's *Refugees and Rescue: The Diaries and Papers of James G. McDonald 1935–1945*, ed. by Richard Breitman, Barbara McDonald Stewart, and Severin Hochberg, Bloomington and Indianapolis: Indiana University Press, 2009, p. 29, cite Philippe Burrin, *Hitler and the Jews: The Genesis of the Holocaust*, New York: Hodder Arnold, 1994, pp. 48–49 (verified in the edition with the same title, London, Melbourne, Auckland: Edward Arnold, A member of the Hodder Headline Group, 1994).

57 McDonald, *Refugees*, pp. 43–45.

There was no sustained, concerted, or at all widespread opposition to the regime's anti-Jewish policies. There were eruptions from time to time: The theologian Dietrich Bonhoeffer published a critique entitled 'The Church and the Jewish Question' in two separate periodicals in June and September 1933 (Goebbels' control of other than mainstream publications was not yet complete);[58] on 4 June 1936, the Provisional Board of the German Evangelical Church and the Council of the German Evangelical Church/Confessing Church, a secession from the established Lutheran Church, sent Hitler a memorandum that deplored antisemitism and anti-Jewish policies;[59] Julius von Jan in a sermon on 16 November 1938 condemned the pogrom; the Old Prussian Confessing Church Synod's Council of Brethren instructed all its pastors to read from the pulpits on Repentance Day in November 1943 a text including the statement that it was wrong 'to kill men because they are regarded as unworthy to live, or because they belong to another race'.[60]

In the summer of 1936, after the Franco-Russian Pact of 1935 was ratified in 1936, after the re-militarisation of the Rhineland, after the outbreak of the Spanish Civil War, and during the Olympic Summer Games in Berlin, Hitler dictated his second Four-Year Plan. He predicted war against the Soviet Union and possibly against France and Britain. Therefore, the German economy and Armed Forces must be ready for war in four years, the war economy must be independent of imports as much as possible and develop all domestic resources regardless of cost, and raw materials and foodstuffs will be secured by the expansion of living space (*Lebensraum*) – war will create the supplies needed for more war. Hitler explicitly rejected any suggestion of limiting national re-armament, and he rejected Economics Minister Schacht's objection that the armaments costs would be economically too damaging.[61] When the main features of

[58] Hoffmann, *Behind Valkyrie*, pp. 137–55; cf. Dietrich Bonhoeffer, *Dietrich Bonhoeffer Works*, vol. 12, Philadelphia: Fortress Press, 2009, pp. 361–70.

[59] Hoffmann, *Behind Valkyrie*, pp. 101–16.

[60] Eberhard Bethge, *Dietrich Bonhoeffer: Theologian, Christian, Contemporary*, London: Collins, 1970, p. 613.

[61] Treue, 'Hitlers Denkschrift', pp. 184–210; *Völkischer Beobachter* 10 September 1936, pp. 1–2; Schacht in 'Niederschrift des Ministerrates am 12.5.36, 17 Uhr', and 'Niederschrift des Ministerrates am 27.5.36, 11³⁰ Uhr', in *Prozess* 27 (1948): 135–43–48. Schacht went so far, on 2 September 1936, before Hitler spoke at the annual *NSDAP* Nuremberg rally, as to implore Colonel Georg Thomas, the head of Armed Forces Economic Staff and Weaponry (*Wehrwirtschaftsstab und Waffenwesen [W]*, later *Wehrwirtschafts- und Rüstungs-Amt im Oberkommando des Heeres*), to ask the war minister, Field Marshal von Blomberg, to impress upon the *Führer* that telling the world that Germany was going it alone economically was 'to choke our own throat', and that domestic raw materials were

Hitler's plan were published in September, one of the points in Hitler's memorandum was not published; it contained one of Hitler's most fanatically pursued aims:

> But I further consider it necessary to make an immediate investigation into the outstanding debts in foreign exchange owed to German business abroad. There is no doubt that the outstanding claims of German business are today quite enormous. Nor is there any doubt that behind this in some cases there lies concealed the contemptible desire to possess, whatever happens, certain reserves abroad which are thus withheld from the grasp of the domestic economy. I regard this as deliberate sabotage of our national self-assertion and of the defence of the Reich, and for this reason I consider it necessary for the Reichstag to pass the following two laws:
>
> 1) A law providing the death penalty for economic sabotage, and
> 2) A law making the whole of Jewry liable for all damage inflicted by individual specimens of this community of criminals upon the German economy, and thus upon the German people.[62]

The first of these laws was promulgated on 1 December 1936. It stated that 'whoever, for base motives and contrary to law shifts assets to foreign countries or leaves assets in foreign countries and thereby severely damages the German economy, shall be punished by death'.[63] As far as is known, the second law was never drafted. It was not necessary. That Jews were economic saboteurs had been proclaimed year after year.

On 5 November 1937, Hitler announced to the commanders in chief of the army (General Werner Freiherr von Fritsch), the navy (Admiral Erich Raeder), and the air force (General Hermann Göring), and to the war minister (Field Marshal Werner von Blomberg) and the foreign minister (Konstantin von Neurath), that he would incorporate Austria and wage war against Czechoslovakia in the near future. Hitler's *Wehrmacht* adjutant, Colonel Friedrich Hossbach, wrote minutes, hence the meeting became known as the 'Hossbach Conference'. All except the commander-in-chief of the navy expressed reservations about Hitler's programme. By 4 February 1938, intrigues had eliminated the foreign minister, the commander-in-chief of the army, and the war minister and

'much too expensive to be used in export and export alone enabled further armaments'; Thomas, 'Notiz', *Prozess* 27 (2 September 1936): 155–56. Cf. Wolfgang Michalka, ed., *'Volksgemeinschaft' und Grossmachtpolitik*, Munich: Deutscher Taschenbuch Verlag, 1985, pp. 187–88.

62 *Documents on German Foreign Policy 1918–1945. Series C (1933–1937)*, vol. 5, London: HMSO, 1966, (*DGFP C V*), no. 490, pp. 853–62, here p. 861; *Völkischer Beobachter* (10 September 1936): 1–2.

63 *Reichsgesetzblatt. Teil I. Jahrgang 1936*, Berlin: Reichsverlagsamt, 1936, p. 999.

his position altogether. Hitler as *Führer* now combined the war ministry with the chancellorship and the presidency. The commander-in-chief of the army was replaced by a general willing to do Hitler's bidding.

Hitler's next steps, the annexation of Austria on 12 March 1938 and the annexation of the Sudeten Land from Czechoslovakia in October 1938, were peaceful armed invasions, the first one accompanied by Austrian cheers and half-hearted protests from some powers, the second by British and French threats of military intervention and then by international approval in the Munich Agreement of 30 September 1938. On 15 March 1939, Hitler broke the agreement and had troops occupy the rest of Czechia. On 31 March 1939, Prime Minister Neville Chamberlain announced in the House of Commons that His Majesty's government would 'at once lend the Polish government all support in their power' if, in the event of any action that clearly threatened Polish independence, the Polish government considered it vital to resist with their national forces.[64]

Hitler hoped to deter British and French intervention and lay to rest any Soviet apprehensions through making a pact with Stalin to divide Poland with him. But when he attacked Poland on 1 September 1939, Britain, France, Australia, India, and New Zealand declared war on Germany on 3 September, the Union of South Africa on 6 September, and Canada on 10 September. On 17 September the Soviet generals Kovalev with an army group of four armies and Timoshenko with three armies invaded Poland and advanced to the agreed line. Britain refused to acquiesce to this state of affairs, so that Hitler decided to 'eliminate' France and Britain before embarking upon his main war against the Soviet Union and the Jews, although he seemed barely able to wait before launching a comprehensive campaign of murder against the Jews, as events in Poland indicate.

In May and June 1940, German forces invaded Luxembourg, Belgium, the Netherlands, and France. After the defeat of France, after having failed to defeat Britain, Hitler began his main war for *Lebensraum* against the Soviet Union on 22 June 1941. Initial successes notwithstanding, the offensive stalled and faltered. A last desperate assault on Moscow began on 2 October 1941 as 'Operation Taifun'. It caused the Soviet government to evacuate to Kuibyshev, but Stalin remained in Moscow. Mud, then frost, slowed the German advance. By 2 December the German Army Group

[64] *The Parliamentary Debates*, 5th series, vol. 345: *House of Commons, official report*, London: His Majesty's Stationery Office, 1939, col. 2415.

Centre reached the outskirts of Moscow, but the troops were exhausted. On 2 December temperatures dropped to –25° C, and on 5 December to –38° C. The German armies in Russia were barely able to survive.

The United States of America meanwhile provided support to Britain, including naval incidents designed to provoke German reactions. President Roosevelt told Prime Minister Winston Churchill during their meetings in Placentia Bay in August 1941 that 'he would wage war, but not declare it, and that he would become more and more provocative', and that 'he would look for an 'incident' which would justify him in opening hostilities'.[65] The Atlantic Charter of 14 August 1941 that Roosevelt and Churchill signed in Placentia Bay threatened Germany with disarmament. After Japan's attack upon Pearl Harbor (7 December 1941), Germany declared war on the United States (11 December 1941). Hitler hoped Japan would keep America from intervening in Europe until he had defeated Russia, but he knew that this was a faint hope and that he could not win the war.

The crimes of the National Socialist dictatorship in Germany from 1933 to 1945 prompted the elaboration of opposing concepts based upon the rule of law and resulted in the resistance of a socially and politically representative although numerically small group of Germans with the goal of terminating Hitler's criminal regime.

Resistance emerged in many forms, both passive and active, at all levels of society. Some civil servants sought to modify decrees and laws in an effort to protect some of the persecuted, clergymen insisted on their pastoral prerogatives and duties, and labourers and intellectuals engaged in underground agitation against the regime and its policies.[66] The resisters were a small minority, diminished by the tens of thousands of regime opponents murdered or imprisoned in concentration camps. Joseph Goebbels, *Reich* minister for public enlightenment and propaganda, complained in his diary in October 1941 that 'our intellectual and society classes have suddenly re-discovered their humanitarian feelings for the wretched Jews', referring to widespread disapproval of the deportations from Berlin. The minister also noted that 'the Jews are still

[65] Martin Gilbert, *Winston S. Churchill*, vol. 6, London: Heinemann, 1983, p. 1168.

[66] Peter Longerich, *'Davon haben wir nichts gewusst!' Die Deutschen und die Judenverfolgung 1933–1945*, Munich: Pantheon, 2007, pp. 183–85, cites Goebbels' diary for 28 October 1941; see Joseph Goebbels, *Die Tagebücher von Joseph Goebbels. Teil II. Diktate 1941–1945. Band 2. Oktober-Dezember 1941*, Munich, New Providence, London, Paris: K.G. Saur, 1996, pp. 194–95 (28 October 1941). Cf. Anne Nelson, *Red Orchestra*, New York: Random House, 2009.

finding powerful protectors in the highest national authorities', and that the deportations were unpopular in Germany.[67] There was, however, no mass disaffection. Effective resistance could come only from inside the higher levels of government, and military support would be indispensable for any chance of removing the dictatorship.

Motivations for resistance had a common denominator: removal of a pernicious regime. While Communists, however, aimed at replacing one dictatorship with another, the non-Communist resistance was concerned above all to restore the rule of law, civil liberties, social justice, and the integrity of the national existence and territory. The persecution of the Jews was a concern to most. These Germans saw the persecution, mistreatment, and eventual systematic murder of the Jews as the most heinous crime of the National Socialist state. While the *SS* (*Schutzstaffel*), Secret State Police (*Geheime Staatspolizei*, *Gestapo*), and other agencies involved in the mass murder of the Jews tried to keep their operations secret, many in the army during the war in the Soviet Union and many bystanders in German towns and in the countryside were witnesses and often enough accomplices. In an attempt to make the population as a whole accomplices in the regime's murderous enterprises, official and semi-official public statements indicated what the regime was doing.[68] On 27 February 1942, the party newspaper *Völkischer Beobachter* quoted Hitler: 'The Jew will be exterminated!' Goebbels said in his weekly lead article of 14 June 1942 in *Das Reich*: 'The Jews play their malicious game in this war, and they will have to pay for it with the extermination of their race in Europe and perhaps far beyond it'.[69] There were many such public references, and there were reports from soldiers on leave who had seen massacres, such as the execution of an entire trainload of Jews in open terrain in Poland. Too few had the moral conviction and courage to risk being themselves sent to a concentration camp and murdered to dare to protest openly – although some did: The Scholl Group of students in 1942/1943 and the spouses of Jews who protested outside a deportation-collection house in Rosenstrasse in Berlin in March 1943 are examples.[70] In the anti-Hitler conspiracy that culminated in the 20

[67] Goebbels, *Tagebücher, Teil II, Diktate 1941–1945*, 2, pp. 194–95 (28 October 1941).

[68] Longerich, *Davon*, pp. 182–262; p. 200 cites Hitler's message commemorating the founding of the party on 24 February 1920 in *Völkischer Beobachter* 27 February 1942, under the headline 'Der Jude wird ausgerottet werden!'

[69] Longerich, *Davon*, pp. 201, 213.

[70] Cf. C.Moll, 'Acts of Resistance: The White Rose in the Light of New Archival Evidence', in Michael Geyer and John W. Boyer, eds., *Resistance Against the Third Reich, 1933–1990*, Chicago: University of Chicago Press, 1994; Inge Scholl, *Students Against Tyranny*,

July 1944 coup d'état, there were regime opponents who acknowledged a 'Jewish Problem' and a need to deal with it, and others who were uncompromising in their opposition to any discrimination against the Jews, but all of them deprecated the regime's crimes and methods. The *Gestapo*, after months of interrogations and investigations following the 20 July 1944 coup d'état, summarised its findings:

> The entire inner alienation from the ideas of National Socialism that characterised the men of the reactionary conspiratorial circle expresses itself above all in their position on the Jewish Question [...] they stubbornly take the liberal position of granting to the Jews in principle the same status as to every German.[71]

Carl Goerdeler was among these, 'the men of the reactionary conspiratorial circle'.

The following three chapters will establish the background and antecedents of the situation in which Goerdeler conceived his rescue plan for the Jews. Chapter 2 will sketch Goerdeler's career, and Chapter 3 will set the scene for and describe Goerdeler's activities on behalf of the Jews. Chapter 4 will establish the context of the conspiracy whose civil leader was Goerdeler. Chapters 5, 6, 7, and 8 will contain the text of the plan, the examination of its meaning, and the resulting conclusions.

Middletown: Wesleyan University Press, 1970; Annette E. Dumbach, *Shattering the German Night: The Story of the White Rose*, Boston: Little, Brown, 1986; Nathan Stoltzfus, *Resistance of the Heart: Intermarriage and the Rosenstrasse Protest in Nazi Germany*, New York: W.W. Norton, 1996; Antonia Leugers, ed., *Berlin, Rosenstrasse 2–4. Protest in der NS-Diktatur: Neue Forschungen zum Frauenprotest in der Rosenstrasse 1943*, Annweiler: Plöger, 2005.

71 *Spiegelbild einer Verschwörung: Die Kaltenbrunner-Berichte an Bormann und Hitler über das Attentat vom 20. Juli 1944: Geheime Dokumente aus dem ehemaligen Reichssicherheitshauptamt*, Stuttgart: Seewald Verlag, 1961, pp. 449–50, 457, 471; see below at p. 132n33; Hans Mommsen, 'Der Widerstand gegen Hitler und die nationalsozialistische Judenverfolgung', in Hans Mommsen, *Alternative zu Hitler: Studien zur Geschichte des deutschen Widerstandes*, Munich: Verlag C.H. Beck, 2000, pp. 386–91. Hans Mommsen, *Alternatives to Hitler: German Resistance under the Third Reich*, London, New York: I.B. Tauris, 2003, pp. 258–62, esp. 259.

2

Carl Goerdeler

Carl Friedrich Goerdeler was born in Schneidemühl in Posen on 31 July 1884 as the son of a circuit judge.[1] He grew up in Schneidemühl (now Piła in Poland), and from the age of six in Marienwerder, an administrative town in the province of West Prussia, now Kwidzyn in northern Poland, where his father was transferred. His father also represented the district in the Prussian Legislative Assembly (*Landtag*) for the Free Conservative Party (*Freikonservative Partei*), a party of the elite that generally supported the government; after the First World War, its members and supporters tended to find themselves in the German National People's Party (*Deutschnationale Volkspartei, DNVP*). There prevailed in the Goerdeler home an atmosphere of the old-Prussian conservative civil-service value system of duty, frugality, integrity, and confidence in the consolidated power of the Prussian monarchy. History and politics held centre stage in day-to-day family discourse, but literary and other cultural interests were not neglected. From 1902 Goerdeler studied law in Tübingen for three semesters, then moved to the University of Königsberg, where he completed his studies in 1905. He then served in Königsberg's No. 16 Field Artillery Regiment. When he had passed his law examinations and by 1911 completed a dissertation on the concept of legal responsibility, he volunteered in a bank formerly named *Preussische Seehandlung*, from 1904 *Königliche Seehandlung* (after 1918 *Preussische Staatsbank*).

[1] The following overview of Goerdeler's education and early career is based on Gerhard Ritter, *Carl Goerdeler und die deutsche Widerstandsbewegung*, Stuttgart: Deutsche Verlags-Anstalt, 1954, pp. 21–46.

He decided against a career as a judge and chose municipal administration instead. Here he saw scope for his creative energy, his desire to improve peoples' lives, his profound sense of compassion as well as justice, and his faith in the employment of fiscal and economic rationality. On 1 October 1911, he began working in the municipal administration of Solingen in the west German industrial region, soon rising to deputy mayor. In the First World War, from 4 August 1914 to 31 January 1919, he served on the eastern front, at its end with the rank of captain in 10th Army staff under its Commander-in-Chief General Erich von Falkenhayn.[2] Here Goerdeler was charged with the administration of White Russia and Lithuania, where he restored the finances – the Bolsheviks had emptied the coffers – and provided for the material and cultural needs of the population to such an astonishing degree that General von Falkenhayn praised his brilliant work and great humanity as most exceptional. Goerdeler had direct knowledge of some of the anti-Jewish atrocities in Poland. The killings in the years 1918–1921 were in many cases condoned or even encouraged by the respective governments.[3] Whether or not Goerdeler was aware of the high number of murders in these years, he was certainly surrounded in Poland throughout these years by widespread, continuing pogroms, beatings, lootings, destruction, and murders committed against Jews. Twenty-three years later, Goerdeler's 1918 experiences heightened his outrage at the brutal mistreatment of the Russian population by German occupiers.

In the spring of 1919, he returned from his post on the Dnjepr. The monarchy to which he had felt attached had vanished, and he hesitated

[2] Gerhard Ritter, *The German Resistance: Carl Goerdeler's Struggle against Tyranny*, Salem NH: Ayer Company, 1992 (reprinted from New York: Praeger, 1958), pp. 18–20; Ines Reich, *Carl Friedrich Goerdeler: Ein Oberbürgermeister gegen den NS-Staat*, Cologne, Weimar, Vienna: Böhlau Verlag, 1997, pp. 73–74. Falkenhayn died in 1922; Henning von Tresckow married Falkenhayn´s daughter Erika in 1926.

[3] Trude Maurer, *Ostjuden in Deutschland 1918–1933*, Hamburg: Hans Christians Verlag, 1986, pp. 51–57 bases the number of 150,000 killed on Salo W. Baron, *The Russian Jew under Tsars and Soviets*, New York, London: Macmillan, 1964, pp. 219 et seq., and in the 2nd ed. (New York: Macmillan, 1976; London: Collier Macmillan, 1976, p. 184), the numbers given are for Ukraine ('easily exceeding 50,000 slain') and including those who later died from wounds and illnesses contracted in the disturbances 'may well have reached 150,000'. Chimen Abramsky ('The Biro-Bidzhan Project, 1927–1959', in Lionel Kochan, ed., *The Jews in Soviet Russia since 1917*, 3rd ed., Oxford, London, New York: Oxford University Press, 1978, pp. 64–66) accepts an estimate of 200,000 killed in pogroms in the Ukraine alone in 1917–1921; Helmut Pieper (*Die Minderheitenfrage und das Deutsche Reich 1919–1933/34* [D 7 Göttinger philosophische Dissertation], Hamburg: Alfred Metzner Verlag, 1974, pp. 10–11) merely cites Paul Mantoux, *Les délibérations du Conseil des Quatre (24 mars–28 juin 1919): Notes de l'Officier Interprète*, vol. 1, Paris: Éditions du Centre National de la Recherche Scientifique, 1955, pp. 440–41.

to serve in the republic – especially in the west German industrial heartland, where radicals were numerous and British occupation was a heavy burden – before he did after all resume his work in Solingen in April 1919. In June 1919 in the weeks before the signing of the Treaty of Versailles, he took leave to go to his West Prussian homeland. There were parliamentary action committees, multipartisan people's councils, and militia formations, all seeking to prevent the cession of territory to the newly created Poland. The Social-Democrat *Reich* commissar for the East, August Winnig, on 15 June called upon the population to resist the treaty and if necessary to take up arms to save their honour. Some considered secession, an independent state; the mood in XVII Army Corps Command was martial. These conditions drew Goerdeler home. He and his brother Fritz reported for duty with No. 71 Field Artillery Regiment, but he was immediately dispatched to XVII Army Corps Command under Lieutenant-General (*General der Infanterie*) Otto von Below in Danzig as political liaison officer between Corps Command and Parliamentary Action Committee. When XVII Army Corps chief of staff Lieutenant-Colonel Stapff asked his view of the Eastern Question on 13 June, Goerdeler promptly composed his first 'Resistance' memorandum addressed to the XVII Army Corps Command staff officers:

1. The peace will be signed according to sentiments known to me in the West.
2. The only possibility of saving Germandom in the East and the East March for the *Reich* is the military defeat of Poland.
3. The necessity for the East to act independently follows from 1 and 2.
4. This action, if timely and militarily successful, will carry along the population even if the party leaders now are temporising.[4]

The matter was urgent; by 23 June the *Reichstag* had to decide whether to sign the treaty. Goerdeler kept urging all concerned to 'act', if need be against the authority of Supreme Army Command and the republican government. No 'action' materialised. Goerdeler was motivated by patriotic idealism (nowadays described with the pejorative 'nationalism') – by

[4] Goerdeler's memorandum on the territorial finances in the occupied territory of 10th Army from 20 February to 30 November 1918 (Die Landesfinanzen im besetzten Gebiet der X. Armee vom 20.2. bis 30.11.1918), Bundesarchiv Koblenz N 1113/11; Goerdeler's June 1919 memorandum – see Ritter, *Carl Goerdeler*, p. 27; also in Gillmann and Mommsen, *Politische Schriften*, pp. 191–98, with Goerdeler's report on his work from 13 to 26 June 1919 (Bundesarchiv, Nachlass Goerdeler N 1113 Band 10 Bll. 5–17).

faith in what he considered moral principles – and he showed not only his characteristic courage and uncompromising apodicticity, but also his tendency to pursue illusory aims.

In 1920 he returned to his career in municipal administration, for a few months in Solingen, but he wanted to be nearer his home, where he believed 'Germandom' (*Deutschtum*) must be upheld and defended. He applied unsuccessfully for the position of city treasurer in Königsberg, then successfully for the post of deputy mayor in that city. The Social Democrats suspected him of being a conservative nationalist and wanted a Social Democrat, but the city council elected him. At his induction on 11 February 1920, the Social Democrats left the assembly hall, but in the ten years he held the post, his work and his accomplishments thoroughly won them over.[5]

Goerdeler confessed later that he had been brought up in 'a narrow kind of nationalism' (*in einem Nationalismus enger Art*)[6] that he outgrew after 1930, as mayor of Leipzig, when he had much contact with foreigners and foreign countries. He accepted and supported the republic, after the initial pain of change and the loss of the patriarchic monarchy that had been politically and socially 'home'. He wrote in prison, in 1944, that it was unfair to simply say the republic had 'failed'; had it not, after all, beaten down the revolution? Soon after the shock and upheavals of the collapse of 1918–1920, Goerdeler and other administrators and politicians, as he put it,

> worked, worked, worked, forgot the family, slaved to master the turmoil, to cleanse the administration, to order, to modernize, to order the finances, to restore law, decency and duty, to remove housing shortages, to repair transport and utility services, to habituate to steady work those who had become unused to it, to remove the dictate of Versailles. How unjust is it, to overlook particularly this work and the successes achieved by Stresemann! There was nothing to be done with force, without an army, there remained only prudence![7]

Goerdeler continued his engagement in the *DNVP* in the 1920s, resigning his membership only in December 1931 because the party's platform conflicted with his responsibilities as *Reich* prices commissioner.[8] He did agitate against the 'Corridor', the Polish territory separating East Prussia from the rest of Germany, the effects of which he felt keenly

[5] Ritter, *Carl Goerdeler*, pp. 29–30.

[6] Ritter, *Carl Goerdeler*, p. 30; Gillmann and Mommsen, *Politische Schriften*, p. 1225.

[7] Gillmann and Mommsen, *Politische Schriften*, p. 1214; Ritter, *Carl Goerdeler*, p. 31.

[8] Gillmann and Mommsen, *Politische Schriften*, pp. 200–13.

as deputy mayor of East Prussia's capital. Königsberg was an outpost of 'Germandom' in the East, and focal point of German chancellor Gustav Stresemann's foreign policy. It was also the command centre of Military District I (*Wehrkreiskommando I*) and the 1st Division of the small German Army. The divisional commanders were Major-General (*Generalleutnant*) Wilhelm Heye (1923–1926); Major-General Friedrich Freiherr von Esebeck (1926–1929)[9]; and Brigadier, subsequently Major-General, Werner von Blomberg (1929–1930).[10] Ernst Siehr was the governor (*Oberpräsident*) of East Prussia (1920–1932). Goerdeler thus met and established contacts with important personages. He knew the later war minister, General von Blomberg; the later Commander-in-Chief of the Army (1934–1938) Brigadier Werner Freiherr von Fritsch; and the Chief of the General Staff of the Army (1933–1938) General Ludwig Beck from the time when Beck was artillery commander IV in Dresden.[11] He served on regional and national administrative bodies, including the German Cities' Conference (*Deutscher Städtetag*). As deputy chair of the Employers' Association of German Municipal Associations, he was involved in difficult wage negotiations, frequently having to travel between Königsberg and Berlin, and he came in contact with labour organisations and trades unions and became acquainted with their concerns. His engagement in efforts to reform the Prussian and German bureaucracy made him known and recognised nationally.[12] In 1930 his qualifications and extraordinary reputation as a municipal administrator in Königsberg secured him his election as mayor by the city council of Leipzig, one of the largest and economically most important German cities.

He served here, with growing links to all levels of German politics and administration, until his resignation in 1936 and departure from office in 1937. He advised the president of the republic, Paul von Hindenburg, as *Reich* prices commissioner (*Reichskommissar für die Preisüberwachung*) from December 1931 to December 1932. When Hindenburg dropped Chancellor Heinrich Brüning in May 1932, Brüning's successor Franz

9 *Genealogisches Handbuch der freiherrlichen Häuser: Freiherrliche Häuser A*, vol. 9, Limburg a.d. Lahn: C.A. Starke Verlag, 1975, p. 102.

10 Reichwehrministerium (Heeres-Personalamt), ed., *Rangliste des Deutschen Reichsheeres: Nach dem Stande vom 1. April 1923* [same title for 1 May 1927–1930], Berlin: E.S. Mittler and Sohn, 1923, 1927–30.

11 Gillmann and Mommsen, *Politische Schriften*, p. 1233; Klaus-Jürgen Müller, *Generaloberst Ludwig Beck: Eine Biographie*, Paderborn, Munich, Vienna, Zurich: Ferdinand Schöningh, 2008, p. 95 (Goerdeler mentions Beck as then-commander of the Infantry School in Dresden).

12 Ritter, *Carl Goerdeler*, pp. 31–32.

von Papen and President von Hindenburg urged Goerdeler to join Papen's cabinet as economics and labour minister. Goerdeler refused because of his lack of confidence in Papen. At the request of Hitler, he served again as *Reich* prices commissioner in 1934–1935.[13] In December 1932, he was mentioned as a successor to Papen as chancellor; but *Reichswehr* minister Major-General (*Generalleutnant*) Kurt von Schleicher had intrigued to make himself chancellor, not Goerdeler.[14] Goerdeler served on the boards of twenty-one organisations, on seven of them as chairman; they included the German Library (*Deutsche Bücherei*) in Leipzig, the German Municipal Conference (*Deutscher Gemeindetag*), the *Gewandhaus* executive, the German Mining Company at Olsnitz (*Gewerkschaft Deutschland*), the Saxon Music Conservatory (*Landeskonservatorium der Musik zu Leipzig*), municipal banking associations, the Permanent Settlement Advisory Board in the *Reich* Labour Ministry, and municipal housing associations.[15] From 1938 onward he was the recognised political leader of the clandestine opposition to Hitler and their candidate for chancellor.

Goerdeler had a powerful role in the government at its highest level. He had access to all cabinet ministers. On 30 June 1934, upon a request from the commander of No. 11 Infantry Regiment in Leipzig, Colonel Erich Friderici,[16] who had received an order to keep all troops in barracks and wanted to know whether the garrison was being used for political ends, Goerdeler rushed to see the war minister, Field Marshal von Blomberg,

[13] 10 December 1931–17 December 1932 and 5 November 1934–1 July 1935; *Die Regierung Hitler: Band II: 1934/35*, Munich: R. Oldenbourg Verlag, 1999, p. 133n4, p. 149n4; *Die Regierung Hitler: Band III: 1936*, Munich: R. Oldenbourg Verlag, 2002, p. 565n3; Ritter, *Carl Goerdeler*, pp. 21–30, 47, 57–60, 76. Reich (*Carl Friedrich Goerdeler*, p. 104) asserts that Goerdeler did not join the cabinet because his demand that two to three National Socialists be included was not adopted and cites as evidence Goerdeler's handwritten London account of 9 July 1937, Bundesarchiv Koblenz N 1113 B. 43 (Reich cites NL 1113 B. 12; the account is printed in Gillmann and Mommsen, pp. 240–59); but this, Goerdeler's account, does not say that. Goerdeler wrote (leaves 29–31), as one of three demands (none of which was adopted), that 'two to three cabinet posts should be offered to the N.S.D.A.P., and if it co-operated, so much the better'. Furthermore, Goerdeler wrote in his account (leaves 31–32), that he explained his refusal to join the cabinet to President von Hindenburg face to face by saying that Papen was unsuitable to head the government 'in such hard times'.

[14] Goerdeler, London account, leaves 38–43; Herbert Grundmann, *Die Zeit der Weltkriege* (Bruno Gebhardt, *Handbuch der deutschen Geschichte*, vol. 4), Stuttgart: Union Verlag, 2nd rev. repr., 1961, p. 173; Leo Just, *Handbuch der Deutschen Geschichte*, vol. 4, 1st part, Frankfurt: Akademische Verlagsgsellschaft Athenaion, 1973, p. 177.

[15] Minute, 28 January 1937, Stadtarchiv Leipzig, Kap. 10 G Nr. 685 Bd. 1.

[16] Reichwehrministerium (Heeres-Personalamt), ed., *Rangliste des Deutschen Reichsheeres: Nach dem Stande vom 1. Mai 1932*, Berlin: E.S. Mittler and Sohn, 1932.

Reich Chancellor Adolf Hitler at the foundation-stone-laying for the Richard Wagner National Monument in Leipzig on 6 March 1934. From left to right: *Reich* Postmaster and Minister of Transport Paul Freiherr Eltz von Rübenach; Chief of *Reich* Chancellery State Secretary Dr Hans-Heinrich Lammers; Vice Chancellor Franz von Papen; Frau Winifried Wagner; *Reich* Chancellor Adolf Hitler; Mayor of Leipzig Dr Carl Goerdeler; Saxon *Reich* Governor and Gauleiter Martin Mutschmann; *Reich* Minister for Popular Enlightenment and Propaganda Dr Joseph Goebbels. Bundesarchiv Bild 147-15591.

and was received by him on that day at 3:00 P.M.[17] When he asked for RM 2,400 per annum for expenses, Hitler decided that he was to be given the same expenses allowance as *Reich* ministers, RM 4,800 per annum.[18] Hitler received him on several occasions. Once, after a conference with Hitler in which he convinced the dictator to follow his, Goerdeler's, advice, in March 1935, Hitler then and there ordered the minister of the interior Wilhelm Fritsch to incorporate Goerdeler's points in a draft law, and then invited Goerdeler to lunch with him.[19] At a meeting with Hitler and Schacht at the end of June 1935 that Goerdeler had requested, Schacht and Goerdeler disagreed on financial policy, and Hitler essentially told them to work it out. Goerdeler said he needed his authority

[17] Gillmann and Mommsen, *Politische Schriften*, pp. 1211–12.
[18] *Regierung Hitler* 2, p. 111.
[19] Gillmann and Mommsen, *Politische Schriften*, pp. 1209–10.

expanded, and Hitler immediately agreed.[20] Goebbels called Goerdeler 'a clever head' and wanted Hitler to place him above the minister for agriculture, Walter Darré, whom Goebbels did not care for. In October 1936 he wanted Hitler to re-appoint Goerdeler as *Reich* prices commissioner.[21] In light of such experiences, it seemed reasonable to Goerdeler to expect that, given the chance, he could convince Hitler again.

He frequently gave advice, solicited and unsolicited, during and between his two terms as *Reich* prices commissioner, at times sarcastically tearing to shreds the draft proposals of others if he considered them unsound.[22] He commented upon unemployment benefits, energy management and prices, agricultural prices, a directed versus free economy, wages in the construction industry, housing, export, dumping, national railways, world supply of commodities, and municipal self-government. He always wrote and reasoned with the confidence of a man who knew his own expertise and superior understanding of fundamental human nature and of the forces driving the economy. He argued on the supposition that the government was open to rational argument, and that it wished to increase revenues and foreign-currency returns by exports. After the end of his second term as *Reich* prices commissioner, Goerdeler continued to write letters and memoranda. He wrote a letter to Hitler in April 1936 to protest against the destruction of the principle of municipal self-government, and he invoked the legacy of the reformer of Prussia in the Napoleonic era, Heinrich Friedrich Karl Freiherr von und zum Stein.[23]

When Hitler had prepared his long memorandum for the second Four-Year Plan, he charged Göring with the economic and armaments tasks set out in it (2 September 1936) and officially named him '*Reich* Commissioner for the Implementation of the Four-Year Plan' (*Reichskommissar für die Durchführung des Vierjahresplanes*) on 18 October. The new Four-Year Plan had been in preparation during the summer. *Der Herr Generaloberst*, as Göring was referred to in minutes of cabinet meetings, on 7 August 1936 requested memoranda on economic issues from several experts including

[20] To A.P. Young, (*The 'X' Documents*, ed. Sidney Aster, London: Andre Deutsch, 1974, p. 153). Young, who dated the meeting at 29 June; in his notes of January 1945 (Gillmann and Mommsen, *Politische Schriften*, p. 1210) he dates it at '27 or 28 June 1935'.

[21] Goebbels, *Tagebücher I Band 3/I*, pp. 132 (8 November 1934), 278 (19 August 1935), 279 (21 August 1935), 282–83 (25 and 27 August 1935); Goebbels, *Die Tagebücher von Joseph Goebbels*, part 1: *Band 3/II*, Munich: K.G. Saur, 2001, pp. 30 (2 March 1936), 105 (13 June 1936), 204 (6 October 1936).

[22] *Die Regierung Hitler*, part 1: *1933/34* [titles inconsistent within series], Boppard am Rhein: Harald Boldt Verlag, 1983, pp. 34, 343–49, 501–3, 1183–84; *Regierung Hitler II*, pp. 1141–42.

[23] *Regierung Hitler III*, pp. 242–44.

Goerdeler, retired State Secretary Ernst Trendelenburg, and Colonel Georg Thomas, the head of Armed Forces Economic Staff and Weaponry (*Wehrwirtschaftsstab und Waffenwesen (W)*, later *Wehrwirtschafts- und Rüstungs-Amt im Oberkommando des Heeres*).[24] Goerdeler was the first of them to send Göring an advance version of his memorandum, dated 31 August 1936, in which he argued for 'significant limitations of armaments'. When Göring presented the new Four-Year Plan in a ministerial council meeting on 4 September 1936, he said Goerdeler's memorandum was the only one received at that time and that it was 'completely useless'.[25]

No wonder: Goerdeler, whose homeland was East Prussia, acknowledged the need for Germany to re-arm; he strongly approved of the need to use armed force to regain the Polish Corridor and to resolve Germany's Eastern Question (*die Rückgewinnung des Korridors und die Bereinigung der deutschen Ostfrage*); he said the 'division of Germany into two separate territories' was intolerable. The resolution of the 'German Eastern Question cannot be achieved unless Germany could deploy the concentrated force of our nation'.[26] 'Which German whose homeland had become Polish would not give his life to remove this state of affairs? Never will the Pole, not even by way of compromise, voluntarily give up so much as a foot of the land that he now possesses'. But he wanted re-armament to be slowed in the interest of sound fiscal policy, balanced budgets, and sufficient exports to secure the necessary goods and raw materials required for re-armament, industrial and agricultural production, and the necessities of consumption.[27] The final version of

[24] Göring's appointment: 'Verordnung zur Durchführung des Vierjahresplanes [*sic*]. Vom 18. Oktober 1936', *RGBl. I. 1936*, p. 887; 'Gesetz zur Durchführung des Vierjahresplans – Bestellung eines Reichskommissars für die Preisbildung. Vom 29. Oktober 1936', *RGBl. I. 1936*, pp. 927–28; 'Erlass über die weiteren Aufgaben des Beauftragten für den Vierjahresplan. Vom 18. Oktober 1940', *RGBl. I. 1940*, Berlin: Reichsverlagsamt, 1940, p. 1395; 'Zweiter Erlass über die weiteren Aufgaben des Beauftragten für den Vierjahresplan. Vom 20. September 1944', *RGBl. I. 1944*, Berlin: Reichsverlagsamt, 1944, p. 211; Erich Gritzbach, *Hermann Göring: Werk und Mensch*, Munich: Zentralverlag der NSDAP, Franz Eher Nachf., 1939, pp. 160–61; Wolf Keilig, *Das deutsche Heer 1939–1945: Gliederung – Einsatz – Stellenbesetzung*, Bad Nauheim: Verlag Hans-Henning Podzun, 1956-[1970], pp. 211/339; Goerdeler, memorandum on the foreign-exchange, raw-materials, and currency situation, typed, with penciled corrections in Goerdeler's hand, 31 August 1936, in the author's possession.

[25] *Regierung Hitler III*, pp. 500–4.

[26] Goerdeler, memorandum 31 August 1936, esp. p. 12; Gillmann and Mommsen (*Politische Schriften*, p. 411) say that another copy is 'in the private possession of the Goerdeler family'; the full-length memorandum of 17 September 1936 is printed in Gillmann and Mommsen, *Politische Schriften*, pp. 411–64; see esp. 445, 447–48.

[27] Bundesarchiv Koblenz, N 1113 Band 26, titled 'Anlage', pp. 11–13; Gillmann and Mommsen, *Politische Schriften*, pp. 448, 1202, 1214–16.

the memorandum, submitted on 17 September, had as little impact as the preliminary version of 31 August. Both papers, however, contained Goerdeler´s strongest-yet proposals regarding the Jewish Question, and they will be further examined in Chapter 3.

Goerdeler resigned as mayor of Leipzig in the fall of 1936 in circumstances that also will be examined in Chapter 3. Robert Bosch, the company founder and an opponent of National Socialism, employed Goerdeler as a consultant residing in Berlin.[28] Goerdeler conducted business for Bosch with the Wallenberg brothers, Marcus and Jacob, the owners of Stockholms Enskilda Bank. The Wallenbergs' Stockholms Enskilda Bank succeeded Fritz Mannheimer of Mendelssohn & Company in Berlin and later Amsterdam as custodian of Bosch interests, and in 'cloaking' assets of Bosch, particularly shares of American Bosch Corporation in Springfield, Massachusetts, against confiscation in case of war. After the war, the Wallenberg brothers had assistance from John Foster and Alan Welsh Dulles in efforts to recover assets for Bosch.[29] In office or out of office, Goerdeler still had extraordinary connections. Since he had to travel at least ten times to Stockholm on business, he had a cover for his attempts to prevent and later to end the war and the crimes and outrages committed by the National Socialists.[30] He warned foreign governments of Hitler's intentions and drew up peace proposals. These had little weight coming from one without standing in the German government; after the war had begun, they were incompatible with Allied war aims.[31]

Fearless and untiring, Goerdeler worked to assemble a coalition of opponents of the regime, including military commanders.[32] His involvement in preparations for the overthrow of the regime reached a feverish pitch by December 1941, as he was composing a ninety-nine-page memorandum called 'The Aim' (*Das Ziel*) to lay the foundations for the post-Hitler state. This memorandum contains Goerdeler's plan

[28] Joachim Scholtyseck, *Robert Bosch und der liberale Widerstand gegen Hitler 1933 bis 1945*, Munich: C.H. Beck Verlag, 1999, pp. 188–224.

[29] Gerard Aalders and Cees Wiebes, 'Stockholms Enskilda Bank, German Bosch and IG Farben: A Short History of Cloaking', *The Scandinavian Economic History Review* 33 (1985): 25–50; Ulf Olsson, *Furthering a Fortune: Marcus Wallenberg: Swedish Banker and Industrialist 1899–1982*, Stockholm: Ekerlids Förlag, 2001, pp. 203, 236; Håkan Lindgren, *Jacob Wallenberg 1892–1980: Swedish Banker and International Negotiator*, Stockholm: Atlantis, 2009, pp. 281–84, 290–91, 304, 309; Scholtyseck, *Robert Bosch*, pp. 283–302.

[30] Scholtyseck, *Robert Bosch*, pp. 265–82.

[31] Cf. Peter Hoffmann, 'The Question of Western Allied Co-operation with the German Anti-Nazi Conspiracy, 1938–1944', *The Historical Journal* 34 (1991): 437–64.

[32] See Ritter, *Carl Goerdeler*, pp. 322–24.

Carl Goerdeler on trial in the People's Court, Berlin, 7 September 1944. Goerdeler was sentenced to death and was hanged on 2 February 1945. Bundesarchiv Bild 102-1276.

for a secure status of the Jews. It will be presented and explained in Chapters 5–7.

A survey of some of the developments affecting the status of the Jews in the world at the time will provide the background for the memorandum, placing it in the context of the time.

Later, in the years 1937 to 1939, when Goerdeler travelled in Europe, North America, and Palestine, he recorded his observations of anti-Jewish (with a religious emphasis) and antisemitic (racial) 'movements', to which he refers again in the following years and which required 'a new order for the status of the Jews' in the entire world.[33] The 'movements' existed in the National Socialist war against the Jews, and elsewhere, as in Poland, where there were waves of anti-Jewish riots and pogroms, which became antisemitic in the later 1930s.[34]

[33] Fritz Kieffer, 'Carl Friedrich Goerdelers Vorschlag zur Gründung eines jüdischen Staates', *Zeitschrift der Savigny-Stiftung für Rechtsgeschichte* 125 (2008): 476, cites Gillmann and Mommsen, *Politische Schriften*, pp. 525–634. 'Anti-Jewish' indicates a religious and cultural objection; 'antisemitism' connotes race.

[34] Emanuel Melzer, *No Way Out: The Politics of Polish Jewry 1935–1939*, Cincinnati: Hebrew Union College Press, 1997, pp. 53–70 and passim; Melzer (p. 182n2 and pp. 69–70) mentions three 'waves' of pogroms: 1918–1920, 1929–1930, and 1935–1937/38; Joseph Marcus, *Social and Political History of the Jews in Poland, 1919–1939*, Berlin, New York, Amsterdam: Mouton Publishers, 1983, passim.

3

Antecedents

In the regions that after 1918 formed the new state of Poland following the removal of the Russian, Austrian, and German authorities, and also in the other Eastern European countries, pogroms occurred, and there were atrocities and mass killings of Jews during the years 1918 to 1921. While Goerdeler was in Eastern Europe, about one hundred Polish towns experienced bloody anti-Jewish pogroms.[1] At least 150,000 Jews were murdered in Eastern Europe between 1918 and 1921. The murders in Lemberg (Lwów) on 22–24 November 1918, and in Pińsk, Vilna, Lida, and Minsk in April 1919, were notorious.[2]

On 15 March 1919, representatives of Jewish communities in Eastern Europe formed the 'Comité des Délégations Juives auprès de la Conférence de la Paix'. The Comité submitted to the Peace Conference at Paris *A Report on the Pogroms in Poland*, by Israel Cohen, and a memorandum entitled 'Les Droits Nationaux des Juifs en Europe Orientale' by Léo Motzkin, the Comité's secretary general. The memorandum stated that there were approximately 6,500,000 Jews in Congress Poland, 2,250,000 in Austria-Hungary, 240,000 in Romania, and 9,000,000 in the Turkish Empire, in Greece, Bulgaria, 'etc.'. When Léo Motzkin wrote his memorandum, reliable demographic statistics did not exist; his numbers were estimates.[3]

[1] Kieffer, *Goerdelers Vorschlag*, p. 477, cites Maurer, *Ostjuden*, pp. 51, 54–55.

[2] Frank Golczewski, *Polnisch-jüdische Beziehungen 1881–1922*, Wiesbaden: Franz Steiner Verlag, 1981, pp. 158–71, 174, 219–33, 246–64, 290–97, 341–47; Abramsky, 'The Biro-Bidzhan Project', pp. 64–66, accepts an estimate of 200,000 killed in pogroms 1917–1921; cf. Carole Fink, 'The Paris Peace Conference and the Question of Minority Rights', *Peace and Change* 21 (1996): 277–79.

[3] Cf. Golczewski, *Polnisch-jüdische*, pp. 172, 174, 176–78, 181–217.

The best currently available estimates for the numbers of Jews in those countries are 2,845,300 Jews in Poland in 1921, 667,062 in Austria-Hungary in 1910, 128,859 in Austria in 1925, 756,900 in post-Trianon Romania in 1930, 473,400 in post-Trianon Hungary, around 10,000 in Greece before 1914, 43,232 in Bulgaria in 1920, and a minimum of 187,073 (in reality an estimated 220,000, allowing for the usual undercount) in the Ottoman Empire in 1914.[4]

The Comité's memorandum concluded,

Taking into account the abnormal situation of the Jews in the countries in which they have been oppressed, as well as their dispersal throughout the world, which prevents them from forming a majority in any given country, it is fitting to assure to the 15 million Jews participation in the League of Nations. This participation should be linked to the recognition of the national community of Judaism.

(Tenant compte de la situation anormale des Juifs dans les pays où ils ont été opprimés, ainsi que de leur dispersion à travers le monde, laquelle les empêche de former une majorité dans un pays quelconque, il convient d'assurer aux quinze million de Juifs une participation à la Ligue des Nations. Cette participation devra être liée à la reconnaissance de la communauté nationale du Judaïsme.)

General elections among Jews were to result in a Jewish World Congress (*Congrès juif mondial*), which in turn was to elect members to represent the Jews in the League of Nations.[5]

[4] The numbers not available in *Statistik des Deutschen Reichs* are taken from *The YIVO Encyclopedia of Jews in Eastern Europe*, entries 'Population', 'Hungary', 'Romania'; *YIVO Encyclopedia* lists 1,003,000 Jews in Austria-Hungary in 1900, and 911,227 in Hungary alone in 1910; *Encyclopaedia Judaica*, entry 'Bulgaria'; *Statistik des Deutschen Reichs, Band 240: Die Volkszählung im Deutschen Reiche am 1. Dezember 1910*, Berlin: Verlag von Puttkammer und Mühlbrecht, Buchhandlung für Staats- und Rechtswissenschaft, 1915, pp. 27, 134–53, 204, 210; neither *YIVO Encyclopedia* nor *Encyclopaedia Judaica* have numbers for the Ottoman Empire; *Encyclopaedia Judaica* gives 79,454 for Turkey in 1927, the year of the first census in the Republic of Turkey; an authoritative source for pre–First World War numbers, however, is demography specialist Kemal H. Karpat, *Ottoman Population 1830–1914: Demographic and Social Characteristics*, Madison: University of Wisconsin Press, 1985, p. 188; Kemal H. Karpat, *Studies on Ottoman Social and Political History: Selected Articles and Essays*, Leiden, Boston, and Cologne: Brill, 2002, p. 157, 161.

[5] Kieffer, *Goerdelers Vorschlag*, p. 477, refers to Israel Cohen, *A Report on the Pogroms in Poland*, [London]: Central Office of the Zionist Organisation, April 1919, pp. 1–36; brochured together with Cohen's report, without a separate title page, is Léo Motzkin, 'Les revendications nationales des juifs', pp. 7–27, here esp. pp. 7–8 and 20–23; the context makes clear that the fifteen million Jews are those in Eastern Europe and parts of the dissolving Ottoman Empire; see also Fritz Kieffer, *Judenverfolgung in Deutschland – eine innere Angelegenheit? Internationale Reaktionen auf die Flüchtlingsproblematik 1933–1939*, Stuttgart: Franz Steiner Verlag, 2002; Philipp Caspar Mohr, *Kein Recht zur*

On 1 May 1919 at 11 A.M., in a meeting of the 'Big Three' – President Woodrow Wilson, Ministerpresident George Clemenceau, and Prime Minister David Lloyd George – the American president took up the persecution of the Jews as one of the matters that disturbed the peace of the world: '*Un des éléments qui troublent la paix du monde est la persécution des Juifs*'.[6] The Jews were being especially badly treated in Poland, and they were deprived of citizenship rights in Romania. Wilson pointed out an opportunity to intervene: 'In the treaty with Germany, we stipulate concerning Poland'.[7] There were also millions of Germans in the territory of Poland; there must be national-minority guarantees and religious-minority guarantees. Lloyd George said that 'the Jews want to form a sort of state within the state. Nothing will be more dangerous'. Wilson proposed convening a small committee of experts to write the necessary clauses, and the 'Big Three' agreed that such clauses be included in the treaties that were to be signed.[8] The Committee for New States and the Protection of Minorities was formed on 1 May 1919. The 'Big Three' imposed the obligation to accord protection to ethnic, racial, and religious minorities within their states upon Poland, Czechoslovakia, Yugoslavia, Romania, Greece, Austria, Bulgaria, Hungary, and Turkey. Germany had to accept provisions concerning the to-be-partitioned parts of Upper Silesia but was not forced to sign the minorities treaty, nor was Germany required to make a declaration concerning the protection of minorities when it was admitted into the League of Nations in September 1926.[9] The minorities treaty did place upon 'new' states obligations that older established states did not have to accept.[10] Articles 86 and 93 of the Peace Treaty with Germany foresaw that Czechoslovakia and Poland would include in a future treaty with the Allied and Associated Powers

Einmischung? Die politische und völkerrechtliche Reaktion Großbritanniens auf Hitlers 'Machtergreifung' und die einsetzende Judenverfolgung, Tübingen: Mohr Siebeck, 2002, pp. 122–25. See also Marcus, *Social and Political History*, pp. 293–311; Fink, 'Paris Peace Conference', p. 278.

6 Goerdeler invoked the same concern, as will be seen below in Chapter 5.

7 Golczewski, *Polnisch-jüdische*, pp. 303–9, describes Poland's – mostly negative – reaction to the imposed minority-protection treaty of 28 June 1919.

8 Mantoux, *Les délibérations*, pp. 440–41.

9 Mohr, *Kein Recht zur Einmischung*, pp. 122–25. Mohr, p. 123, cites Hugo Wintgens, 'Der völkerrechtliche Schutz der nationalen, sprachlichen und religiösen Minderheiten in Polen', in Fritz Stier-Somlo, ed., *Handbuch des Völkerrechts Band 2, 8: Abteilung*, Stuttgart: W. Kohlhammer, 1930, p. 115, for Clemenceau's, Wilson's, and Lloyd George's wish to include in the protection not merely national minorities but particularly the Jews; see also Fink, 'Paris Peace Conference', pp. 273–88.

10 Cf. Fink, 'Paris Peace Conference', pp. 280–81.

stipulations for the protection of the interests of national, linguistic, and religious minorities.[11] On 28 June 1919, immediately after the German representatives had signed the Treaty of Versailles, the representatives of the state of Poland, the state that had been brought into being minutes earlier by the signing of the Treaty of Versailles, signed with the Allied and Associated Powers – under protest – a treaty whose first twelve articles dealt with the rights of minorities in Poland.[12] Jews from radical assimilationists to autonomists short of Zionism were disconcerted and worried. The German Zionists rejected the idea of a national-minority status with defined civil rights.[13] In Romania the government had consistently since the nineteenth century denied Jews the protections provided by its constitution, not to mention minority status, and continued to violate its obligations under minority clauses.[14]

The definition of citizenship in the minorities treaty was complicated by Jewish and German fears of spoliation and expulsion from territories that had changed hands, and spoliation of those who had fled during the war or had served in one of the involved armies. Jews and Germans wanted a date in August 1914 as the determining date, while the Poles wanted the latest possible date in order to exclude as many 'non-Poles' (Jews and Germans) as possible. A compromise satisfactory to neither side referred to 'habitual residents' and to those born on Polish soil who were not nationals of another state. That left out large groups of Russian Jews and ethnic Germans. Claims to national-cultural autonomy were rejected.[15] The League of Nations Council was responsible for the enforcement of the minority treaty. In cases of complaints from minorities, the council favoured the new states over their minority populations. After Germany had joined the League of Nations, German

[11] *The Treaty of Peace between the Allied and Associated Powers and Germany, The Protocol Annexed Thereto, the Agreement Respecting the Military Occupation of the Territories of the Rhine, and the Treaty between France and Great Britain Respecting Assistance to France in the Event of Unprovoked Aggression by Germany: Signed at Versailles, June 28th, 1919*, London: His Majesty's Stationery Office, 1919, Articles 86, 93.

[12] *Treaty with Poland: Treaty of Peace between the United States of America, the British Empire, France, Italy, and Japan and Poland: Signed at Versailles on June 28, 1919*, Washington: Government Printing Office, 1919.

[13] Francis R. Nicosia, *Zionism and Anti-Semitism in Nazi Germany*, Cambridge and New York: Cambridge University Press, 2008, p. 54, cites Yehuda Reinharz, 'The Zionist Response to Antisemitism in Germany', *Leo Baeck Institute Yearbook* 30 (1985): 118–19.

[14] Cf. Geoff Gilbert, 'Religio-nationalist Minorities and the Development of Minority Rights Law', *Review of International Studies* 25 (1999): 392, 402.

[15] Fink, 'Paris Peace Conference', pp. 281–82.

submissions on behalf of her minorities in Poland got no satisfaction, and her proposal to make the league more active on behalf of minorities was defeated by Britain and France.[16] Hitler, appointed *Reich* chancellor on 30 January 1933, was more interested in robbing and expelling the Jews from Germany than in protecting ethnic Germans abroad.[17] In October 1933, Germany withdrew from the Geneva disarmament conference and from the League of Nations over French obstruction against relaxing the armaments clauses in the Treaty of Versailles[18] and in 1934 made common cause with Poland in a nonaggression treaty. Poland renounced the minority treaty on 13 September 1934.[19] Hitler merely used such issues as opportune instruments, as in his attempt to take over Czechoslovakia in 1938 and Poland in 1939. In 1939 he needed to secure his southern flank in case of war with France and Britain; abandoning the ethnic German South Tyroleans, he agreed with Mussolini to have them 'transferred', that is, expelled, from the South Tyrol.[20]

Later attempts to protect minorities, particularly Jews, through international action, fared no better. On 14 July 1933, a law was promulgated in Germany for the repeal of naturalisations and the withdrawal of citizenship. The law was directed against 'Eastern' Jews in particular.[21]

[16] Fink, 'Paris Peace Conference', pp. 283–84.

[17] *Akten zur deutschen auswärtigen Politik 1918–1945: Band* 6, Baden-Baden: Imprimerie Nationale, 1956, pp. 77–78.

[18] Cf. Edward W. Bennett, *German Rearmament and the West, 1932–1933*, Princeton: Princeton University Press, 1979, pp. 471–90.

[19] Hans Roos, *Geschichte der Polnischen Nation 1916–1960*, 2nd ed., Stuttgart: W. Kohlhammer Verlag, 1964, p. 139. Hans Roos, *A History of Modern Poland*, London: Eyre and Spottiswoode, 1966, p. 137; Fink, 'Paris Peace Conference', p. 284.

[20] Legationsrat Junker, minute 16 August 1939, *Akten zur deutschen auswärtigen Politik 1918–1945*, vol. 7, Baden-Baden: Imprimerie Nationale, 1956, pp. 77–78; cf. Ulrich von Hassell, *Die Hassell-Tagebücher 1938–1944: Aufzeichnungen vom Andern Deutschland*, ed. Friedrich Freiherr Hiller von Gaertringen and Klaus Peter Reiss, Berlin: Siedler, 1988 (cited Hassell 1988), pp. 94–96; Gerhard L. Weinberg, *The Foreign Policy of Hitler's Germany: Starting World War II 1937–1939*, Chicago and London: University of Chicago Press, 1980, p. 565.

[21] For this and the following account and quotations, see 'Gesetz über den Widerruf von Einbürgerungen und die Aberkennung der deutschen Staatsangehörigkeit. Vom 14. Juli 1933', and 'Verordnung zur Durchführung des Gesetzes über den Widerruf von Einbürgerungen und die Aberkennung der deutschen Staatsangehörigkeit. Vom 26. Juli 1933', *RGBl. I 1933*, pp. 480, 538–39. *Parliamentary Debates, Fifth Series–Volume 280: House of Commons: Official Report*, London: His Majesty's Stationery Office, 1933, c. 2604–6 and vol. 282 (General Index for Session 1932–1933), London: His Majesty's Stationery Office, 1934; *Bills, Public: Three Volumes. Session 22 November 1932–17 November 1933*, vol. 3 (the Bill 'Nationality of Jews. 163. Bill to Promote and Extend Opportunities of Citizenship for Jews Resident outside the British Empire' is here listed for page 5 but was not printed).

Twelve days later, on 26 July 1933, a British member of Parliament, Commander Oliver Locker-Lampson, introduced a private member's bill in the House of Commons. Presenting the bill, Locker-Lampson said that he had advocated fair treatment for Germany after the last war and had been persuaded to do so 'by the German Jews who pleaded best for Germany, who day in and day out, tried to get England to be fair to Germany. And those citizens of Germany, the most eloquent and the most patriotic, are now being driven out'. His proposed bill addressed the issue directly, as its title indicates: The 'Nationality of Jews Bill, to promote and extend opportunities of citizenship for Jews resident outside the British Empire', was 'ordered to be brought in by Commander Oliver Locker-Lampson, Rear-Admiral M.F. Sueter, Viscount Elmley, Sir Wilfrid H. Sugden, Mr. B. Janner, Mr. G.W. Holford Knight, Mr. P.H. Hannon, and Mr. W.J. Stewart' and had its first reading on the same day. Second reading, scheduled for 7 November 1933, never took place. The bill was not even printed in the relevant volume of *British State Papers*. The introduction of the bill had been a response to what Goerdeler later called anti-Jewish 'movements'. Its failure was a symptom of the worldwide xenophobia and ethnophobia in the 1930s, reenforced by the impact of the Great Depression.

When in March 1938, in the wake of the annexation of Austria, large numbers of mostly Jewish refugees sought a safe haven, and many more were expected to follow, the question of offering 'certain Austrian citizens who have resided in this country for some time the opportunity of becoming British citizens immediately' was raised in the House of Commons. The home secretary, Sir Samuel Hoare, in his reply on 22 March 1938, did not close the door to refugees but declared that there needed to be controls, and indiscriminate admission 'would not only create difficulties from the police point of view but would have grave economic results in aggravating the unemployment problem, the housing problem and other social problems', whereas he proposed 'to pursue a policy of offering asylum as far as is practicable' without creating the impression that the door was 'open to immigrants of all kinds'.[22]

[22] A.J. Sherman, *Island Refuge: Britain and Refugees from the Third Reich 1933–1939*, London: Paul Elek, 1973, pp. 92–93, cites *Parliamentary Debates, Fifth Series, Volume 333, House of Commons: Official Report*, London: His Majesty's Stationery Office, 1938, 22 March 1938, c. 990–96, for his statement that Colonel Josiah Wedgwood, M.P., introduced a motion in the House of Commons to admit refugees from Austria for a period of six months and to grant British nationality to those of them who might request it, and that the House rejected such a sweeping proposal; there is no reference to the motion in the questions put and answers given on 22 March 1938.

'Movements' against the Jews were thus in progress in many places in the 1930s. To many observers they were most visible and shocking in their manifestations in Germany. From 30 January 1933, the day of Adolf Hitler's appointment as chancellor, the German government continually increased and intensified its discrimination and persecution of Jews in Germany, through published discriminatory laws, through unpublished directives to government agencies and bureaucrats, and in the form of brachial brutalities, a process of which the pogrom of 9 November 1938 was an intermediate culmination and the murder of near six million Jews the outcome. Few people could imagine anything like the Holocaust, which the Nazis later carried out. James McDonald, for one, had a sense of what was coming when he predicted in 1933 and 1935 that in case of war, there would be wholesale slaughter of Jews.[23]

On 12 and 26 October 1933, after months of discussions and lobbying, and just as Germany was leaving the League of Nations, the League of Nations Assembly and Council appointed, as high commissioner for refugees coming from Germany, the American James Grover McDonald, a Christian perhaps more than a Catholic, without a budget, with further severe limitations upon his activities: He was to deal only with refugees already outside Germany; there was no financial support from the league; he could not report to the league assembly or council but only to the commission's governing body, which consisted of the representatives of the governments involved; he could not criticise Germany; there was to be no discussion of the cause of the refugee problem; and the German government would have nothing to do with the High Commission.[24] The League of Nations secretary general, Joseph Avenol, ruled that private organisations (on whom the high commissioner depended for funding) could only have an advisory role. Any appearance of the High Commission being a Jewish institution would compromise its potential effectiveness, particularly in its relations with Germany.[25] McDonald had to be extremely careful in choosing his staff.

The reasons for all this, if not the causes, were clear enough. McDonald explained them to a group of the (American) Federal Council of Churches in New York on 3 November 1933, the eve of his departure for Europe:

What is happening in Germany is something so terrible, so shocking, that it is difficult to give to any one who has not been there an adequate sense of it [...]

[23] McDonald, *Advocate*, p. 69; McDonald, *Refugees*, pp. 43–45.
[24] McDonald, *Advocate*, p. 125.
[25] McDonald, *Advocate*, pp. 152–53.

You must use brutal, cold, contemptuous language to show what the Nazis feel toward the Jew [...] But what is important is that what is happening today in Germany may happen next week or next month in Austria. And if this thing becomes the rule in Germany and Austria and on the whole succeeds in its policy, then I think life for the Jews anywhere on the continent between France and Russia may become impossible. Even in our own country we see from time to time evidences of prejudice that may disquiet the most conservative among us.[26]

At the same time, the British government tried to bar the High Commission from any jurisdiction in Palestine. All this meant that neither the League of Nations nor the countries of refuge were prepared adequately to deal with the Jewish Question.[27]

Discussing the High Commission for Refugees Coming from Germany with Dr Chaim Weizmann in Geneva on 12 November 1933, McDonald explained to Weizmann his 'sense of horror at the Nazi attitude' and his 'fear that this example might be followed elsewhere'. Weizmann replied

that he was convinced that the danger to world Jewry was fully as grave as I thought; that there was immediate danger in Poland the instant [Polish leader Josef] Piłsudski was removed from the scene, and that in Austria and Hungary and Romania the danger was also imminent. Even in Great Britain, the United States, and France there could be no real assurance of the future. The Jews had always survived through the remnants of the race, and they might have to do so again. Despite these evident dangers, the bulk of the well-to-do Jews in the West failed completely to sense the realities of the situation.[28]

In April 1934, Withold Chodzko, Polish representative on the governing body of the High Commission for Refugees Coming from Germany, communicated to McDonald the same point about the danger in Poland as Weizmann had done.[29]

Concerning British insistence that Palestine was outside the jurisdiction of the High Commission for Refugees Coming from Germany, Weizmann advised McDonald to first of all see Lord Robert Cecil, one of the 'fathers' of the League of Nations, whom McDonald had known since the early 1920s, to try to overcome the resistance of the British Colonial Office. Weizmann envisaged the High Commission 'as playing a large role' in Palestine.[30]

[26] McDonald, *Advocate*, pp. 142–43; ellipses ibid.
[27] McDonald, *Advocate*, p. 145.
[28] McDonald, *Advocate*, pp. 152.
[29] McDonald, *Advocate*, p. 354.
[30] McDonald, *Advocate*, pp. 107n28, 152.

After speaking with Jewish leaders, diplomats, and government and League of Nations officials in London, Paris, Geneva, Vienna, Prague, and Warsaw in April 1934, McDonald sent a telegram to the American Foreign Policy Association:

EVERYWHERE PARIS VIENNA PRAGUE WARSAW OVERWHELMING PROOF IMPERATIVE NEED CORPORATION GENEROUS SCALE STOP DYNAMIC SITUATION DEMANDS ACTION STOP WISH YOUR COLLEAGUES COULD SEE PRESENT TRAGEDY AND SENSE DANGER CATASTROPHE.[31]

Carl Goerdeler found himself in this 'dynamic situation'. In April 1933, when *SA* thugs were maltreating Jews in Leipzig, Goerdeler as mayor of Leipzig went in formal dress to a Jewish quarter of his city to protect Jews and their businesses, and he used the city police to free Jews who had been detained and beaten by *SA* stormtroopers.[32]

In the same month, the government issued anti-Jewish laws and a cluster of anti-Jewish decrees, such as the earlier-mentioned civil-service law that barred Jews from government and administrative positions at every level and of every kind, from teaching positions in all educational and scientific establishments, from primary schools to universities and academies, and barred converted former Jews from the Catholic and Lutheran clergy.[33] A decree excluded 'non-Aryan' physicians who (or whose fathers and sons) were not World War veterans and Communist physicians from practice under the public health system.[34] In May 1934 the government excluded from *approbation* physicians who had one or more Jewish grandparents, and also non-Jewish physicians who were married to a 'non-Aryan'; physicians *previously* admitted to practice under public health-insurance plans did not lose their approbation.[35] In July 1934, when a national law required the establishment of a 'race authority' within the municipal health commissions, Goerdeler resisted official and unofficial pressures for several months, but was finally forced in January 1935 to accept this

[31] Quoted from McDonald Papers in United States Holocaust Memorial Museum, Washington, in McDonald, *Advocate*, p. 365.

[32] Marianne Meyer-Krahmer, *Carl Goerdeler und sein Weg in den Widerstand: Eine Reise in die Welt meines Vaters*, Freiburg im Breisgau: Herder Taschenbuch Verlag, 1989, p. 73.

[33] 'Gesetz zur Wiederherstellung des Berufsbeamtentums. Vom 7. April 1933', *RGBl. I 1933*, pp. 175–77; 'Erste Verordnung zur Durchführung des Gesetzes zur Wiederherstellung des Berufsbeamtentums. Vom 11. April 1933', *RGBl. I 1933*, p. 195.

[34] 'Verordnung über die Zulassung von Ärzten zur Tätigkeit bei den Krankenkassen. Vom 22. April 1933', *RGBl. I 1933*, p. 222.

[35] 'Verordnung über die Zulassung von Ärzten zur Tätigkeit bei den Krankenkassen. Vom 17. Mai 1934', *RGBl. I 1934*, pp. 399–410.

since it was the law.[36] On 9 April 1935, Goerdeler received a complaint from the Central-German Association of the Central Association of German Citizens of Jewish Faith (*Landesverband Mitteldeutschland des Centralvereins deutscher Staatsbürger jüdischen Glaubens e.V.*) against the Leipzig deputy mayor, Rudolf Haake, a National Socialist, who had advised all municipal administrators and employees against consulting Jewish physicians.

Here Goerdeler immediately acted against this unlawful boycott attempt. On 11 April 1935, he signed a list of 'non-Aryan' physicians who were *not* excluded by law from practice under public health-insurance plans and of those who were legally excluded, and he circulated the list in the Leipzig municipal administration.[37] Goerdeler could not break the law, regardless of whether he considered it just, but he could and did confirm the legal position and the protection it provided for those whom the law had not excluded from practice or approbation.

In 1936 the matter of access for Jews to municipal public baths became an issue. There had been restrictions on access to public baths imposed on Jews as early as 1933 in Tübingen, Plauen, Nuremberg, Erlangen, and Munich. The central government in Berlin and the *NSDAP* leadership at the time opposed the general expansion of measures separating Jews from non-Jews out of internal and foreign-political considerations. The *NSDAP* leadership ordered the repeal of these restrictions, to little effect, but they tolerated local initiatives restricting access to public baths, sports facilities, libraries, and hospitals. The *Deutsche Gemeindetag* ignored the lack of a positive government directive and told inquiring municipalities that they could make any rules they wished. When the *Völkischer Beobachter* of 19 July 1936 reported that the mayor (*Oberbürgermeister*) of Breslau, Dr. Hans Fridrich, had forbidden German Jews the use of municipal baths, numerous municipalities followed the example.[38] The

[36] Verhandlungen der Stadtverordneten zu Leipzig 1935, Stadtarchiv Leipzig, Band I, 30 Jan. 1935; 'Gesetz zur Vereinheitlichung des Gesundheitswesens. Vom 3. Juli 1934', *RGBl. I 1934*, pp. 531–32; 'Erste Durchführungsverordnung zum Gesetz über die Vereinheitlichung des Gesundheitswesens. Vom 6. Februar 1935', *Reichsgesetzblatt Teil I 1935*, Berlin: Reichsverlagsamt, 1935 (citation: *RGBl. I 1935*), pp. 177–80.

[37] Stadtarchiv Leipzig, Kap. 1 Nr. 122.

[38] Wolf Gruner, *Öffentliche Wohlfahrt und Judenverfolgung*, Munich: R. Oldenbourg Verlag, 2002, pp. 69, 77, 140–43 (no reference to Goerdeler); Wolf Gruner, 'Die NS-Judenverfolgung und die Kommunen. Zur wechselseitigen Dynamisierung von zentraler und lokaler Politik', *Vierteljahrshefte für Zeitgeschichte* 48 (2000): 85–86, 92, 94–98; Rüdiger Fleiter, *Stadtverwaltung im Dritten Reich: Verfolgungspolitik auf kommunaler Ebene*, Hannover: Hahnsche, 2006, pp. 142, 148, 186 (no references to Goerdeler).

files in the Leipzig City Archives reveal that Haake sought to give force to that unofficial practice in Leipzig. The ultimate responsibility here rested with Goerdeler. From a post-Auschwitz point of view, one may wish that Goerdeler had taken a more principled position in this matter, but we do not know his considerations, only that the restriction had been issued without his approval. He may have decided not to resign yet, or not over this issue rather than one of potentially greater public appeal; he certainly still hoped to influence government policy at a higher level and in larger issues. The records reveal no further personal involvement by Goerdeler other than his answer on 19 September 1936 to an inquiry from the Saxon section of the National Conference of Municipalities. He wrote, using the passive voice in the third person, that from the end of July 1935, Jews had been prohibited from using the Leipzig municipal summer baths, indoor pools, and other communal baths.[39] The date of Goerdeler´s reply may help to explain its mild form; it was four days after he had received the complaint, and two days after he had submitted his long memorandum on the economy to Göring.[40] Goerdeler was a prominent figure on the national political stage. From 1934 to 1935, he held 'high national office' in the economic-policy field. He ultimately renounced the possibility of regaining his office as *Reich* prices commissioner when Hitler did not meet his demands for expanded authority.[41]

In the summer of 1934, he wrote a memorandum on internal policy in which he demanded the consolidation of German racial policies.[42] He addressed it to the *Reich* chancellor, as Goerdeler's biographer Gerhard

[39] Stadtarchiv Leipzig, Kap. 1 Nr. 122.

[40] See below at p. 50.

[41] Ritter, *Goerdeler*, pp. 70, 79, writes that Goerdeler declined an offer of 'high national office' in the economic-policy field when his conditions were not met; in fact, Hitler eventually decided not to extend Goerdeler's mandate after July 1935 when he saw fractious rivalries involved in Goedeler's demands for expanded authority for the office of *Reich* prices commissioner; see *Regierung Hitler II*, pp. 663–64, 671, 676–77, 689–92, 705–6, 790–92.

[42] The editors of his principal political works date 'August/September 1934'; Gillmann and Mommsen, *Regierung*, p. 342. Theodore S. Hamerow, *On the Road to the Wolf's Lair: German Resistance to Hitler*, Cambridge, London: The Belknap Press of Harvard University Press, 1997, p. 128, apparently following Ritter, *Goerdeler*, 2nd ed. 1956, p. 75 (Hamerow cites the 1954 1st ed., p. 64; Gillmann and Mommsen also cite the 1st ed., p. 68), describes the memorandum as addressed to Hitler, which is what Ritter must have read on a copy at his disposal since he quotes in quotation marks 'An den Reichskanzler', but Ritter cites no evidence; Gillmann and Mommsen, p. 342, consider unconfirmed that Goerdeler had addressed the memorandum to Hitler, since they could not find any copy with this heading or notation; see also Ritter, *Goerdeler*, p. 72.

Ritter quotes, '*An den Reichskanzler*'. Ritter describes this memorandum as 'a first, still quite openly prosecuted attack against the party regime in the "Third Reich"'.[43]

The social and political discourse in the years before the mass murder of Jews by the National Socialist dictatorship tolerated attitudes and judgments that have since become unacceptable. International concerns, and defences against unwanted immigrants, had been heightened by Germany's annexation of Austria and the Sudeten region. The notes that the United Kingdom, France, and the United States of America handed to the Hitler government in October 1938, acknowledging 'Germany's entire right to take measures of internal effect with regard to the political opinions, the religious beliefs and the racial organisation of its citizens', indicated the international norms in such matters. The United Kingdom and the United States had their own laws restricting immigration on racial grounds. Approximately 120,000 Jewish immigrants settled in Great Britain between 1880 and 1914. Agitation in the United Kingdom against Jewish immigration gave rise to the British Aliens Act of 1905.[44] An American law excluded 'members of the yellow race' and Hindus from naturalisation.[45] The theologian Dietrich Bonhoeffer, in April 1933, rejected from a Christian standpoint any racial view of Judaism; but at the same time he acknowledged that

> [w]ithout doubt one of the historical problems that must be dealt with by our state is the Jewish question, and without doubt the state is entitled to strike new paths in doing so. It remains for the humanitarian associations and individual Christian men who know themselves called upon to do so, to make the state aware of the moral aspect of the measures it takes in this regard, that is, should the occasion arise, to accuse the state of offenses against morality.[46]

[43] Ritter, *Goerdeler*, p. 72.

[44] David Feldman, 'Was the Nineteenth Century a Golden Age for Immigrants? The Changing Articulation of National, Local and Voluntary Controls', in Andreas Fahrmeir, Olivier Faron, and Patrick Weil, eds., *Migration Control in the North Atlantic World: The Evolution of State Practices in Europe and the United States from the French Revolution to the Inter-war Period*, New York and Oxford: Berghahn Books, 2003, 2005, pp. 167, 170.

[45] Berthold Schenk Graf von Stauffenberg, 'Die Entziehung der Staatsangehörigkeit und das Völkerrecht: Eine Entgegnung', *Zeitschrift für ausländisches öffentliches Recht und Völkerrecht* 4 (1934): 270. According to Weil, *Migration Control*, pp. 271–97 (quotation on p. 272), 'the racialist approach' officially dominated American immigration policy 'from the 1920s through to 1965'; see also Patrick Weil, *Qu'est-ce un Français?* Paris: Bernard Grasset, 2002, pp. 72–90, 93, 97–134.

[46] Bonhoeffer, *Works* 12, pp. 363, 368.

He would not have written this after 1940. He took an unequivocal position in favour of saving the Jews during the war and was at the end of it, on 9 April 1945, hanged for his commitment and Resistance activities.

The position of Johannes Popitz, the Prussian minister of finance, illustrates the complexity of efforts to exert a moderating influence upon Hitler's anti-Jewish policies. Like *Reich* economics minister and *Reichsbank* president Schacht in his Königsberg speech on 18 August 1935, Popitz saw in the anti-Jewish persecutions a danger to Germany's international standing in the financial markets and to Germany's foreign trade, yet Popitz had deeper concerns. Popitz' and Goerdeler's positions must be seen against the background of the worldwide anti-German boycott that the Polish delegation had suggested during the World Jewish Congress in Geneva in August 1932, half a year before the National Socialists came to govern Germany.[47] Begun after Hitler's appointment as chancellor, it was led and organised by Jewish Boycott Committees; a Central Committee for Anti-Nazi Economic Action was established in Poland at the beginning of 1933 for the development and coordination of a boycott campaign.[48] In September 1935, a world conference of Polish Jews abroad met in London and passed a resolution to boycott German goods, to boycott 'everything and anything emanating from present-day Germany'.[49] Further, the antisemitic attitudes in America and anti-Jewish and antisemitic persecutions in Poland, Hungary, and Romania formed a part of the background for Popitz' position.[50] In view of German atrocities against the Jews during the Second World War that resulted in nearly six million murders attended by the most brutal cruelties, it may appear inappropriate to refer anti-Jewish events in other countries. Yet it is necessary to view Goerdeler's, Popitz' and others' positions in the 1930s from *their* perspective and point of view, which was a point of view *without* the knowledge of the subsequent millionfold mass murder of Jews. From this perspective, German measures against Jews during the early 1930s were limited compared with the atrocities and pogroms that swept a country like Poland.

[47] Alfred Wiślicki, 'The Jewish Boycott Campaign against Nazi Germany and Its Culmination in the Halbersztadt Trial', in *Polin: Studies in Polish Jewry*, vol. 8, London and Washington: Littman Library of Jewish Civilization, 1994, pp. 282–83; cf. *Encyclopaedia Judaica*, vol. 21, p. 219.

[48] Wiślicki, 'Jewish Boycott', pp. 282–83.

[49] *The Times* 13 September 1935, p. 14.

[50] Cf. Jerzy Tomaszewski, 'The Civil Rights of Jews in Poland 1918–1939', in *Polin: Studies in Polish Jewry*, vol. 8, London and Washington: Littman Library of Jewish Civilization, 1994; cf. Melzer, *No Way Out*.

Popitz, who lost his life for his part in the 20 July 1944 plot, was a jurist, from 1919 in the *Reich* Ministry of Finance, from 1925 to 1929 as state secretary, in 1932–1933 as *Reich* minister without portfolio, and from April 1933 to 20 July 1944 Prussian minister of finance. He is not on record as having questioned the government's right to define its citizens, but chaotic and unlawful arbitrariness was abhorrent to him. In 1933, 1934, and 1935, Popitz was concerned with the rule of law and orderly procedures, and with ending the extralegal and unpredictable hooliganism of *SA* troopers and individual party functionaries. An uncompromising protest against these persecutions could have led only to retirement and inactivity; the chance of achieving anything lay in attempting to work within the existing system.

In March 1933 Popitz sent a draft for the 'Law for the Restoration of the Professional Civil Service' to Vice Chancellor Franz von Papen (a different version became law on 7 April 1933). Apparently Popitz agreed that the government should have the ability, if it wished to do so, to remove Communists and Jews from the civil service. A meeting of ministers on 5 May 1933 including Popitz and chaired by the Prussian ministerpresident Hermann Göring discussed details of the law's implementation, and the protocol declared unanimous agreement with the proposals, in particular with Popitz' suggestion that civil servants could be retired with full pension rights but without being given reasons, so that neither political nor 'racial' reasons would be given, thereby avoiding any defamation.[51]

In discussions preceding and during the preparations for the Nuremberg Race Laws, on 20 August 1935, Popitz said he wished 'that the government set a clear limit – it did not matter where – for the treatment of the Jews, but then firmly see to it that the limit be respected'.[52] In stark contrast with this seemingly conformist position, Popitz wrote his deep

[51] Hans Mommsen, *Beamtentum im Dritten Reich*, Stuttgart: Deutsche Verlags-Anstalt, 1966, pp. 39–42; Popitz to Ministerialdirektor im Preussischen Staatsministerium Dr. Friedrich Walter Landfried 23 March 1933, Geheimes Staatsarchiv, Berlin, HA Rep. 90 Nr. 469; Protokoll über die Chefbesprechung am 5. Mai 1933 of Ministerpresident Göring (in the chair), Staatsminister Kerrl, Professor Dr. Popitz, Rust, Staatssekretäre Körner (d.St.M.), Dr. Wiskott (Landw.), Grauert (Min.d.Inn.), Ministerialdirektor Dr. Schellen (Min.d.Inn.), Ministerialrat Bergbohm als Protokollführer, Leiter der Pressestelle des St.M. Oberregierungsrat Sommerfeldt, Geheimes Staatsarchiv, Berlin, HA Rep. 90a B III 2 b Nr. 6 Bd 182 Bl. 130–35.

[52] Otto Dov Kulka, 'Die Nürnberger Rassengesetze und die deutsche Bevölkerung im Lichte geheimer NS-Lage- und Stimmungsberichte', *Vierteljahrshefte für Zeitgeschichte* 32 (1984): p. 617.

convictions into constitutional drafts and laws prepared about 1940 for the time after Hitler's fall, toward which he conspired with others; here Popitz stipulated the complete removal of the measures discriminating against Jews.[53]

After his arrest for having participated in the conspiracy to overthrow the regime, the *Gestapo* quoted Popitz as having agreed that the Jews should be removed from positions in the state and in the economy, but that he had recommended a more gradual method, especially because of foreign-policy considerations.[54] Whether Popitz had personally agreed with and approved restrictions upon Jews does not, on close scrutiny, emerge from this summary interrogation report. It contains Popitz' acknowledgment of the position he had taken in 1935. The vulgar language of the German *Gestapo* report shows, however, that it contains the formulations of the interrogator; only under torture could Popitz have signed or agreed to them. His alleged expression of his 'approval of the National Socialist state in every way' is blatantly incorrect; Popitz himself contradicted it in his testimony at his trial in the 'People's Court' on 3 October 1944, saying that 'the manner and speed of the solution of the Jewish Question' had caused his 'inner detachment from National Socialism'.[55] He disagreed with the manner of the 'solution of the Jewish

[53] 'Gesetz über die Wiederherstellung geordneter Verhältnisse im Staats- und Rechtsleben. (Vorläufiges Staatsgrundgesetz)', Bundesarchiv Koblenz, Nachlass Johannes Popitz, N 1262/Popitz 79. Although the editor of the 1988 edition of Hassell's diaries stated that the included version of Popitz' 'Gesetz über die Wiederherstellung geordneter Verhältnisse im Staats- und Rechtsleben. (Vorläufiges Staatsgrundgesetz)' followed the copy in the Bundesarchiv, this edition (Hassell 1988, p. 461), like the older one (Ulrich von Hassell, *Vom andern Deutschland. Aus den nachgelassenen Tagebüchern 1938–1944*, Zurich: Atlantis Verlag, 1946, p. 392), does not contain subpoints (a) and (b) of point 6 in the copy in Bundesarchiv Koblenz; it reads merely, 'Insofar as the laws and ordinances for Jews contain special regulations, these regulations will be suspended until the definitive settlement. This applies also for the regulation of § 25 of the *Reich* Civil Service Law and for § 15 of the Defence Law' ('Soweit die Gesetze und Verordnungen für Juden besonders bestimmen, werden diese Bestimmungen bis zur endgültigen Regelung ausgesetzt. Dies gilt auch von der Bestimmung des § 25 des Reichsbeamtengesetzes und des § 15 des Wehrgesetzes') Cf. Hoffmann, *Behind Valkyrie*, p. 35.

[54] *Spiegelbild*, S. 448–49: 'Ich bejahe in jeder Weise den nationalsozialistischen Staat und sehe in ihm die geschichtliche Notwendigkeit gegenüber dem Internationalismus und der Verjudung der Systemzeit und gegenüber den unerträglichen Krisen der parlamentarischen Parteien, das deutsche Volk in seinen gesamten nationalen Grenzen zu einen und es so zu regieren, wie es nach seiner geographischen Lage allein regiert werden kann [...] In der Judenfrage war ich als recht eingehender Kenner der Zustände in der Systemzeit durchaus der Auffassung, daß die Juden aus dem Staats- und Wirtschaftsleben verschwinden müßten. In der Methode habe ich mehrfach ein etwas allmählicheres Vorgehen empfohlen, insbesondere aus Rücksichten der äußeren Politik'.

[55] IV g 10 b 57/44 gRs, 4. Okt. 1944, A.W. Dulles Papers, Princeton University.

Question', namely, discrimination, humiliation, robbery, forced emigration, mistreatment, and mass murder. He disagreed with the method and therefore with the 'solution'. Popitz was hanged on 2 February 1945, on the same day as Carl Goerdeler.[56]

Goerdeler demanded, in his 1934 memorandum on German internal policy, adherence to Bismarck's maxim that all internal-policy actions must be examined for their foreign-policy consequences. He demanded a 'consolidation' of German racial policies and insisted that decisions about internal actions and their desirability from the foreign-policy point of view must be the domain of the Foreign Ministry, not, for example, of the Propaganda Ministry, and he concluded: 'What the law has put in place will be understood as self-protection and barely questioned abroad, if in this framework everything now transacts itself with iron discipline and avoiding excesses and pedantism'.[57] In view of international law and the positions taken by the Western Powers in this matter, Goerdeler's assumption that 'what the law has put in place will be understood as self-protection and barely questioned abroad' was no doubt realistic. At the same time, he made clear his general rejection of racial policies by laughing at them: 'If in the field of art, for example, we dislike Mendelssohn's composition "The Creation", we should not perform it, but we should not announce that for reasons of racial policy it must be replaced by another. We might badly embarrass ourselves here, for it is rather possible that no living German composer could produce a better composition'.[58] On the

[56] Ritter, *Goerdeler*, pp. 411–45.

[57] Gillmann and Mommsen, *Politische Schriften*, p. 368; Gillmann and Mommsen, p. 342, date the memorandum 'August/September 1934'.

[58] Gillmann and Mommsen, *Politische Schriften*, p. 368. In Peter Hoffmann, 'The German Resistance to Hitler and the Jews: The Case of Carl Goerdeler', in Dennis B. Klein, Richard Libowitz, Marcia Sachs Littell, and Sharon Steeley, eds., *The Genocidal Mind: Selected Papers from the 32nd Annual Scholars' Conference on the Holocaust and the Churches*, Saint Paul: Paragon House, 2005, pp. 278–79, and other articles, I have cited evidence against branding Goerdeler a conservative dissimilationist anti-semite (Hoffmann, 'The German Resistance and the Holocaust', pp. 105–26; Peter Hoffmann, 'The German Resistance to Hitler and the Jews', in David Bankier, ed., *Probing the Depths of German Antisemitism: German Society and the Persecution of the Jews, 1933–1941*, Jerusalem, New York, and Oxford: Yad Vashem, Leo Baeck Institute, Berghahn Books, 2000, pp. 463–77; Peter Hoffmann, 'The Persecution of the Jews as a Motive for Resistance Against National Socialism', in Andrew Chandler, ed., *The Moral Imperative: New Essays on the Ethics of Resistance in National Socialist Germany, 1933–1945*, Boulder and Oxford: Westview Press, 1998, pp. 73–104; Peter Hoffmann, 'The German Resistance, the Jews, and Daniel Goldhagen', in Franklin H. Littell, ed., *Hyping the Holocaust: Scholars Answer Goldhagen*, East Rockaway: Cummings and Hathaway, 1997, pp. 73–88). Now I am profoundly indebted to Fritz Kieffer for his

whole, however, in the interest of gaining acceptance for his moderate and rational ideas, Goerdeler attempted to strike a sympathetic note in his memorandum, as when he welcomed Hitler's expressed wish to avoid conflict with the Catholic Church.[59] Confident of his access to the highest levels of power, that is, to Hitler, particularly during his second term as *Reich* prices commissioner, 5 November 1934–1 July 1935, Goerdeler nevertheless expressed his criticisms clearly.[60]

On 7 August 1936, General Hermann Göring, ministerpresident of Prussia, asked Goerdeler for his views on the foreign-currency and raw-materials situation. Goerdeler submitted a preliminary memorandum on 31 August, and a longer, more elaborate version on 17 September. In both he advised austerity, slowing re-armament, and fiscal responsibility. Now he fell out of favour.

In his memoranda of 31 August/17 September 1936, Goerdeler also said that he saw a 'grand opportunity' to end the international currency turmoil and to win a great moral victory by reaching agreement with the Western Powers, particularly England and France. He declared himself convinced that England and France would make available to Germany, at low interest rates, the necessary gold to stabilise the German currency, but that they would not come to an agreement with Germany unless certain other issues were also resolved. He made this point in the preliminary version of his memorandum, explicitly citing, in the following order, the Jewish Question, the Free-Masons Question, legal security, the Church Question (*die Judenfrage*, *die Logenfrage*, *die Rechtssicherheit*, *die Kirchenfrage*), and even more explicitly and strongly in the long version: One must reckon with 'very decided wishes' on the part of England and France.

> I do not doubt that England and France have certain wishes in another area. I could imagine that we must bring into a certain greater agreement with imponderable views of other nations some questions such as the Jewish Question, the Free-Masons´ Question, legal security, the Church Question. But I assert that these sacrifices are nothing vis-à-vis the course of events that begins if we do not now come to the only decision for which an alternative decision of any kind does not at all exist.

analysis of Goerdeler's proposals on behalf of the Jews. Kieffer accepts Mommsen's and Gillmann's dating of the memorandum for the end of 1941 and beginning of 1942; this bears upon its meaning, and Kieffer examines the context as well as the juridical aspects of the passage in Goerdeler's memorandum dealing with the status of the Jews in the world; Kieffer, 'Goerdeler's Vorschlag', pp. 474–500.

[59] Gillmann and Mommsen, *Politische Schriften*, p. 369.

[60] Ritter, *Goerdeler*, p. 76.

German fiscal soundness and an orderly budgetary and debt management were indispensable. It will be necessary temporarily to reduce the tempo of re-armament.

But, he declared in the longer version, the wishes of England and France will go farther.

It is a fact that there are in place governments with other views there, and there are issues in which great discord has emerged. Well known are the concerns about the treatment of the Jewish Question, the Free-Masons Question, the Church Question. But, since in the experience of world history it has commonly always been less a question of fundamentals than of method, and since the honour, liberty and existence of the German people are priorities, since moreover apparently there now exists the possibility to bring up for negotiation with good prospects of success our colonial demands, and since in any case we need time for quiet re-armament, so certain sacrifices in forms seem to me nothing considering the course of events which will occur with certainty if we do not now reach the decision which is now required. Having reviewed my preliminary report, I cannot see that there could be any alternative decision which was apt to lead us out of our situation. It is the same in economic and political life as in the military. Certain situations demand *one* decision and none other. If the one is not taken, success will not be achieved. More, however, is at issue here; it is not the question of achieving or not achieving a success, but the issue is that every wrong decision must bring us into ever more untenable positions. Almost daily now I am receiving emergency messages from businesses of the free economy and from my administration which point to the consequences of the increasing scarcity of raw materials.[61]

Goerdeler knew that Göring was in charge of the Four-Year Plan, and that this plan included some form of autarky policy. He knew also that the plan aimed at achieving the utmost speed in war preparations. He agreed that military intervention against Poland would be necessary to regain formerly German territory, and he conceded that armaments were necessary. He tried to show, however, that they could not be accomplished without changing the treatment of the Jews and other groups who had incurred the hatred of the Nazis. He put the Jews first in his list. The boycott against German business and industry had an effect, of course, but Goerdeler did not cite this, as he very well could have done. He chose to cite 'very decided wishes' on the part of England and France that went beyond any insistence on German fiscal soundness and an orderly budgetary and debt management. 'It is a fact that there are in place governments with other views [in England and France], and

[61] Gillmann and Mommsen, *Politische Schriften*, pp. 445–46.

there are issues in which great discord has emerged. Well known are the concerns about the treatment of the Jewish Question, the Free-Masons Question, the Church Question'. But if 'the honour, liberty and existence of the German people are priorities', a modification of methods was a small sacrifice to make.

According to Goerdeler in his memorandum for Göring, armaments depended upon a balanced national budget, a balanced national budget depended upon an accommodation with England and France about currency and economic questions, and an accommodation with England and France depended upon changes in 'the treatment of the Jewish Question, the Free-Masons Question, the Church Question'.

To reiterate, in the circumstances, Goerdeler had to use arguments that at least remotely promised to be effective. But his main concern was not the economic impact of the anti-German boycott. His main concern was to change German policy with regard to the 'Jewish Question, the Free-Masons Question, the Church Question'. This is additionally illustrated by the fact that Goerdeler later, in August 1938, continued to make this argument, namely, that Britain should threaten to withhold economic concessions, and eventually, that Britain should break relations with Germany, if the persecution of the Jews continued; only in 1938, he directed it to the British government rather than the German government in the hope of influencing the German government through British pressure.[62] Acting *Reich* economics minister Schacht had used the same list of concerns in the same order a year earlier in his Königsberg speech of 18 August 1935: Jews, Free-Masons, clergy.[63]

There are two reasons why Goerdeler cannot have known the contents of the passage in the new Four-Year Plan containing the threat of extermination against the Jews. First, there is no evidence that Göring read that passage in the ministerial meeting of 4 September 1936. Schacht, who was present, later wrote that Göring had read 'only a few harmless sentences' from Hitler's memorandum.[64] The second reason is that, with his bluntness, and sometimes foolhardy courage, and in view of the uncompromising directness with which Goerdeler advocated war against Poland to recover formerly German territory, it is implausible that he would have confined himself in 1936 to the mild criticism in his memorandum, had he been aware of Hitler's lethal threat against the Jews.

[62] See pp. 76–82 below.
[63] Schacht, *Königsberger Rede*, p. 9.
[64] Treue, 'Hitlers Denkschrift', pp. 184–210, here p. 196n25.

In the same summer of 1936, the Olympic Games took place in Germany. The National Socialists in Leipzig, particularly the deputy mayor, Rudolf Haake, wanted to remove the statue of Felix Mendelssohn-Bartholdy that stood in front of the Leipzig *Gewandhaus* concert hall.

Mendelssohn founded the Leipzig Conservatory, conducted the *Gewandhaus* Orchestra from 1835 to 1847, and developed the choir of St Thomas' Church. King Friedrich Wilhelm IV of Prussia sought to bring him to Berlin. In 1841 Mendelssohn accepted an appointment but returned to Leipzig after fourteen months, in September 1842.[65] Felix Mendelssohn-Bartholdy was the grandson of the philosopher Moses Mendelssohn, a friend of Gotthold Ephraim Lessing and an advocate of Jewish enlightenment and acculturation. He was baptised a Christian, but the National Socialists regarded him as a Jew.[66]

Goerdeler insisted that the statue be left in place. Openly and directly, he confronted the National Socialists with a position diametrically opposed to their declared views and policies: He insisted that the statue for a man they considered a Jew be left standing. When he was about to leave on a trip to Finland on behalf of the German Chamber of Commerce, he assured himself in the Propaganda Ministry that the minister, Goebbels, and Hitler himself approved of his decision to leave the statue where it was, and he instructed his deputy Haake accordingly. When Goerdeler was out of town, Haake had the statue removed. Upon his return, Goerdeler on 14 November demanded an explanation. Haake wrote to Goerdeler on 16 November and accused him of having resisted from 1933 onward every single renaming of a street that bore the name of a Jew, and of having from 1933 onward obstructed every effort to remove the Mendelssohn-Bartholdy statue 'because of his attitude in the Jewish Question', and because he did not share the Party's view about the Jews. After Goerdeler's last instruction to leave the statue in place, Haake decided, as he wrote, without telling Goerdeler, 'on the next occasion to act as [Goerdeler's] legal deputy and to assume the responsibility', because his 'conscience as a National Socialist no longer allowed a compromise in this question'. He had become convinced, he continued, that 'in this

[65] Peter Mercer-Taylor, *The Life of Mendelssohn*, Cambridge: Cambridge University Press, 2000, pp. 165–75.

[66] Gillmann and Mommsen, *Politische Schriften*, p. 1223; Hoffmann, 'The German Resistance to Hitler and the Jews', pp. 280–81; cf. W.A. Lampadius, *Life of Felix Mendelssohn Bartholdy*, republication of the ed. of 1865, Road Town and Boston: Longwood Press, 1978, p. 14; Vera Forester, *Lessing und Moses Mendelssohn: Geschichte einer Freundschaft*, Hamburg: Europäische Verlagsanstalt, 2001.

question Goerdeler out of his inner self would never understand him and his fellow Party members'. In the matter of the Mendelssohn monument, 'it was not material but ideologic principles that were decisive'. He asserted that the Leipzig Party officials and city council were unanimous on his, Haake's, side and that they and the public were incensed about Goerdeler's resistance and considered his resistance 'weakness'. Haake stressed that 'the real cause lay in Dr Goerdeler's world-view which was the opposite of National Socialism', that Goerdeler had criticised and opposed most National Socialist policies since 1933 – and that the issue of the statue was 'only the outward occasion of the conflict'.[67]

It might be argued that Haake used these accusations to justify his own insubordination, and that Haake only construed a link between Goerdeler's attitude in the Jewish Question and the Mendelssohn-Bartholdy statue. Goerdeler, however, had used the example of Mendelssohn earlier, in 1934, in the context of his rejection of racial policies.[68] Even more important is the fact that Goerdeler had taken his position on the Mendelssohn-Bartholdy statue *before* it had become an issue of his authority over that of his deputy through Haake's insubordination. And in the same time frame, in September 1936, Goerdeler had demanded a change of policy in the Jewish Question at the highest level of government. This fact, that the larger context of Goerdeler's actions aimed at protecting Jews, makes the argument that it was a matter of injured authority untenable.[69]

Haake, for his part, wrote from conviction. On 4 December 1936, he wrote to the Saxon governor (*Reichsstatthalter*) and the Party's regional leader (*Gauleiter*) Martin Mutschmann that, from the beginning of his association with Mayor Goerdeler, he noted 'again and again that the latter made an effort to work within the thought system of National Socialism, but that he never quite succeeded', and that Goerdeler lacked

[67] Acta, das Felix Mendelssohn-Bartholdy-Denkmal btr. Ergangen vor dem Rathe der Stadt Leipzig 1859–1947, Stadtarchiv Leipzig, Cap. 26A Nr. 39; Goerdeler personnel file Stadtarchiv Leipzig, Kap. 10 G Nr. 685 Bd. 1 and 2. Manfred Unger, 'Die "Endlösung" in Leipzig: Dokumente zur Geschichte der Judenverfolgung 1933–1945', *Zeitschrift für Geschichtswissenschaft* 11 (1963): 944, cites Goerdeler as saying only that the matter could be examined; Unger, who was at the time head of the Stadtarchiv and had full access to all the records, suppressed the accusations against Goerdeler of having opposed the National Socialist anti-Jewish policies. See also Goerdeler to Mutschmann 23 November 1937, Stadtarchiv Leipzig, Kap. 10 G Nr. 685 Bd. 2. Cf. Hoffmann, 'The German Resistance to Hitler and the Jews', pp. 277–90.

[68] See p. 49 above.

[69] Hans Mommsen's judgment in *Alternative zu Hitler*, p. 389, that Goerdeler resigned mainly because of the loss of his authority misses the point: Goerdeler had lost his authority here because of his opposition to the National Socialists' Jewish policy.

'the great faith' that National Socialists own in all decisive questions; just as Goerdeler in 1933 doubted that the National Socialist government would last long, so he also doubted the appropriateness of the various measures – whether it was re-armament, the remilitarisation of the Rhineland, or economic decisions, Dr Goerdeler was invariably pessimistic. From the middle of the year, Dr Goerdeler had been increasingly pessimistic. He had criticised the national financial policies most severely, predicting a catastrophe, and considered the foreign-currency and raw-materials situation as particularly dire. Haake, he continued, had read Goerdeler's memorandum for Göring, and it reflected the same pessimistic mentality. For any measure to be taken, Goerdeler wanted at least a 51 percent chance of success. National Socialists cannot work with such a man in view of the great tasks that must be accomplished in future. Goerdeler showed no understanding for the National Socialist position in the churches question.

Dr Goerdeler's attitude in the Jewish Question had been revealed extraordinarily clearly in the matter of the Mendelssohn-Bartholdy statue. As I wrote, he has made extraordinary difficulties not only in the matter of the Mendelssohn monument, but in all cases of re-naming streets named after a Jew. If he now took the occasion of the matter of the Mendelssohn monument to ask to be pensioned, I am firmly convinced that the causes lie much deeper.

Haake also surmised that Goerdeler's frustrated ambition to again be named *Reich* prices commissioner was involved, and that Goerdeler may have felt in the face of the successes of National Socialism that his own very different views were no longer sustainable.

When Mutschmann installed Goerdeler's successor, the Leipzig National Socialist county leader (*Kreisleiter*) Walter Dönicke, he said that Leipzig as a world-rank city had to have a National Socialist mayor. Goerdeler wrote to Mutschmann from New York on 23 November 1937 to explain the reasons for his resignation, listing first the removal of the Mendelssohn-Bartholdy statue and the refusal of the Saxon Ministry of the Interior to take the action against Haake that Goerdeler had to demand to preserve his authority. In consequence, Goerdeler concluded, he was forced to resign his office.[70] He had not the power to simply have the statue brought back, and so he had lost both a point of principle and his authority. The issue of his authority forced him to resign, although, of course, it was not the primary cause of the conflict. When

[70] Goerdeler to Reichsstatthalter Martin Mutschmann 23 November 1937, Stadtarchiv Leipzig, Kap. 10 G Nr. 685 Bd. 2.

Haake proposed that the city council approve Goerdeler's request to be relieved of his office with pension, not one of the thirty councillors who were present rose to say a word of thanks, or in Goerdeler's defence.[71]

After his resignation as mayor of Leipzig in the autumn of 1936, effective in April 1937, Goerdeler worked in Berlin as a consultant and agent for the Robert Bosch Company of Stuttgart.

Robert Bosch and his company executives, particularly Hans Walz and Albrecht Fischer, gave support and assistance to Jews in the 1930s in many forms through community organisations and the like. In December 1936, Karl Adler, the Jewish head of the Conservatory for Music in Stuttgart, wrote in an appeal to Hans Walz that Robert Bosch's help in critical times was 'today support and assistance for thousands of the despairing German Jews'.[72] In the case of a Frankfurt jewellery store whose Jewish co-owners wished to sell their shares and emigrate, Bosch paid a generous price and facilitated the transfer of the proceeds of the sale via Switzerland to the United States.[73] When Karl Adler was arrested in connection with the 9 November 1938 pogrom, Robert Bosch caused Hans Walz to intervene, and Adler was released on condition that he increase the speed of Jewish emigration as manager of the Stuttgart bureau of the Agency for Adult Education (*Mittelstelle für Erwachsenenbildung*) that Martin Buber had founded in 1934. Adler's task was enormously complicated, particularly by the fact that most assets of Jews had been confiscated, and also because the *Gestapo* had set up an office of their own in the agency. Robert Bosch supported Adler's work with 'substantial sums' from 1938 to 1940. This had to be done in secret, in sealed envelopes

[71] Nichtöffentliche Beratung des Bürgermeisters mit den Ratsherren am Mittwoch, den 2. Dezember 1936, 18 Uhr, im Sitzungssaal, Leipzig C 1, Neues Rathaus, 2. Obergeschoss, Zi. 386/8, Stadtarchiv Leipzig, Kap. 10 G Nr. 685 Bd. 1. One of the councillors, Otto Wolf, wrote on 7 December 1936 to Party authorities that Goerdeler had in 1934 severely criticised Hitler's actions 'in the Röhm affair' and said that the courts of law should have been employed, and that it was impossible for him to wear the Party badge if he received one; that Goerdeler had resisted every renaming of a street named after a Jew; that Mrs Goerdeler had herself driven in the mayor's official automobile to Jewish stores to do her shopping; that in May 1936, faced with the *Führer*'s and the government's confidence in Goerdeler, the council renewed Goerdeler's appointment as mayor, but since then he had ever more displayed his economic pessimism, particularly in connection with the new Four-Year Plan; and that we are scandalised now, in the matter of the Mendelssohn monument, that we the councillors asked Mayor Haake to remove it in Dr Goerdeler's absence, that Dr Goerdeler, a non-National Socialist, now invokes discipline toward him from National Socialists in a fundamentally National Socialist matter, while he has not enough discipline to support the measures of the *Reich* government.

[72] Scholtyseck, *Robert Bosch*, pp. 265–69.

[73] Scholtyseck, *Robert Bosch*, p. 270.

containing between RM 500 and 3,000. Many Jews had to be smuggled across the border, at a cost of about RM 1,000 per person. In one spectacular case, the police and *SS* extorted an exorbitant sum for allowing a group of Jews to cross the Rhine into France.[74]

In August 1937 Goerdeler travelled to Canada and the United States.[75] Goerdeler wrote for Hitler two reports about his visit to Canada, and one lengthy one about his travels in America. He called his first report on Canada, dated 27 September 1937, a 'Special Report'. In it, he stressed Canadian views on German policies toward the Jews and the churches, devoting one and a half pages of the not quite four pages of the report to Canadians' conspicuously large interest in Germany's treatment of the Jewish Question:

> Strikingly, the treatment of the Jewish Question meets with greater interest in Canada than in Western Europe. This astonished me all the more since I did see negroes in Canada but no Jews. [...] If, nevertheless, a conspicuously high interest is focused in Canada upon the treatment of the Jews in Germany, it is because this young country [Canada] displays an uncommonly high respect for the values of humanity.[76]

Goerdeler thus characterised German policy toward the Jews as inhuman. He concluded that, if German policy makers hoped to influence the Canadian government, they must know these facts and must accommodate the critical views of Canadians in the Jewish Question, the Church Question, and the Rule-of-Law Question.

In a report on America, dated 2 January 1938 – for Robert Bosch, Gustav Krupp von Bohlen und Halbach, Hermann Göring,[77] Hitler's adjutant Fritz Wiedemann, and Generals Werner Freiherr von Fritsch, Ludwig Beck, Franz Halder, and Georg Thomas – Goerdeler wrote that the Americans were generally understanding and friendly toward Germany. The boycott movement (initiated by the American Jewish Congress) was less noticeable the farther removed one was from its centre in New York. One had to keep in mind 'that there was barely a club in the United States that admitted Jews, that Jews are not allowed into some hotels, and that apparently in all universities the percentage of Jewish students has been tacitly set'. Goerdeler's anecdotal observations prove to

[74] Scholtyseck, *Robert Bosch*, pp. 271–73.

[75] Ritter, *Goerdeler*, p. 163.

[76] Typed carbon copy in the possession of the author; not in Gillmann and Mommsen, *Politische Schriften*.

[77] Air minister, commander-in-chief of the air force, Prussian minister-president, and interior minister, plenipotentiary for the Four-Year Plan.

have been accurately representative. According to opinion polls, at least three-fifths of the American public was antisemitic in the years 1938–1940, and anti-Jewish feeling in America increased during the war years. Although the American public was not subject to massive anti-Jewish propaganda, over one-third believed that Jews had too much power; the same proportion, one-third, were prepared to support a general antisemitic campaign, one third were opposed to an antisemitic campaign, and one-third 'would have been little concerned' by such action.[78] For purposes of immigration and restrictions upon immigration, the United States government's Immigration and Naturalization Service used the concept of the 'Jewish race'.[79]

Goerdeler continued,

> In my view the entire boycott movement will be over at the moment in which Germany makes it known in practice that she is concerned with the *principle*, but that the *individual* Jew within the law will not by extraordinary means be deprived of every opportunity of existence. If Germany, however, takes the occasion of the development of the Jewish Question in Eastern Europe to suggest a positive solution of the Jewish Problem among all involved and interested states – Palestine is not sufficient – then every reservation connected with this issue, also in the United States, would be removed because then the greatest interest of all [states] in a positive solution would have to reveal itself.[80]

There are several points requiring comment. First, one year after his demand to take into account the 'very decided wishes' of England and France in 'the Jewish Question, the Free-Masons´ Question, legal security, the Church Question', and his resignation over an issue of anti-Jewish

[78] David S. Wyman, *Paper Walls: America and the Refugee Crisis 1938–1941*, Amherst: University of Massachusetts Press, 1968, p. 22, cites Charles Herbert Stember et al., *Jews in the Mind of America*, New York and London: Basic Books, 1966, pp. 53–55, 121, 123–24, 127–28, 84–85, 130–33, 208–10, 214–15.

[79] Wyman, p. ix.

[80] Gillmann and Mommsen, *Politische Schriften*, pp. 578–79: '*Meines Erachtens ist die ganze Boykottbewegung zu Ende in dem Augenblick, in dem Deutschland praktisch zu erkennen gibt, dass ihm am* Grundsatz *gelegen ist, daß aber der* einzelne *Jude im Rahmen des Gesetzes nicht mit außerordentlichen Mitteln um jede Existenzmöglichkeit gebracht werden soll.* Wenn *aber Deutschland die Entwicklung der Judenfrage in Osteuropa zum Anlass nimmt, eine positive Lösung des Judenproblems – Palästina reicht nicht aus – unter allen beteiligten und interessierten Staaten anzuregen, so würde sofort jede Hemmung, die mit dieser Frage in Verbindung steht, auch in den Vereinigten Staaten beseitigt sein, da sich dann das grösste Interesse aller an einer positiven Lösung offenbaren müsste*'. While Jewish organisations in the 1930s considered Madagascar as at least a possible supplemental receiving area for Jewish settlers, the island does not appear in Goerdeler's proposals; cf. Magnus Brechtken, '*Madagaskar für die Juden*': *Antisemitische Idee und politische Praxis 1885–1945*, Munich: R. Oldenbourg Verlag, 1997, pp. 116–19.

policy in Germany, Goerdeler again took the issue of anti-Jewish policies to the highest level of government in Germany and urged international consultations and negotiations about it. Goerdeler addressed his memorandum to the most powerful person in Germany, Hitler, through the dictator's personal adjutant, Wiedemann, and to the other most powerful persons in Germany: Hitler's designated successor, Göring,[81] and the heads of the army, the dominant military service in Germany. Goerdeler pressed the German government to make a decisive move.

Second, Goerdeler argued that *if Germany*, the country currently with the most virulent anti-Jewish policies but also a country that met with much understanding and friendliness in America, if this Germany took an initiative in a positive direction, the world would listen. *If Germany* took up 'the development of the Jewish Question in Eastern Europe to suggest a positive solution of the Jewish Problem among all involved', then it would likely, so Goerdeler believed, lead to a positive solution in the 'interest of all'. Germany would not in the first instance have to recant and change her policy toward the Jews. This did not mean that Goerdeler agreed with the regime's general policies toward the Jews, only that the regime could retain its hostile attitude toward the Jews while opting for measures less harmful to the Jews as well as to German commercial and foreign-policy interests. Knowing how adamant, indeed fanatical, Hitler was about the matter, and in light of the state of international law and racially based policies in numerous nations, Goerdeler could not with any hope of success in this memorandum oppose the regime's anti-Jewish policies more fundamentally.[82]

What Goerdeler was suggesting with a view to 'the development of the Jewish Question in Eastern Europe' was a relaxation of restrictions on Jewish immigration from Eastern Europe, to the United States and other countries and territories. Goerdeler did not suggest any easing of the obstacles to Jewish emigration from Germany to America, only that the boycott would end if Germany participated in a positive manner in international consultations to solve 'the Jewish Question'. The 'Jewish Question' encompassed the issues raised by the Comité des Délégations Juives auprès de la Conférence de la Paix in 1919.

Germany could take a position in favour of the protection of the Jews in Eastern Europe. If Germany suggested a positive solution 'among all

[81] Hitler's decree based on the law concerning the *Führer*'s succession of 13 December 1934 in Bundesarchiv Nachlass Hitler/23 and R 43 II/1660 (Reichskanzlei, Registratur Dr. Lammers).

[82] Cf. pp. 75–6 below.

involved', that would include Germany itself, with the implication that Germany changed its policy toward the Jews. Germany would show itself as lawful and reasonable. Then 'every reservation connected with this issue', the 'Jewish Problem', would 'be removed'. The economic issues, such as the boycott movement, would cease to exist.

Goerdeler was optimistic, but not naive. His many ideas and proposals were in fact part of the international search for a solution to 'the Jewish Question'. He was one of very, very few in Germany who concerned themselves to this extent with the condition of the Jews. He anticipated and moved far beyond the efforts and results of the international conference at Évian-les-bains, months before President Roosevelt initiated the conference. No one else proposed and formulated what Goerdeler advocated from 1938 to 1941. This will be addressed in Chapters 5 and 6.

There had been, in the twentieth century, various schemes to find a 'solution' to the 'Jewish Question'. Colonisation in other regions than Russia and Eastern Europe had been a topic before 1933. There had been efforts, from 1906 to 1928, to settle Jewish refugees in Cyprus. Their prospects depended upon international cooperation, and upon funding. Neither of these conditions found much support. American Jewish communities and organisations were best able to provide funding. Support from the American Colonization Association, however, was weak. Efforts in 1935 to revive the Cyprus idea were headed by Max Warburg's brother Felix Warburg, one of the most important American Jewish leaders; they failed, as had earlier attempts. Felix Warburg offered a mere U.S. $10,000 toward the Cyprus project.[83]

On 23 October 1935, at the end of a luncheon that McDonald had with the bishop of Chichester, George Bell, Lord Lothian (Philip Henry Kerr, eleventh marquess of Lothian, under-secretary of state for India 1931–1932) came along, and McDonald told him that he had a responsibility to use his influence on Germany. Lord Lothian replied that he doubted anything could be done until Germany raised a question such as the return of the colonies. Then the British government could say, 'We cannot sit down with you until you have changed your policy of intolerance'.[84] But when McDonald went to see Assistant Under-secretary Sir Orme B. Sargent in the Foreign Office and told him Lord Lothian's suggestion, Sargent said that first of all, it might be months or years

[83] McDonald, *Refugees*, p. 9.
[84] McDonald, *Refugees*, p. 56.

before Germany raised the question of colonies, and second, the British government would not engage in such bargaining – and, if the British government agreed to discuss such a German proposal, Germany might ask Britain to take a definite quota of emigrants from Germany.[85]

The third of Goerdeler's points that require comment is that he was seeking a method to settle 'the Jewish Question in Eastern Europe', and he added that Palestine was 'not sufficient'. He was undoubtedly aware of the 'growing concern' among British members of Parliament caused by 'the development of antisemitism in Eastern Europe', and also with the position of the British Mandatory government.[86] Several million East European Jews could not be settled in Palestine in a limited time frame, and within the terms of British Palestine policy.

The British government had issued a statement of policy dated 2 November 1917, in the form of a letter from Foreign Secretary Arthur James Balfour to Baron Walter Rothschild. It is known as the Balfour Declaration, which stated:

> His Majesty's government view with favour the establishment in Palestine of a national home for the Jewish people, and will use their best endeavors to facilitate the achievement of this object, it being clearly understood that nothing shall be done which may prejudice the civil and religious rights of existing non-Jewish communities in Palestine, or the rights and political status enjoyed by Jews in any other country.[87]

The Balfour Declaration and the Mandate for Palestine were later incorporated into the Treaty of Peace with Turkey, signed at Sèvres on 10 August 1920. The treaty contained this stipulation:

> The Mandatory will be responsible for putting into effect the declaration originally made on November 2, 1917, by the British Government, and adopted by the other Allied Powers, in favour of the establishment in Palestine of a national home for the Jewish people, it being clearly understood that nothing shall be done which may prejudice the civil and religious rights of existing non-Jewish communities in Palestine, or the rights and political status enjoyed by Jews in any other country.[88]

[85] McDonald, *Refugees*, p. 64.

[86] *The Times* 7 July 1937, p. 16.

[87] *Documents on British Foreign Policy 1919–1931: First Series*, vol. IV, no. 242, pp. 340–49 ('Memorandum by Mr. Balfour [Paris], respecting Syria, Palestine, and Mesopotamia, August 11, 1919').

[88] *Treaty of Peace with Turkey: Signed at Sèvres, August 10, 1920. [With Maps.] Presented to Parliament by Command of His Majesty [Cmd. 964.]*, London: His Majesty's Stationery Office, 1920 (brackets on title page), section 7, articles 94–97.

British geopolitical interests in the eastern Mediterranean were evident, near the Suez Canal, the road to India, and the oil around the Persian Gulf. At the time of the Balfour Declaration, the impending demise of the Ottoman Empire was equally obvious. The possibility of creating an ally in the region cannot have been far from the thoughts of the concerned civil servants in the Foreign Office. In any case, the British government, chosen by the Allied and Associated Powers as the Mandatory, needed to balance conflicting interests of Arabs and Jews in Palestine and was obliged, particularly after disturbances in 1930, to assert that it 'will continue to administer Palestine in accordance with the terms of the Mandate, without discriminating between persons on the ground of religion or race'.[89] This was proving difficult in face of pressures from many quarters.

The White Papers of 1922 and 1930 restricted Jewish immigration into Palestine.[90] In response to Jewish pressure, the British government in 1931 cancelled the restrictions of 1930. With the outbreak of the Arab Revolt (1936–1938), however, the restrictions were again put in place.

The influential British president of the Zionist Organisation, Chaim Weizmann, had aims that conflicted with British policy. He told the League of Nations high commissioner for refugees coming from Germany in 1933 that he was anxious to buy 'a substantial tract of land in Syria at the corner where it joins Trans-Jordania and Palestine', and that he was negotiating with France about the purchase. This would be a 'bridgehead in the Jordan valley'. If it could be 'occupied with 5,000 families sufficiently armed to protect themselves against marauding Bedouins, the way would have been opened for mass colonization in Trans-Jordania'. On that basis Weizmann foresaw a cohesive Jewish community of as many as five million.[91]

The fourth point that emerges is that Goerdeler was, of course, aware of the worldwide ethnophobia and resistance to Jewish immigration. A year before the Évian Conference, almost two years before the ill-fated voyage of the *St Louis*, Goerdeler believed that Germany had only slightly to change its policy to defuse the situation in a large part of the world.[92] He was looking for a secure status of the Jews in the entire world even

[89] *The Times* 14 February 1931, p. 12.

[90] Dalia Ofer, *Escaping the Holocaust: Illegal Immigration to the Land of Israel, 1939–1944*, New York and Oxford: Oxford University Press, 1990, pp. 5–7.

[91] McDonald, *Advocate*, p. 153.

[92] Sarah A. Ogilvie and Scott Miller, *Refuge Denied: The St. Louis Passengers and the Holocaust*, Madison: University of Wisconsin Press, 2006.

then, in 1937. He could not say this *expressis verbis*, considering to whom the memorandum was directed.

The fifth is that, as early as 1937, Goerdeler advanced the concept of an international agreement:

> If Germany, however, takes the occasion of the development of the Jewish Question in Eastern Europe to suggest a positive solution of the Jewish Problem among all involved and interested states – Palestine is not sufficient –, then every reservation connected with this issue, also in the United States, would be removed because then the greatest interest of all [states] in a positive solution would have to reveal itself.[93]

Goerdeler suggested that the German government use the situation of the Jews in Eastern Europe for an international dialogue. This would be capable of removing 'every reservation connected with this issue, also in the United States'. America was obviously the country best able to receive large numbers of immigrants. The expectation of a positive attitude of the United States toward the situation in Eastern Europe was reasonable in view of President Wilson's stance at the Paris Peace Conference of 1919. In a memorandum of 1 December 1937 to be published in America whenever he gave a signal for its publication, or 'in case something happened to him', Goerdeler said he was disturbed by the equanimity with which many outside Germany received the news of the Hitler regime's atrocities.[94]

There had indeed been a good deal of publicity about the plight not only of German Jews, but also of those in East European countries. In 1936 the Polish government felt ready to raise the question of African colonies for Poland. In this connection the Polish government sought to enable Jewish emigration from Poland to Madagascar and generally to increase Jewish emigration to 100,000 annually. The idea of Polish–Jewish colonisation in Madagascar was not new; the former French undersecretary of state Gratien Candace had mentioned it in an interview in May 1935.[95] The debate in Poland became more intense when in

[93] Gillmann and Mommsen, *Politische Schriften*, pp. 578–79: '*Wenn aber Deutschland die Entwicklung der Judenfrage in Osteuropa zum Anlass nimmt, eine positive Lösung des Judenproblems – Palästina reicht nicht aus – unter allen beteiligten und interessierten Staaten anzuregen, so würde sofort jede Hemmung, die mit dieser Frage in Verbindung steht, auch in den Vereinigten Staaten beseitigt sein, da sich dann das grösste Interesse aller an einer positiven Lösung offenbaren müsste*'. While Jewish organisations in the 1930s considered Madagascar as at least a possible supplemental receiving area for Jewish settlers, the island does not appear in Goerdeler's proposals; cf. Brechtken, *Madagaskar*, pp. 116–19.

[94] Ritter, *Goerdeler*, pp. 167–68.

[95] Brechtken, *Madagaskar*, p. 102.

August 1936 the British Mandatory power curtailed Jewish immigration to Palestine.[96] In Geneva on 2 October 1936, the Polish foreign minister Józef Beck mentioned to the president and cofounder of the World Jewish Congress (WJC), Nahum Goldman, who was the WJC's representative at the League of Nations, that Jewish emigration from Poland was the most important constructive means for the solution of the Jewish Question in Poland. Beck said that besides Palestine, other territories must be found, and he asked Goldman to ask the French government to enable the immigration of Polish Jews to Madagascar. A few days later, Beck put the same proposal to the French ministerpresident Léon Blum; the French foreign minister Yvon Delbos favoured the idea.

These 'thoughts' were not secret, there were reports in the press.[97] The Comité pour la Défense des Droits des Israélites en Europe Centrale et Orientale in November 1936 submitted to the French Foreign Ministry a note concerning settlement of Jews from East and Central Europe in the French overseas territories of Madagascar and New Caledonia. The extremely difficult situation of the Jews in Germany, Romania, Lithuania, Russia, and Poland, the Comité stated, made the provision of colonial territories for the emigration of the persecuted a necessity. Jewish aid organisations, such as the American Joint Distribution Committee and the New York Refugee Economic Corporation, were prepared to provide generous financial support. In view of the tremendous barriers to Jewish immigration in Argentina and Brazil (countries where the political and economic climate was 'laden with anti-Semitism'[98]), and in the United States of America, other territories should be considered, such as Madagascar and New Caledonia.[99] Numbers were not mentioned, but the persecuted Jews in all of Central and Eastern Europe were in question.[100]

In January 1937, the French ministre des colonies, Marius Moutet, said in an interview that the Jews represented a serious settlement element, and that the governor of Madagascar had expressed himself favourably on the subject of settlers for the island, but at the same time warned against exaggerated hopes for rapid mass colonisation, as the *Israelitisches*

[96] Brechtken, *Madagaskar*, pp. 81–164, esp. 88–91. Brechtken, p. 82, attempts in tortuously obscure argumentation to declare the Polish settlement plan decidedly different from the National Socialist considerations of 1940 because the Poles had not pursued a 'race-ideological state aim'.

[97] Brechtken, *Madagaskar*, pp. 97–99.

[98] McDonald, *Advocate*, p. 800.

[99] Brechtken, *Madagaskar*, p. 100.

[100] Brechtken, *Madagaskar*, p. 101.

Familienblatt reported for its German readers on 21 January 1937.[101] The French Ambassador in Warsaw reported that information about a possible Jewish colonisation in French territories 'provoquent à Varsovie une sensation'. Expectations were soon dampened when the undersecretary of state in the French Colonial Ministry, Paul Bouteille, informed the Jewish Agency, and the press, that in 1937 ten families at most could be placed in the French colonies, and perhaps thirty in 1938, and fifty in 1939. In the weeks following, Moutet and other government officials made clear that they were in principle well disposed toward plans for Jewish settlement, but that the opportunities were extremely limited, only a few hundred persons could be settled in Madagascar, and every settler would have to have at least £1,000; the Ministry for the Colonies had no funds for the purpose.[102] Therefore, these plans would in no case amount to an evacuation of Jews from Poland, he said, and the hopes of other countries that Moutet's suggestions would make possible the evacuation of Jews from their territories were baseless; in the first instance, it was a question of settling refugees already in France. The relevant agencies in the French government calculated that 300,000 francs per immigrant would have to be invested for settlement in the New Hebrides, and that the plantations in their first years would be highly deficitary. It was a question of finances, and neither the French nor the Polish government, nor the Jewish organisations, was now able or prepared to underwrite such enterprises.[103] The Polish government pursued the matter with the French government in January 1938, but by the end of May 1938, the whole project of settling a substantial number of Jews in any French colonies had collapsed, in part because of unfavourable conditions in Madagascar, and in part because the government in France kept changing at the rate of four different administrations in the year 1938 alone, including three different ministers for the colonies.[104]

The Polish Jewish press commented that there were no serious settlement opportunities in the territories that had been mentioned, and Jews could not settle in 'deserts'; the American Jewish press unanimously rejected colonial-settlement schemes for Jews.[105] In Germany, the *Jüdische Rundschau* in January 1937 commented with the noncommittal statement that the matter must be monitored with careful attention; the

[101] Brechtken, *Madagaskar*, p. 103; the paper had an edition of 36,500 in 1935.

[102] Brechtken, *Madagaskar*, pp. 103–6.

[103] Brechtken, *Madagaskar*, pp. 105–6.

[104] Brechtken, *Madagaskar*, pp. 129–37, 142–47.

[105] Brechtken, *Madagaskar*, pp. 106–7.

C.-V. Zeitung in the same month cited the rejection of the idea by the Polish Jewish press and proposed opening Transjordania and Syria to Jewish settlement, adding that there were far better settlement conditions in Argentina and Australia than in the proposed desert regions.[106] Reports and comments in the Jewish and non-Jewish press continued for over two years. In 1937 and 1938, mainstream papers such as the *Berliner Börsenzeitung*, *Berliner Tageblatt*, *Danziger Neueste Nachrichten*, *Deutsche Rundschau*, *Fränkische Tageszeitung*, *Neue Zürcher Zeitung*, *The Times*, and the National Socialist Party paper *Völkischer Beobachter* all carried stories about the settlement ideas for Madagascar and other territories.[107]

On 12 March 1938, Germany occupied and then-annexed Austria (*Anschluss*). Adolf Eichmann, *SS* specialist in Jewish affairs, moved into Vienna immediately, raided Jewish community centres, and began to organise a Central Office for Jewish Emigration in Vienna for the purpose of driving out as many Jews as possible as rapidly as possible. The office officially opened on 20 August 1938. Between August 1938 and June 1939, it 'facilitated' the emigration or expulsion of 110,000 Jews.[108] But the Jews' exodus had begun immediately after 12 March. There was at the time no visa requirement for crossing the German–Swiss border, and many Viennese Jews took advantage of this.[109]

The League of Nations Covenant did not provide any mechanism for intervention in the internal affairs of a foreign state, in order, for example, to protect a minority. Article 15 in essence declared that members of the League of Nations or the League of Nations Council would not intervene

[106] Brechtken, *Madagaskar*, p. 107, cites *Jüdische Rundschau* 19.1.37, p. 1, 'Judensiedlungen in französischen Kolonien?' *C.-V. Zeitung* 21.1.37, 'Ansiedlungsmöglichkeiten in französischen Kolonien?' *Israelitisches Familienblatt* 21.1.37, p. 2, 'Ansiedlung in französischen Kolonien'; *Israelitisches Familienblatt* 28.1.37, p. 1, 'Ein neues Kolonisationsprojekt'; *Der Israelit* 21.1.37, p. 2, 'Französische Kolonien für Judensiedlung' and p. 5, 'Wieder Madagaskar?'

[107] Brechtken, *Madagaskar*, pp. 312–18.

[108] Donald Nieweyk and Francis Nicosia, *The Columbia Guide to The Holocaust*, New York: Columbia University Press, 2000, p. 8; 'Adolf Eichmann', United States Holocaust Memorial Museum *Holocaust Encyclopedia*, *http://www.ushmm.org/wlc/en/article.php?ModuleId=10007412*; see also the overview and documentation of the persecution and expulsion of Jews in Wolf Gruner, ed., *Die Verfolgung und Ermordung der europäischen Juden durch das nationalsozialistische Deutschland 1933–1945. Band 1. Deutsches Reich 1933–1937*, Munich: Oldenbourg Verlag, 2008, passim; and Susanne Heim, ed., *Die Verfolgung und Ermordung der europäischen Juden durch das nationalsozialistische Deutschland 1933–1945. Band 2. Deutsches Reich 1938-August 1939*, Munich: R. Oldenbourg Verlag, 2009, pp. 13–63 and passim.

[109] Hilberg, *Destruction*, p. 174.

in 'a matter which by international law is solely within the domestic jurisdiction' of a party or member.[110] The issue became one of such international concern, however, that some governments decided to react.

Immediately upon the *Anschluss* of Austria to Germany, the Polish government and public feared that as many as 30,000 Viennese Jews would wish to return to their homeland in formerly Austrian Galicia, now a part of Poland, or to Warsaw or other parts of Poland.[111] The government introduced a draft act in the Polish Parliament (*Seym*) on 15 March 1938 and had it passed into law on 31 March.[112] The law aimed to deprive certain categories of nonresident Poles of Polish citizenship. It was intended to prevent the immigration (re-migration) of Jews to Poland.[113] At the same time, the Consular Department in the Polish Foreign Ministry promoted mass emigration of Jews from Poland.[114] On 15 June 1938, the Polish Telegraphic Agency reported that Jews from Vienna who had succeeded in entering Poland were to be put into the Polish concentration camp of Bereza Kartuska.[115]

On 14 March 1938, the British Home Office confidentially advised the Foreign Office that the expected great increase 'of refugees of Jewish race or ancestry' necessitated a visa system to control admissions. Although the refugees might not be individually undesirable, the memorandum explained, their numbers might 'create social and labour problems'.[116] On 15 March, when six persons holding Austrian passports arrived at Folkestone, a tightening of conditions for admission already appeared to apply.[117] On 16 March, the Cabinet, upon the insistence of the home

[110] 'If there should arise between Members of the League any dispute likely to lead to a rupture', which is not submitted to arbitration by a court agreed to by the parties to the dispute, the members agree that they will submit the matter to the League of Nations Council. 'If the dispute between the parties is claimed by one of them, and is found by the Council to arise out of a matter which by international law is solely within the domestic jurisdiction of that party, the Council shall so report, and shall make no recommendation as to its settlement'. *The Covenant of the League of Nations with a Commentary Thereon: Presented to Parliament by Command of His Majesty: June 1919*, London: His Majesty's Stationery Office, 1919, pp. 6–7.

[111] Karol Jonca, 'The Expulsion of Polish Jews from the Third Reich in 1938', in *Polin: Studies in Polish Jewry*, vol. 8, London and Washington: Littman Library of Jewish Civilization, 1994, p. 256. Jonca gives no numbers of Jews in Germany who were regarded as Jews by whatever criteria, or of non-Jewish Poles in Germany in 1938.

[112] Jonca, 'Expulsion', pp. 256, 258.

[113] Jonca, 'Expulsion', p. 261; *The Times* 30 March 1938, p. 13.

[114] Tomaszewski, 'Civil Rights', p. 126.

[115] Yehuda Bauer, *My Brother's Keeper: A History of the American Jewish Joint Distribution Committee, 1929–1939*, Philadelphia: Jewish Publication Society of America, 1974, pp. 244.

[116] Sherman, *Island Refuge*, p. 87.

[117] *Parliamentary Debates* 333, c. 990.

secretary, Sir Samuel Hoare, discussed the abrogation of the 1928 British–German agreement for the mutual abolition of visas. The Home Office had reasons to fear not merely a large influx of refugees and resulting social and labour problems, but also a German intention of inundating Britain with refugees to create a Jewish Problem in Britain.[118]

On 17 March 1938, a member of the British House of Commons, the Hon. R.D. Denman, asked whether the motion could be debated that 'in the opinion of this House, immigration of Jews into Palestine in accordance with the principle of economic absorptive capacity should be resumed from the end of March, 1938'. The prime minister replied that he was 'afraid that the Government have no time at their disposal' for such a debate. When Colonel Rt.Hon. J.C. Wedgwood asked whether the prime minister could not 'get some modification made in the immigration schedule which has recently been put up, as the policy of this Government on Palestine', the speaker balked at allowing the question.[119]

On 22 March, the home secretary stated the government's policy in the House of Commons: He was sure, he said, that there was a general desire 'to maintain the traditional policy of this country of offering asylum to persons who for political, racial or religious reasons have had to leave their own country'. However, indiscriminate admission would create difficulties from the police point of view and also have 'grave economic results in aggravating the unemployment problem, the housing problem and other social problems'. Sympathetic consideration would be given to 'Austrians' seeking admission to Britain, and to 'Austrians' who were already in the country and applied for naturalisation. At the same time, overcrowding had to be avoided even in the professions, and 'in the sphere of business and industry the social and economic difficulties must be taken into account'.[120] Neither the government nor Parliament agreed to wholesale admission and naturalisation for refugees.[121] Visa requirements went into effect. On 21 April the British ambassador in Berlin, Sir Nevile Henderson, formally notified the German government of his government's intention to terminate the visa agreement of 1928. On 27 April the British Foreign Office circulated British consulates with criteria for granting visas to German and Austrian travellers.[122]

[118] Sherman, *Island Refuge*, pp. 87–93.
[119] *Parliamentary Debates* 333, c. 584; speaker of the house was Captain Right Hon. Edward A. FitzRoy, M.P.
[120] *Parliamentary Debates* 333, c. 991–92.
[121] Sherman, *Island Refuge*, p. 93.
[122] Sherman, *Island Refuge*, pp. 89–90.

On 22 March 1938, reacting to the *Anschluss* of Austria, President Roosevelt, who had been sympathetic to the fate of the Jews in Germany but had refrained from any action to increase immigration from Germany into the United States, was now willing to consider some remedies. Without consulting the Department of State, he decided to ask a number of governments, on 24 March, including those in the United Kingdom and in France, whether they would cooperate in setting up a 'special committee composed of representatives of a number of Governments for the purpose of facilitating the emigration from Austria, and presumably from Germany, of political refugees'; the emigration would have to be financed solely by private organisations. Some of the president's advisers had advocated a 'Napoleonic' approach, McDonald told members of the British delegation on 1 July; the idea of the Évian conference was an 'intuitive' proposal of the president. McDonald supported it.[123] Secretary of State Cordell Hull had to 'catch up'. The American note with the president's question was handed to the Foreign Office in Whitehall on 24 March.[124]

The American note did not say whether the United States intended to enlarge its own immigration quotas, it did not say where and how the refugees could be accepted, and it proposed to expand the authority of the League of Nations high commissioner for refugees coming from Germany to refugees coming from Austria. Combined with its reference to private funding, its vague and broad phrasing, and its lack of clarity about the president's motives, the note suggested to the Foreign Office that pressure from certain metropolitan constituencies in this midterm election year might be a factor and that the diplomatic and technical aspects had not been thought through. The note referred to persons as refugees who had not yet left Germany or Austria but who desired to emigrate because of persecution to which they might be subjected on political, racial, or religious grounds.[125] Roger Mellor Makins reported McDonald's scepticism, and R.A. Butler summarised the Foreign Office view with his comment: '"Intuition", "Napoleonic gestures" are always dangerous, especially when buried in the convenient sand of private organisations which have no money'.[126]

[123] McDonald and Myron C. Taylor (see below) appear to have given their support after Roosevelt had decided to launch the proposal; Sherman, *Island Refuge*, pp. 113–14; McDonald, *Refugees*, p. 122.

[124] Sherman, *Island Refuge*, pp. 95, 113; McDonald, *Refugees*, p. 122.

[125] Sherman, *Island Refuge*, pp. 95–96, 100–1.

[126] Sherman, *Island Refuge*, p. 114.

The initiative embarrassed the American government. The public and Congress would not tolerate any liberalisation of the immigration laws. Even if Austrian Jews were allowed to take unused places in the German quota, if there were any unused places – the combined total of the German and Austrian quotas would admit 27,370 in any one year – the numbers of Jewish immigrants who could be admitted still would be small. There was no government financing available, the private Jewish organisations were not unified, and in any case they were advised to keep in the background to avoid irritations. Very little if anything could be accomplished without German cooperation.[127]

At the same time, the British government welcomed the American government's willingness to involve itself in international and League of Nations affairs.[128] They had few illusions that war could be avoided in this or the next year, and it could be vital to encourage the United States to engage itself in Europe.[129] During the conference at Évian, the British delegation learned that President Roosevelt was convinced that no single country could escape from the effects of war if it came. The conference, in the president's view, ought also to 'promote Anglo-American cooperation and assist oppressed peoples'.[130]

The League of Nations Council took up the matter of extending the authority of the high commissioner for refugees coming from Germany at its meeting on 9 May and accepted a British motion to extend the high commissioner's authority to refugees coming from Austria.[131]

There was no more information coming from the American convenor for a while, concerning plans, structure, and agenda for the conference, except for the bare announcement that Mr Myron C. Taylor, formerly president of United States Steel Corporation, would chair the conference, with Mr James G. McDonald as his deputy. The Foreign Office's reaction to this was uncomplimentary, especially regarding McDonald, whom R.M. Makins of the Foreign Office Central Department apostrophised as 'not a success as High Commissioner' and a 'very tiresome individual'.[132] At the same time, it was realised that the German government's policy of

[127] McDonald, *Refugees*, pp. 121–24; Sherman, *Island Refuge*, pp. 114–15.

[128] Sherman, *Island Refuge*, pp. 96, 102, 114–15, 121.

[129] The president's quarantine speech in Chicago on 5 October 1937 had been an encouraging indication; *The Public Papers and Addresses of Franklin D. Roosevelt: 1937 Volume: The Constitution Prevails*, ed. Samuel I. Rosenman, New York: Macmillan, 1941, pp. 406–11.

[130] Sherman, *Island Refuge*, p. 121.

[131] Sherman, *Island Refuge*, p. 97.

[132] Sherman, *Island Refuge*, p. 100.

despoiling and expelling its Jewish population raised 'questions of world-wide importance'.[133]

Various ideas were being floated and continued to be raised during and after the Évian Conference, for the settlement of Jews somewhere in the world. Thomas J. Watson, founder and chairman of International Business Machines (IBM), wrote to Secretary of State Hull on 31 March 1938 that contributing money for temporary relief will not 'answer the Jewish problem as it exists today' – that it was the responsibility of the world to provide a permanent home for the Jewish refugees who had to leave Germany and Austria, and also for those who may find it necessary to leave other countries; Germany, England, France, and the United States should cooperate 'to turn over the former German colonies as a country for the Jews', in fact for all Jews who were prepared 'to participate in the building of a Jewish nation'; and Germany would have to request that England and France turn over the colonies, and the United States could participate by making concessions regarding international debts.[134]

The high commissioner for refugees, Sir Neill Malcolm, presented a proposal to the League of Nations Council on 9 May, that a small state be created, in North Borneo, in which stateless persons could become nationals and acquire the necessary documents to establish their legal status in countries of refuge. The Foreign Office considered a fictitious state 'rather impracticable' and incapable of improving refugees' chances of emigration and settlement.[135]

Settlement of Jewish refugees in British African colonies or mandates was discussed variously, but the British Colonial Office held out little hope that a very few refugees could be settled in Kenya, Tanganyika, and Northern Rhodesia; of the self-governing dominions in the empire, Australia might receive a few refugees; Canada did not even encourage British immigrants; New Zealand could not absorb any; and there was anti-Semitism in South Africa. The Treasury maintained that British government financial assistance to refugees was 'almost out of the question'.[136] Kenya was mentioned frequently in the context of potential settlement in the British Empire, but as in the cases of other colonies, there was really 'no room' for settlement – no large cities, no infrastructure, and far too few candidates among the Jewish refugees who could farm. The Colonial

[133] Sherman, *Island Refuge*, p. 113.

[134] The editors of McDonald, *Refugees*, p. 149, quote this from National Archives Record Group 59, Lot File 52D408, Alphabetical Subject File, Box 6, Jewish Refugees.

[135] Sherman, *Island Refuge*, pp. 95–97.

[136] Sherman, *Island Refuge*, p. 103.

Office explained to the Foreign Office in September 1938 that Kenya could receive at the most a total of 150 settlers. Australia advised the Dominions Office that she could accept up to 5,000 settlers per annum – if they were able to bring with them some capital.[137]

On 16 November 1938, Henry Morgenthau Jr., the American secretary of the Treasury, spoke to President Roosevelt of the suggestion of Constantine McGuire, an influential lawyer and Catholic layman, whom Morgenthau had recruited for the refugee cause, to trade French and British Guiana for war debts and to buy Dutch Guiana, to gain a territory for settling Jews. Roosevelt said: 'It's no good, it would take the Jews from 25 to 50 years to overcome the fever'; but the same method of debt forgiveness could apply to the Cameroons, a former German colony, about which the president had been speaking to Morgenthau 'for a long time' – the Cameroons had been explored, and that country was ready and had a good climate.[138] On 17 January 1939, the president wrote to Myron Taylor for Prime Minister Chamberlain that 'Angola offers the most favorable facility' for the creation of 'a supplemental Jewish homeland', declaring it 'a step essential to the solution of the Jewish problem'.[139] Later in the year, the American undersecretary of state, Benjamin Sumner Welles, in a memorandum to the president of 29 August, proposed as settlement areas British Guiana, the Dominican Republic, Mindanao, and Angola (by offering Portugal a large sum to purchase Angola, or to create a chartered company). The president's Advisory Committee on Political Refugees considered the same likely settlement places and in addition Northern Rhodesia.[140]

The British delegation to the Évian Conference, headed by Edward Turnour, sixth earl Winterton, M.P., chancellor of the duchy of Lancaster, would take as 'positive' a position as possible, namely, that there were no general restrictions against European immigration to colonial territories, so long as immigrants could demonstrate prospects of employment or other means of subsistence.[141] While the British government did not believe that any approach to the German government would be effective, should that question be raised at Évian, the principle that 'the country of origin should make a contribution to the solution of emigration problems' should be established at Évian; and it should be made clear to

[137] Sherman, *Island Refuge*, pp. 135–36.
[138] McDonald, *Refugees*, pp. 148, 152–54.
[139] McDonald, *Refugees*, p. 160.
[140] McDonald, *Refugees*, pp. 179–81.
[141] Sherman, *Island Refuge*, p. 109.

'other Central European Governments that, if they wish to get rid of their Jewish populations, they will be required to make a contribution to that end'.[142] The unstated fact was that no country in the world wanted to add to its population destitute and demoralised outcasts.[143]

This did not change during the meetings of the conference from 6 to 15 July 1938. The conference agreed to substitute the term 'involuntary emigrants' for the term 'refugees' and to establish an Inter-Governmental Committee for dealing with Germany.[144] The delegates of the thirty-two governments attending all expressed sympathy for the refugees, but none offered to accept any substantial numbers of them, or only those provided with sufficient assets, or qualified as agriculturalists. The Australian delegate, Lieutenant-Colonel Thomas W. White, minister for trade and customs, was blunt: 'It will no doubt be appreciated also that, as we have no real racial problem, we are not desirous of importing one by encouraging any scheme of large-scale foreign migration'.[145] Apart from publicity for the Jewish Question and for the pernicious policy of the German authorities, the practical result of the conference was the establishment of the Inter-Governmental Committee that the American delegation had been insistent about.

Hitler could answer the question why a civilised country would wish to lose so many valuable citizens by pointing out that the critics did not want them either. In his speech on 30 January 1939, in which he predicted the 'annihilation of the Jewish race in Europe' in case of a new world war, Hitler said the world could not find an excuse 'for refusing to receive this most valuable race in their own countries', nor could he, Hitler, 'see a reason why the members of this race should be imposed upon the German nation, while in the States, which are so enthusiastic about these "splendid people", their settlement should suddenly be refused with every imaginable excuse.'[146] On the whole, the German authorities only accelerated the pace and intensified the brutality of their treatment of the Jews. In Vienna, Eichmann's Office for Jewish Emigration heightened the

142 Sherman, *Island Refuge*, p. 110.

143 Sherman, *Island Refuge*, p. 111.

144 McDonald, *Refugees*, p. 139.

145 White said this presumably in his initial address; Michael Blakeney, *Australia and the Jewish Refugees 1933–1948*, Sidney: Croom Helm Australia, 1985, p. 130; *Proceedings of the Intergovernmental Committee, Evian, 6/15 July 1938, Verbatim Record of the Plenary Meeting of the Committee: Resolutions and Reports, London, July 1938*, p. 8, cited by S. Adler-Rudel, 'The Evian Conference on the Refugee Question', *Leo Baeck Institute Yearbook* 13 (1968): 242.

146 Baynes, *Speeches*, pp. 740–41.

pressure by taking some busloads of Jews across the nearest border and dumping them there, ignoring protests.[147]

The problem of German and Austrian Jews, without a financial foundation and without the willingness of other countries to accept these involuntary emigrants, was intractable enough. The American consul in Berlin, Raymond H. Geist, reported to the Department of State on 28 October 1938 that in September 1938, the American consulate in Berlin was overrun by thousands of desperate visa applicants day after day, that the American immigration quota of 27,300 per annum was now 'insufficient' for about 125,000 applicants, that new applicants now must wait three or four years, and that many of them 'are sure they cannot survive'.[148]

A much greater problem was the situation of the Jewish populations in Poland, Romania, and Hungary. Poland, for example, had since 1936 been searching for a scheme of emigration for its Jews and expected financial assistance from Britain. If the Évian Conference agreed upon any emigration and settlement schemes, it would encourage East European governments to increase the pressure upon their Jewish populations. This could involve millions of migrants. Millions on the move had a different dimension in 1938,[149] when the world's population was two billion, than in 2011, with a world population close to seven billion. Under this aspect alone, the conference was destined to fail – even if it did not fail for lack of a financial arrangement.

Upon the conclusion of the Évian Conference on 15 July, the Inter-Governmental Committee, residing in London, began its work on 3 August. It made recommendations to coordinate 'involuntary emigration' of large numbers of people.[150] This required the cooperation of 'countries of refuge'

[147] Sherman, *Island Refuge*, p. 133.

[148] McDonald, *Refugees*, pp. 143–44.

[149] Sherman, *Island Refuge*, p. 101.

[150] For the following account: Kieffer, 'Goerdeler's Vorschlag', p. 486, cites the U.S. National Archives RG 59, 840, for an American note addressed to the German government in October 1938, and for a similar French note the German Foreign Office Archive (Auswärtiges Amt/Politisches Archiv – AA PA) R 29989; the British Embassy in Berlin handed in a note with more or less the same content; the British note of 17 October 1938, the American note of 18 October 1938, and the French note of 24 October 1938 are also in AA PA R 99366; for minutes recorded by Secretary of State Ernst Freiherr von Weizsäcker and other German Foreign Office officials, see Aufzeichnung des Staatssekretärs 18 Oct. 1938 in *Akten zur deutschen auswärtigen Politik 1918–1945. Serie D (1937–1945). Band V (ADAP D V)*, Baden-Baden: Imprimerie Nationale, 1953, no. 645 pp. 758–59 (see also nos. 646–50 pp. 759–63). Cf. Magnus Brechtken, *'Madagaskar für die Juden': Antisemitische Idee und politische Praxis 1885–1945*, Munich: R.Oldenbourg Verlag, 1997, pp. 193–96; Sherman, *Island Refuge*, p. 119.

and 'the country of origin (Germany including Austria)'. The committee made clear what was meant by cooperation, namely, that the country of origin 'will make its contribution by enabling involuntary emigrants to take with them their property and possessions and emigrate in an orderly manner'. The committee proposed that its director, Mr George S. Rublee, an American citizen, discuss this and related matters with the government of 'the country of origin'. It defined the persons who were intended to benefit from its efforts: '(1) persons who have not already left their country of origin (Germany including Austria) but who must emigrate on account of their political opinions, religious beliefs or racial origin; and (2) persons as defined in (1) who have already left their country of origin and who have not yet established themselves permanently elsewhere'.

In the following months, the British, American, and French governments sought to advance the matter, but the German Foreign Office refused to allow Mr Rublee to come to Berlin for consultations about the modalities of 'involuntary emigration'.[151] On 17, 18, and 24 October 1938, the ambassadors of the United Kingdom, the United States, and France, respectively, who were accredited in Berlin, delivered notes to the German government urging cooperation with the Inter-Governmental Committee. The British note cited the committee's recommendations, which had defined the categories of persons whom its efforts concerned – 'persons who must emigrate on account of their political opinions, religious beliefs or racial origin'; and it named the 'conditions of exodus' as the country of origin permitting the persons it was forcing to leave 'to take with them a reasonable percentage of their property'. The American and French notes made similar statements. 'Countries of refuge' were not prepared to accept Jews without property.

The American note also stated the following: 'The [Inter-Governmental] Committee strictly abstains from any criticism or attempt at interference with Germany's entire right to take measures of internal effect with regard to the political opinions, the religious beliefs and the racial organization of its citizens'. The French note included this assurance: '*Aucun de ces États [represented in the Inter-Governmental Committee] ne conteste au Gouvernement allemande le droit absolu de prendre à l'égard de certains des ses ressortissants des mesures qui relevant uniquement de l'exercice de sa souveraineté*'. None of the three notes objected to expulsions.[152]

[151] *Foreign Relations of the United States. Diplomatic Papers. 1938*, vol. 1, Washington: United States Government Printing Office, 1955, pp. 799–824; there is little evidence of any official reaction to the pogrom of 9 November 1938.

[152] The United Kingdom and the United States had their own laws restricting immigration on racial grounds. Approximately 120,000 Jewish immigrants settled in Great Britain

The American and French notes stated the position of international law. It was not until 10 December 1948 that the United Nations General Assembly adopted the *Universal Declaration of Human Rights*. The *International Covenant on Civil and Political Rights* of 16 December 1966 acquired the force of international law in 1976, after a sufficient number of states had ratified it or acceded to it.[153] It is clear that opponents of the persecution of the Jews in Germany in 1938 could not hope for much support from abroad. What Goerdeler confronted at home, and how he tried to respond to it, will be outlined next.

At the request of the former head of the British Foreign Office, Sir Robert Vansittart, who had been named chief diplomatic adviser to the government at the end of 1937, Arthur Primrose Young, the Scottish engineer and industrialist with ties to the Robert Bosch company, met with Goerdeler on 6 and 7 August 1938 at Goerdeler's country residence in Rauschen Dune in East Prussia.[154] Young reported to Vansittart that Goerdeler expected Hitler's threat of war against Czechoslovakia to lead to 'great internal stress and turbulence consequent upon the reshaping of the government on reasonable and enlightened lines' – in short, a revolution.[155] Young's report continued:

> In discussing the persecution of the Jews X [Goerdeler] said he thought we should be more forceful in expressing our disgust of the Nazi methods. He even went so far as to suggest that we might tactfully indicate that if such practices continued it would make it exceedingly difficult for us to negotiate those "life problems" which awaited solution.[156]

between 1880 and 1914. Agitation in the United Kingdom against Jewish immigration gave rise to the British Aliens Act of 1905. Feldman, 'Nineteenth Century', pp. 167, 170. An American law excluded 'members of the yellow race' and Hindus from naturalisation; Stauffenberg, 'Entziehung', p. 270. According to Patrick Weil, 'Races at the Gate: Racial Distinctions in Immigration Policy: A Comparison between France and United States', in Fahrmeir, Faron, and Weil, eds., *Migration Control*, pp. 271–97 (quotation on p. 272), 'the racialist approach' officially dominated American immigration policy 'from the 1920s through to 1965'.

153 *Treaty Series: Treaties and International Agreements Registered or Filed and Recorded with the Secretariat of the United Nations*, vol. 999, New York: United Nations, 1983, no. 14668, pp. 171–86.

154 For the following, see Young, *The 'X' Documents*, pp. 45–49, 59, 139, 154–62, 177; cf. A.P. Young, 'Record of Conversation with Dr Goerdeler at Rauschen Düne, August 6th, 1938', Churchill College, Cambridge, VNST II 2/19, which is not entirely identical with the printed version, referring to Goerdeler not as 'X' but always as 'Dr Goerdeler'; Peter Hoffmann, *German Resistance to Hitler*, Cambridge and London: Harvard University Press, 1988, pp. 281–82; Hoffmann, 'German Resistance', pp. 73–88.

155 Young, *The 'X' Documents*, pp. 56–57.

156 Young, *The 'X' Documents*, p. 59.

The 'life problems' Goerdeler referred to were 'the Colonial question', the 'problem of Central Europe', the 'currency and gold problems', the 'problem of freer trade', and, associated with it, 'the growing need in all countries to secure a deceleration of armaments'.[157] Goerdeler's warning came four months after the *Anschluss* of Austria and the concurrent eruption of harsh anti-Jewish violence and repression, four months since *SS* and Police Chief Heinrich Himmler's henchmen had been sent to Vienna to drive out the Jews, three weeks after the abortive Évian Conference, two days after General Beck's coup d'état attempt had failed, and at the height of the international crisis over Hitler's threat of war against Czechoslovakia.[158] Much as High Commissioner McDonald had predicted in 1933 and 1935, that in case of war there would be wholesale slaughter of Jews, Goerdeler clearly recognised the trend.[159] In a conversation with Young's representative, Dr Reinhold Schairer, in Switzerland on 6 and 7 November 1938, Goerdeler predicted, a few days before the November pogrom, 'a great increase in the persecution of the Jews and Christians'.[160]

In Young's second meeting with Goerdeler, the question of peace or war dominated their conversation in Zurich on 11 September 1938. Goerdeler advocated, as he had done a month before, that Britain firmly and openly declare her support to France in the event of German aggression against Czechoslovakia, and if as a result France honoured her treaty obligations to Czechoslovakia. Hitler, still determined upon war, must know that war against Czechoslovakia meant war against France and Britain.[161]

Goerdeler concluded his remarks to Young by saying that if we held the peace – meaning, if French and British warnings prevented Hitler from attacking Czechoslovakia – then he, Goerdeler, would go from Switzerland to Turkey and the Balkans. Young already felt that Goerdeler saw himself as the leader of the 'revolution' movement against Hitler; nevertheless, he asked why Goerdeler planned to travel to Turkey and the Balkans. Goerdeler explained that Hitler 'would be forced to realise that victory for the time had gone to X

[157] Young, *The 'X' Documents*, p. 52.

[158] Nicosia, *Zionism*, pp. 137–38; Raul Hilberg, *The Destruction of the European Jews*, New York and London: Holmes and Meier, 1985, vol. I, p. 143; Young, *The 'X' Documents*, pp. 72, 79–84; Peter Hoffmann, 'Ludwig Beck: Loyalty and Resistance', *Central European History* 14 (1981): 332–50.

[159] Cf. Young, *The 'X' Documents*, pp. 83–84. McDonald, *Advocate*, p. 69; McDonald, *Refugees*, pp. 43–45.

[160] Young, *The 'X' Documents*, p. 136.

[161] Young, *The 'X' Documents*, pp. 55, 79.

[Goerdeler]', and therefore it would be 'highly dangerous for him to return immediately'.[162]

On 6 October 1938, the Polish minister for internal affairs, Felicjan Składowski, ordered passports that had been granted by the Polish Foreign Ministry to be submitted for inspection to Polish authorities beginning on 29 October.[163] The German Foreign Office asked the police to deport these persons, or at least as many as possible. They informed the Polish government on 26 October that 'Jews of Polish citizenship will be removed from the *Reich*', unless the Polish government rescinded its order for general passport control and visa stamps for Poles residing in Germany.[164] Without waiting for the Polish answer, which subsequently rebuffed the German ultimatum, the head of Police and *SS* Security Forces, *SS-Gruppenführer* Reinhard Heydrich, on 26 October ordered the arrest and deportation to Poland of Jewish Polish citizens. Polish Jews numbering above 17,000 were forcibly transported across the German–Polish frontier during the night of 27/28 October.[165] When Poland began to expel German citizens and threatened reprisals against Germans living in Poland, the German side suspended the compulsory repatriation of Polish Jews.[166] Only at the end of January 1939 did Germany and Poland reach an agreement allowing the return of the expelled Poles (Polish Jews) to Germany to regulate their affairs, and both sides agreed to desist from the practice of expelling each other's nationals and to reconsider the cases of those already expelled.[167]

There were resident in Germany, according to the 1933 census, 148,092 Polish persons who were not German citizens and most of whom were formally, with papers, or informally Polish citizens. A total of 56,480

162 Young, *The 'X' Documents*, p. 84.

163 Jonca, 'Expulsion', p. 260.

164 Jonca, 'Expulsion', pp. 262–63 (misprint: 16 October); cf. *The Times* 29 October 1938, p. 11.

165 Walther Hofer, 'Die Diktatur Hitlers bis zum Beginn des Zweiten Weltkrieges', in Leo Just, ed., *Handbuch der Deutschen Geschichte* Band IV, 2. Teil, Konstanz: Akademische Verlagsgesellschaft Athenaion Dr. Albert Hachfeld, 1965, p. 94; Bauer, *My Brother's Keeper*, pp. 243–47; Jonca, 'Expulsion', pp. 255–81, here p. 264.

166 *The Times* 31 October 1938, p. 14; *The Times* 4 November 1938, p. 13; on Herschel Grynszpan's assassination of a German Embassy counsellor in Paris, see Helmut Heiber, 'Der Fall Grünspan', *Vierteljahrshefte für Zeitgeschichte* 5 (1957): 134–72; Michael R. Marrus, 'The Strange Story of Herschel Grynszpan', in Michael R. Marrus, ed., *The Nazi Holocaust: Historical Articles on the Destruction of European Jews*, vol. 2: *The Origins of the Holocaust*, Westport and London: Meckler, 1989, pp. 597–607.

167 *The Times* 30 January 1939, p. 11.

of these Polish persons were recorded as Jews (*Glaubensjuden*).[168] In 1938, after the annexation of Austria on 13 March 1938, as the German government actively pressed Jews in Austria, especially in Vienna, to emigrate,[169] Poland was far from willing to welcome them. The Polish foreign minister Józef Beck in Geneva on 13 September 1934 had publicly renounced the Minority Treaty that Poland had signed in 1919.[170]

It appears that a young Jew, Herschel Feibel Grynszpan, who was living in Paris and whose parents were among those deported to Poland, was so upset by this news that he went to the German Embassy on 7 November and shot Counsellor Ernst vom Rath, as it turned out fatally. Rath's death was reported on 9 November.[171] Goebbels and Hitler decided to use the incident to launch nationwide riots against the Jews. These were rapidly orchestrated and carried out mostly by *SA* thugs. Some dozens of Jews were murdered, and over 30,000 were taken to concentration camps. Newspapers reported that Rath's death had so outraged the German population that they engaged in 'spontaneous anti-Jewish demonstrations throughout the *Reich*', that shop windows were smashed and synagogues where the 'subversive and anti-German doctrines were being preached' were burned, and that no looting had occurred and nowhere had a finger been laid upon a Jew.[172]

In his meeting with another emissary of the British government, Dr Reinhold Schairer, who acted at the instance of A.P. Young, on 6 and 7 November 1938, Goerdeler was 'greatly perturbed that there is not yet in evidence any strong reaction throughout the democracies, in the Press, the Church, and in Parliament, against the barbaric, sadistic and cruel

[168] *Statistik des Deutschen Reichs, Band 451,5. Volks-, Berufs- und Betriebszählung vom 16. Juni 1933. Volkszählung. Die Bevölkerung des Deutschen Reichs nach den Ergebnissen der Volkszählung 1933. Heft 5. Die Glaubensjuden im Deutschen Reich. Bearbeitet im Statistischen Reichsamt.* Berlin 1936. Verlag für Sozialpolitik, Wirtschaft und Statistik, Paul Schmidt, Berlin SW 68, p. 13; *Statistik des Deutschen Reichs. Band 470. Die Hauptergebnisse der Volks-, Berufs- und Betriebszählung im Deutschen Reich (einschl. Saarland) auf Grund der Zählung vom 16. Juni 1933 und der Ergänzungszählung im Saarland vom 25. Juni 1935. Bearbeitet im Statistischen Reichsamt.* Berlin 1937. Verlag für Sozialpolitik, Wirtschaft und Statistik, Paul Schmidt, Berlin SW 68 (Nachdruck der Ausgabe Berlin 1937, Otto Zeller Verlag, Osnabrück 1979), p. 10 has 148,787.

[169] Francis R. Nicosia, *Zionism and Anti-Semitism in Nazi Germany*, Cambridge and New York: Cambridge University Press, 2008, pp. 137–39.

[170] Roos, *Geschichte*, p. 139; Roos, *A History of Modern Poland*, p. 137.

[171] Cf. Heiber, 'Der Fall Grünspan', pp. 134–72; Marrus, 'The Strange Story of Herschel Grynszpan', pp. 597–607.

[172] *Deutsche Allgemeine Zeitung* 10 November 1938, p. 2.

persecution of 10,000 Polish Jews in Germany'.[173] Young personally delivered Schairer's account of this meeting to Frank Ashton-Gwatkin, economic counsellor in the Foreign Office, on 10 November 1938.[174] At the end of November, Ashton-Gwatkin asked Young to visit Goerdeler in secret 'and obtain from him the conditions which Germany would desire for close collaboration with Britain', in a possible post-Hitler era, with Goerdeler functioning as Chancellor. Ashton-Gwatkin could hardly have taken this step without being instructed by Foreign Secretary Lord Halifax.[175] On 15 October Goerdeler had told Young that he might have to work with the present German government and play the part of a Talleyrand, but he would not change or modify his attitude to the great fundamental issue at stake.[176]

On 4 December 1938, Young met Goerdeler in a Zurich hotel, to obtain the 'conditions' Ashton-Gwatkin had sent him for. Goerdeler explained that Himmler was the real master of Germany: 'We must recognise that we are dealing with gangsters of the most depraved type'. Germany, said Goerdeler, is controlled by 100,000 of its worst elements, and all others are deeply ashamed of the pogrom. 'The persecution of the Jews will continue with even greater ferocity. The persecution of the Christians will be intensified and then will follow an onslaught on Capital. Hitlerism desires the ultimate destruction of Jews, Christianity, Capitalism'.[177]

Reinhold Schairer, representing Young, again met with Goerdeler on 15 January 1939. Goerdeler gave Schairer information that Hitler had ordered the General Staff to prepare for the occupation of the Netherlands and Switzerland at the same time, as pawns for demands to France and Britain to cede to Germany colonies, loans, and access to raw materials and world markets. When this is secured, the Straits of Gibraltar will be closed, the Suez Canal seized, and the centre of Africa invaded from Libya. The Nazi extremists Ribbentrop, Himmler, and Streicher completely dominate Hitler.[178] On the Jewish Question, Goerdeler asserted, somewhat simplifying, that 'the main point is deep disapproval [in the German population] of the persecution of the Jews and the way in which the Nazi leaders enriched themselves by stealing Jewish property [...] Throughout Germany the cruel and senseless persecution of the Jews

173 Young, *The 'X' Documents*, p. 139.
174 Young, *The 'X' Documents*, p. 141.
175 Young, *The 'X' Documents*, p. 148.
176 Young, *The 'X' Documents*, p. 118.
177 Young, *The 'X' Documents*, pp. 148, 152–53 (Young misdates the pogrom 16 November).
178 Young, *The 'X' Documents*, pp. 158–59.

is more and more deeply resented'. He reported widespread theft and looting of Jewish property,[179] particularly from jewellery shops, and concluded with this advice to the Government of Great Britain:

No further negotiations but action [...] As soon as the planned persecution of the Churches begins, or the new persecution of the Jews is started, it is absolutely essential to break diplomatic relations. The moral front must be strengthened more and more. In every situation, the democracies must move swiftly from a moral defensive to a strong and firm moral offensive. Such tactics are the only methods that Hitler understands and respects. In the first week of January, for example, the German press received instructions to cease their attacks on the USA. Why? Hitler declared that he recognised that the USA meant business.

As Goerdeler explained, the facts of the present situation were the following: '1. Hitler is determined to conquer the world; 2. To achieve this purpose he has decided to destroy Jews – Christianity – Capitalism'.[180]

When Goerdeler met A.P. Young in London on 16 March 1939, the day after the occupation of Czechia by German troops, he stressed 'the vital importance of breaking off all personal and public contacts with leading Nazi officials', he demanded a clear differentiation between the rulers of Germany and the German people, and he declared that Hitler had taken a path that must lead to his destruction and had already passed three 'milestones'. Goerdeler's next statement, naming the 'milestones', underlined the distance between his own moral stance and Hitler's criminality: '1. *The Pogrom against the Jews on November 9 and 10.* Hitler personally

[179] The expelled Jews were allowed to bring with them only 10 Reichsmarks and had to leave behind their other assets and property; *The Times* 3 November 1938, p. 13. Goebbels both hailed and worried about popular reaction to the pogrom (Joseph Goebbels, *Die Tagebücher von Joseph Goebbels. Teil I. Aufzeichnungen 1923–1941. Band 6*, Munich: K.G. Saur, 1998, pp. 178–83, 186). He wrote in his diary on 9 November 1938 'if only one could for once unleash the ire of the people' ('*Wenn man jetzt den Volkszorn einmal loslassen könnte*!'); but on 11 November he noted that the actions had to be controlled and reined in: 'Lassen wir das weitergehen, dann besteht die Gefahr, dass der Mob in die Erscheinung tritt'. And: 'Es kommen Meldungen aus Berlin über ganz schwere antisemitische Ausschreitungen. Jetzt geht das Volk vor. Aber nun muss Schluss gemacht werden'. Goebbels did not record any German criticism of the anti-Jewish violence in the days immediately following the pogrom. But Peter Longerich, *'Davon haben wir nichts gewusst!' Die Deutschen und die Judenverfolgung 1933–1945*, Munich: Pantheon, 2007, pp. 129–44, recorded a great deal of criticism, condemnation, and outrage among the population; Ursula Büttner, '"The Jewish Problem Becomes a Christian Problem": German Protestants and the Persecution of the Jews in the Third Reich', in Bankier, ed., *Probing*, pp. 431–59. David Bankier, *The Germans and the Final Solution: Public Opinion under Nazism*, Oxford and Cambridge: Blackwell, 1992, is a biased treatment; see for example p. 86 on Goerdeler.

[180] Young, *The 'X' Documents*, pp. 160–61.

ordered this pogrom'. The other two milestones were, according to Goerdeler, the dismissal of Dr. Schacht, and the brutal aggression against Czechoslovakia.[181] As in most of his previous statements, the Jews were the first item in Goerdeler's enumeration.

Goerdeler had committed, on behalf of German and non-German Jews, 'treason against the country' (*Landesverrat*) as defined in German law, which carried the death penalty.[182]

The reaction to the pogrom among the German public was mixed. It must be seen in light of the unbloody annexations of Austria and the Sudetenland. In September 1938 when war seemed imminent, the American news correspondent William Shirer wrote in his diary that the people in Berlin had demonstrated with their negative reaction to army troops being marched through Berlin on 28 September that they were 'dead set against the war', that it had been 'the most striking demonstration against the war that I've ever seen'.[183] Now war had been avoided, Hitler's political genius had prevailed, and the success was a splendid one.

Some synagogues are listed as 'not damaged' in November 1938. In Bavaria almost all synagogues or prayer rooms were destroyed or damaged, and a smaller number were burned, as were the synagogues

[181] Young, *The 'X' Documents*, pp. 176–77.

[182] 'Gesetz zur Änderung von Vorschriften des Strafrechts und des Strafverfahrens. Vom 24. April 1934', *RGBl. I 1934*, pp. 341–48 (death penalty for high treason against the *Reich* president, *Reich* chancellor, or 'constitution', and for relations with a foreign government for such a purpose) included the establishment of the 'People's Court' (*Volksgerichtshof*) for deciding cases of high treason and treason against the country and the stipulation that no appeals were allowed against decisions of the 'People's Court'; 'Gesetz gegen heimtückische Angriffe auf Staat und Partei und zum Schutz der Parteiuniformen. Vom 20. Dezember 1934', *RGBl. I 1934*, pp. 1269–71; *Strafgesetzbuch: Strafprozessordnung: Gerichtsverfassungsgesetz nebst den wichtigsten Nebengesetzen*, ed. Reichsjustizministerium, Berlin: C.H. Beck's Verlagsbuchhandlung, 1935, §§ 88–93a, pp. 27–33; *Strafgesetzbuch mit Nebengesetzen und Erläuterungen*, Vierunddreißigste Auflage, Berlin: Walter de Gruyter, 1938, §§ 88–93a, pp. 210–26 (§ 89: 'Wer es unternimmt, ein Staatsgeheimnis zu verraten, wird mit dem Tode bestraft'. P. 210, § 88: Staatsgeheimnisse = Tatsachen oder Nachrichten darüber, 'deren Geheimhaltung vor einer ausländischen Regierung für das Wohl des Reichs, insbesondere im Interesse der Landesverteidigung, erforderlich ist'. 'Verrat im Sinne der Vorschriften dieses Abschnitts begeht, wer mit dem Vorsatz, das Wohl des Reichs zu gefährden, das Staatsgeheimnis an einen anderen gelangen läßt, insbesondere an eine ausländische Regierung oder an jemand, der für eine ausländische Regierung tätig ist, oder öffentlich mitteilt'. Since the 'People's Court' was empowered arbitrarily to use whatever 'evidence' it pleased, the defence of intent, difficult in the best circumstances, was ineffective, as the trials of the conspirators amply demonstrated.

[183] William L. Shirer, *Berlin Diary: The Journal of a Foreign Correspondent, 1934–1941*, New York: Alfred A. Knopf, 1941, pp. 142–43.

in Ansbach, Aschaffenburg, Augsburg, Bad Brückenau, Bad Kissingen, Bamberg; all five synagogues in were burned in Fürth; in Nuremberg one of four synagogues was burned (the main synagogue in Nuremberg had been demolished on 10 August 1938), and one prayer room damaged; and in Munich one of three synagogues was burned, but none of the eight prayer rooms damaged. Twenty-three synagogues or prayer rooms were burned or otherwise destroyed, sixteen were quite damaged, and eighteen were closed in greater Berlin on 9 and 10 November 1938.[184] Ashkenaz House in Jerusalem lists 1,574 synagogues as destroyed in Germany overall.[185]

It was a little awkward to think of criticising 'the *Führer*' in the light of his foreign political 'success'. The *Führer*, moreover, kept aloof, stopped the excesses, was apparently taken aback, and put it about that the pogrom had been carried out without his knowledge. That was the version the army commander-in-chief, General von Brauchitsch, offered in a briefing in which several generals expressed their outrage, and one of them, *Generaloberst* Fedor von Bock, wanted 'that swine, Goebbels' hanged.[186] Indeed, the actions met, as Ian Kershaw put it, 'with little but condemnation even in the highest circles of the regime', including Himmler and Göring.[187] Among the factors that may explain the general passivity of the population was the intimidation and fear created by the dreaded *Gestapo* and the horrors of the concentration camps. Although no doubt there was widespread antisemitism, there was not much approval of violent outrages of this kind. Goebbels' diary entries in the days from 23–30 November 1938 make that clear when he writes (23 November): 'Propaganda briefing re Jewish Question. We will now open a long and intensive campaign. Above all enlighten the middle classes'. And two days later: 'Now begins an antisemitic large-scale battle calculated to last many months', and on 30 November: 'With artists there are some difficulties in the Jewish Question'. Notations that a struggle

[184] http://www.ashkenazhouse.org/synagog/.

[185] http://www.ashkenazhouse.org/memorialcoin.html.

[186] Kershaw, *Hitler 1936–1945: Nemesis*, London: Allen Lane The Penguin Press, 2000, pp. 148–49; Helmut Krausnick, 'Vorgeschichte und Beginn des militärischen Widerstandes gegen Hitler', in Europäische Publikation, ed., *Vollmacht des Gewissens*, Frankfurt and Berlin: Alfred Metzner Verlag, 1960, p. 373, based on both contemporary and post-war testimony. Krausnick, 'Vorgeschichte', p. 373: Bock: '*Kann man dieses Schwein, den Goebbels, nicht aufhängen*?' based on Gen.Liebmann, 'Persönliche Erlebnisse des Gen. d. Inf. a.D. Curt Liebmann i.d.J. 1938/39 (niedergeschrieben im November 1939)', IfZ Zeugenschrifttum Nr. 95.

[187] Kershaw, *Nemesis*, pp. 148–50.

with the churches must not be risked now until the Jewish Question was brought to a conclusion contain the same tendency, that according to reports received, the mood of the population was 'partially positive, partially negative. We must enlighten the people and above all the intellectuals about the Jewish Question'.[188] Hitler ordered the press, speaking to four hundred journalists in Munich on 10 November (the soundtrack has been preserved) with the synagogues still burning, to indoctrinate 'the entire people' that they will begin slowly to scream for violence; the government's true intentions could no longer be camouflaged, he said – the truth had to be brutally stated.[189] Hitler made the point clear in his speech on 30 January 1939: '[I]f international finance Jewry inside and outside Europe should succeed in plunging the nations once more into a world war, the result will not be the bolshevisation of the earth and thereby the victory of Jewry, but the annihilation of the Jewish race in Europe!'[190]

Prime Minister Chamberlain made a statement in the House of Commons on 14 November 1938 confirming press reports 'of action taken against Jews in Germany' and expressing sympathy for those who were being made to suffer for 'the senseless crime committed in Paris', the murder of the German counsellor Ernst vom Rath. Members asked the prime minister what could be done to allow refugees to come into Britain or into Palestine and generally to find a home for these persecuted Jews. Chamberlain answered that he thought the whole matter was receiving the attention of the Inter-Governmental Committee. When he was asked whether the government could 'do something for the victims of this oppression in Germany', Chamberlain replied: 'That is really a question which could not be answered without notice'. Several members kept pressing for more substance. One asked whether the prime minister had considered consultation with the American president about a joint representation to the German government, but received the same answer: 'I should like to have notice of that question'. Another asked about consultations 'with the High Commissioners of the various Dominions of the British Commonwealth as to whether it would be possible to find some place in the British Commonwealth of Nations for these people, considering how relatively few the numbers are in Germany – 500,000, I understand, all of them, men, women and children? Is it impossible to

[188] Goebbels, *Tagebücher*, *Teil I Band 6*, pp. 197–206.
[189] Wilhelm Treue, ed., 'Hitlers Rede vor der deutschen Presse (10. November 1938)', *Vierteljahrshefte für Zeitgeschichte* 6 (1958): 188.
[190] Domarus, *Hitler: Reden und Proklamationen*, p. 1058.

say to the world, "Great Britain will take them and find them a place to start afresh in life"'?

Chamberlain replied that 'any possible way by which we can assist these people' would be taken into consideration. The last question, whether there was not 'a vast Colonial Empire in which something definite could be done by the action of the Government here', received another irrelevant and evasive response: 'That is a matter which is under consideration by the International Committee'.[191]

The Times on 16 November reported under the heading 'Help for Jewish Refugees: Oversea Settlement Discussed' that much interest is taken in the prime minister's statement in the House of Commons on 14 November that the question of finding a place in the Colonial Empire for Jewish refugees from Germany is under consideration by the 'International Refugee Commission', uncertainly referring either to the League of Nations High Commission for Refugees Coming from Germany or to the Inter-Governmental Committee formed at Évian. The report added information that was not in the record of the House of Commons debate: that Lord Winterton was the committee's chairman and Mr Geoerge Rublee, an American, its director, and that 'there has been close cooperation on the Jewish question between Great Britain and the United States, and contacts have been made with France and Holland'.[192] An editorial article in *The Times* of the same date, headed 'Deeds Not Words', commented: 'In this, as in previous cases, deeds not words are required. Fortunately it can now be assumed that something is actually being done. The Prime Minister's statement – that the question of finding a place in the Colonial Empire for Jewish refugees is being studied by the International Commission of which Lord Winterton is chairman – has aroused general interest'. Apart from muddling two different bodies with similar assignments, the article did not say what it was that was 'actually being done', besides the production of more words. The article concluded by saying there was no excuse for unnecessary delay, that surely there was 'room for many of the refugees to settle in some part of the British Colonial Empire' – if two conditions were fulfilled: firstly, the close cooperation of the relevant departments of government (Treasury, Home Office, Foreign Office, Colonial Office), and secondly, that British diplomacy make every possible effort 'to induce the German authorities

[191] *Parliamentary Debates, Fifth Series, Volume 341: House of Commons: Official Report*, London: His Majesty's Stationery Office, 1938, c. 503–6.

[192] *The Times* 16 November 1938, p. 13.

to allow Jews to leave the Reich with a part at least of their capital'. It was merely a partially oblique repetition of the usual obstacles: the lack of places willing to receive Jews, and funding. More discussions and more newspaper coverage followed in England and in Germany. Schemes to settle Jews in colonies or parts of the British Commonwealth were a widely and publicly discussed topic.

On 19 November 1938, Goebbels recorded in his diary: 'London wants to open the former German colonies for the German Jews. A typically English impertinence. But the last word in this has not yet been spoken'.[193] The paper of the *NSDAP*, *Völkischer Beobachter*, on 22 November reported that the debate in the House of Commons was hypocritical and that the English did not really want or feel able to help the Jews, quoting the *Daily Express* as saying that of course the Crown Colonies should be opened to the Jews, and that of course the Jews would not go there where they would have to work very hard, but only to Palestine, which could not accept any more of them.[194] The same paper reported that three hundred prominent Jews in the eastern United States had written to President Roosevelt asking him to persuade the British government to give Palestine entirely to the Jews; the American Jews would have to finance Jewish settlement there, and England could thus all at once dispose of the Jewish Problem for good. The possibilities for saving the German Jews had certainly not improved since the annexations of Austria and the Sudeten region, although the intense persecutions in Germany had brought the issue to the attention of the world more than in the preceding years.

Robert Pell, a State Department official, recorded in February or the first days of March, that repeated attempts by the Inter-Government Committee to contact the German government had failed and had been disrupted by the Sudeten crisis, the murder of legation counsellor vom Rath in Paris, and the events of and following the pogrom of 9/10 November in Germany.

On 15 November the German foreign minister von Ribbentrop informed the American ambassador in Berlin that 'unofficial persons' might discuss refugee questions with Rublee, possibly in the Netherlands. On 8 December Rublee and Pell were to meet with the former Austrian economics minister Hans Fischböck and the journalist Karl-Heinz Abshagen in Brussels. Then Schacht managed, seconded by Göring and with Hitler's blessing, to take charge of this venture, defeating Ribbentrop,

[193] Goebbels, *Tagebücher Teil I, Band 6*, Munich: K.G. Saur, 1998, p. 192.
[194] *Völkischer Beobachter* 22 November 1938, p. 3.

Goebbels, and Himmler in an internal struggle. Schacht solicited an invitation from the governor of the Bank of England, Norman Montagu, and on 15 December met with Lord Winterton and Rublee in London. Schacht proposed that a loan be raised outside Germany to provide the foreign exchange for immediate emigration and settlement needs and that interest payments be financed by additional exports from Germany. Rublee and two advisers went to Berlin in January 1939 and talked with *Ministerialdirektor* Helmut Wohlthat of Göring's staff; Schacht was dismissed as *Reichsbank* president on 21 January 1939, and Göring personally took over the dossier. An exchange of letters on 1 and 2 February 1939 produced a programme that the German government was prepared to adopt, acting independently and unilaterally: to have 150,000 men and single women between the ages of fifteen and forty-five emigrate who were individually capable of earning a living and otherwise fit for emigration, over a period of three to five years; when these people were established abroad, their approximately 250,000 dependants should follow the wage earners, and Germany was to put into a trust 25 percent of the remaining assets of German Jews against emigration needs. On 8 March Pell wrote from London to the Department of State that Göring needed 'ammunition' within two weeks to justify his programme to Hitler, to wit a memorandum on settlement projects, and a financing scheme. At a long secret conference Pell had with the Jewish leaders in Berlin, they declared that they will now force action by sending shiploads of their people without papers to Shanghai, the Mediterranean, and the Caribbean. Pell recorded that he told them that 'they were defeating our efforts to open places in Latin America, but they laughed in my face. After six years of dealing with this problem they are very hard. They do not believe in promises'.[195] This led to the ill-fated voyage when the *SS St Louis*, with 937 mostly Jewish passengers, was barred from landing in Havana on 27 May and anywhere in the United States. Britain, Belgium, France, and the Netherlands eventually divided and absorbed the passengers.[196]

There was hesitation (6 March 1939) 'in Jewish circles', particularly in America, about proceeding along the lines proposed by Göring because this would (1) condone German anti-Jewish policies, including the confiscation of Jewish property and forced emigration; (2) confirm the existence of such a thing as 'international Jewry'; and (3) assist Germany through

[195] Sherman, pp. 194–204; McDonald, *Refugees*, pp. 164–66; Richard Breitman, *The Architect of Genocide: Himmler and the Final Solution*, New York: Alfred A. Knopf, 1991, pp. 59–64.

[196] McDonald, *Refugees*, p. 175.

promotion of exports. Public opinion in America, however, according to a poll taken by *Fortune* magazine, was 83 percent opposed to any increase in immigration quotas.[197] Then, on 15 March 1939, German forces occupied 'Prague', that is, the rest of Czechia. This increased the numbers of potential emigrants. Britian introduced a peace-time draft. The *Gestapo* and *SS* resisted the emigration plan; they were planning to kill the Jews.[198] Wilfrid Israel, in Berlin, told Pell, Sir Herbert Emerson, the director of the Inter-Government Committee, and Max Warburg on 1 May 1939 that he believed Wohlthat sincere, and that all would collapse if the corporation and trust to *finance* emigration were not set up at once; Consul-General Geist reported to the American undersecretary of state, Benjamin Sumner Welles, that unless *places* of settlement were opened up very shortly, the radicals in Germany would again gain control.[199]

The American and British governments and the Jewish organisations except the Zionists agreed to setting up and funding a settlement foundation, but the German side failed to live up to its part, the creation of the trust for 25 percent of remaining Jewish property.[200] With the beginning of the war, all these efforts died. McDonald now concentrated on trying to rescue small numbers of Jews.[201]

In June 1939, with war imminent, Goerdeler travelled to Lybia, Egypt, Palestine, Syria, and Turkey.[202] The situation for the Jews in Germany and in Poland, Romania, and Hungary had become much more precarious than it had been in 1937, during Goerdeler's previous trip to the Middle East.

No doubt he was aware of the official statements and public debate in Britain about her policy in Palestine ever since 1919; of the White Paper of October 1930; of the position Britain took before and during the Évian Conference, namely, that Palestine was not to be mentioned as a potential area that could receive Jewish refugees; of the report of the Royal Commission on Palestine of July 1937 ('Peel Commission', after its chairman, Lord Peel); and of the publication of the resulting White Paper (*Palestine. Statement of Policy*) on 17 May 1939, as British and German newspapers continually reported on them.[203] The Royal Commission

[197] Sherman, pp. 200–2; McDonald, *Refugees*, p. 162.
[198] McDonald, *Refugees*, pp. 168, 171, 333; Breitman, *Architect*, p. 64.
[199] McDonald, *Refugees*, pp. 172–73.
[200] McDonald, *Refugees*, pp. 172–79.
[201] McDonald, *Refugees*, p. 183.
[202] Gillmann and Mommsen, *Politische Schriften*, pp. 627–34.
[203] *The Times* 28 May 1930, p. 15; *The Times* 14 February 1931, p. 12; *The Times* 7 July 1937, p. 16; *The Times* 20 October 1937, p. 13; *The Times* 10 October 1938,

recommended partition as the only solution to the Arab–Jewish antagonisms in Palestine. New anti-Jewish riots by the Arabs followed in September 1937. The White Paper limited Jewish immigration to Palestine to 75,000 for the following five years.[204] The document was laid before Parliament for debate on 17 May 1939 and was approved by a majority. There was resistance to it that continued in debates later in July; particularly the Jewish Agency for Palestine declared that 'the White Paper policy is devoid of moral and legal basis and is calculated to destroy the last and most holy possession of the Jewish people – the National Home'; and the League of Nations Permanent Mandates Commission considered (in a vote of four to three) the policy as not in conformity with the Mandate, whereas the British government insisted that it was.[205] On 30 January 1944, Dr Chaim Weizmann, president of the Jewish Agency for Palestine, declared at the Zionist Federation conference in London that the policy had failed in its objective to appease the Arabs, had reduced Jewish immigration into Palestine to ridiculously small proportions, and had deprived many thousands of a sanctuary that they so needed.[206]

At the same time, by 1939 the situation of Jews in Germany (and in Poland) had become more desperate. Goerdeler now believed that Palestine could receive a large number of Jews.[207]

In his report on Palestine written in the summer of 1939, he argued that Palestine could absorb a large Jewish immigration (*größere Judeneinwanderung*) because the Jewish settlers were competent, industrious, and successful: 'For the solution of the Jewish Question in the world this would only be an advantage' (*Für die Lösung der Judenfrage in der Welt wäre das nur ein Vorteil*). Since the Arabs always opposed whatever the Jews were doing in Palestine, Goerdeler acknowledged the difficulties facing the British Mandate authorities.

p. 14; *Palestine. Statement of Policy. Presented by the Secretary of State for the Colonies to Parliament by Command of His Majesty, May, 1939 (accounts and papers: (12.) state papers. Session 8 November 1938–23 November 1939*, vol. 27), London, 1939; *Völkischer Beobachter* 9 July 1937, pp. 1, 8 ('Die Teilung Palästinas: Der Bericht der Palästina-Kommission in London veröffentlicht'); *Völkischer Beobachter* 23 May 1939, p. 8 ('Judas Ausfälle gegen das Palästina-Weissbuch'). Cf. Bernard Wasserstein, *Britain and the Jews of Europe 1939–1945*, London: Institute of Jewish Affairs, Oxford: Clarendon Press, 1979, p. 17.

204 *Palestine. Statement of Policy*; *The Times* 18 May 1939, p. 9.

205 *The Times* 20 July 1939, p. 16; *The Times* 22 July 1939, p. 9; *The Times* 18 August 1939, p. 10.

206 *The Times* 31 Jan. 1944, p. 2.

207 Gillmann and Mommsen, *Politische Schriften*, pp. 627–34.

In his January 1938 memorandum, Goerdeler had predicted that '[t]he last word about the development in Palestine will be spoken through further European events'. He favoured the formation of a Jewish state in Palestine and predicted that 'the English difficulties' (*die englischen Schwierigkeiten*) with getting Jews and Arabs to cooperate would decrease if Germany came into a 'conflict' (war) with the Western powers.[208] This conflict began in September 1939 with the German attack upon Poland and the declarations of war upon Germany by Great Britain, France, Australia, India, New Zealand, the South African Union, and Canada. In 1940 German forces defeated France and proposed to do the same to the Soviet Union in the following year. By the end of 1941, Hitler had brought about, gambling and blundering as he went, the situation that he had fancied himself cleverly avoiding, when he had drafted his new Four-Year Plan in 1936, a two-front war against the two mightiest powers on earth: Germany was at war with both the Soviet Union and the United States of America. In these changed circumstances, Goerdeler developed ideas for saving the Jews and proposed them in his 1941/1942 memorandum, 'The Aim'. The immediate context will next be described.

[208] Marianne Meyer-Krahmer, *Carl Goerdeler und sein Weg in den Widerstand. Eine Reise in die Welt meines Vaters*, Freiburg im Breisgau: Herder Taschenbuch Verlag, 1989, pp. 127–28; Ritter, *Goerdeler*, p. 211; Gillmann and Mommsen, *Politische Schriften*, pp. 627–34; cf. Scholtyseck, *Robert Bosch*, pp. 260–61. Remarkably little has been published about Goerdeler's trip to Palestine. Reich, *Carl Friedrich Goerdeler*, pp. 270–71, only records a reference to Palestine in Goerdeler's account of his 1937 journey to the United States. Dipper (Christof Dipper, 'Der Deutsche Widerstand und die Juden', *Geschichte und Gesellschaft* 9 (1983): 365, and Christof Dipper, 'The German Resistance and the Jews', *Yad Vashem Studies* 16 (1984): 51–93), whose research was tenuous, and who criticised that Goerdeler had suggested the foundation of the Jewish state in parts of Canada or South America, thought it appropriate to say 'also gerade nicht in Palästina'; Christof Dipper, 'Der 20. Juli und die "Judenfrage"', *Die Zeit* 27 (8. Juli 1994): 20.

4

Conspiracy to Overthrow the Dictator

While German armies were advancing eastward and the Soviet Union seemed on the verge of collapse, President Roosevelt and Prime Minister Churchill met in Placentia Bay in Newfoundland, on each others' ships, the Royal Navy battleship *Prince of Wales* and the American cruiser *Augusta*, and consulted on common war aims, although the United States was not formally a belligerent. Ulrich von Hassell, until February 1938 German ambassador in Rome, one of the best informed among Hitler's German opponents, reacted with dismay to the Atlantic Charter. He noted in his diary that the identification of 'Nazi Regime = Germany', and 'Germany = Hitler' in the preceding months had progressed in rapid strides throughout the world and threatened to destroy every possibility for a post-Hitler government to obtain a tolerable peace.[1] Hitler's removal was the condition for Germany not to be identified with Hitler.

On 18 August 1941, four days after the publication of the Atlantic Charter, Hassell had a conversation with Carl Burckhardt, chair of the *Commission mixte de secours* of the International Committee of the Red Cross. The meeting was arranged by Karl-Ludwig Freiherr von und zu Guttenberg, one of Hitler's underground opponents who worked in Military Counter-intelligence under Admiral Wilhelm Canaris; Guttenberg is said to have put Goerdeler in touch with Hassell in June 1939.[2] They

[1] Hassell 1988, pp. 266–67.

[2] Maria Theodora von dem Bottlenberg-Landsberg, *Karl Ludwig Freiherr von und zu Guttenberg 1902–1945: Ein Lebensbild*, Berlin: Lukas Verlag, 2003, pp. 159–60, 163–64; in Hassell 1988 p. 481n40, the editor says, without citing evidence, that 'in these days', which would be June 1939, Guttenberg had established the contact between Hassell and Goerdeler.

talked about these issues and about 'regime change' in Germany.[3] In the days following, in Berlin, Hassell talked with State Secretary Ernst Freiherr von Weizsäcker about his conversation with Burckhardt. He also met with Popitz and two *Abwehr* officers, Colonel Hans Oster and Hans von Dohnanyi, as well as Lieutenant-General Friedrich Olbricht, chief of General Army Office in Home Army Command. At the time, this was the essential network, the fabric of the conspiracy in high-level positions.

The conspirators were realists. They agreed that 'nothing could be achieved' if it was evident that Germany had no chance of victory.[4] Hassell saw Goerdeler in September 1941 and found his activity pleasing enough, but found his poorly founded prognostications about an impending German collapse and his 'childlike views of planning' worrying.[5] In November 1941 Goerdeler pointed out to his friend Jacob Wallenberg, the Swedish banker who was on the Swedish government's commission for economic relations between Sweden and Germany and held accounts for German firms like Robert Bosch GmbH, that the German forces' defeat outside of Moscow held the chance to bring Hitler down. In February he was still hopeful of the 'possibilities'.[6] At the same time, mass killings of Jews were in progress in German-occupied Soviet territory.

Repeatedly in September, October, and November 1941, Hassell's diary records his own outrage at the news of the mass murder of Soviet prisoners of war and Jews in conjunction with thoughts about methods of bringing down the regime.[7] Together with military and foreign-policy developments, it was Hassell's constant concern. In this atmosphere of despair, anguish, and outrage, there arrived at Hassell's doorstep at the end of September an emissary from Army Group Centre High Command.

Colonel Henning von Tresckow, senior staff officer (operations) in Army Group Centre High Command, was a career officer from the famous No. 9 Potsdam Regiment, and his ancestry included famous generals; General Erich von Falkenhayn, Chief of the Great General Staff in the First World War, was his father-in-law. As a soldier, he faced issues that confronted every soldier whose career had been guided by military honour, the established laws of war, and decency. Was he answering the call of soldierly duty in prosecuting Hitler's war? Were his superior duties

[3] Hassell 1988, p. 267–68.
[4] Hassell 1988, pp. 268, 274–75.
[5] Hassell 1988, p. 273.
[6] Allen Welsh Dulles, *Germany's Underground*, New York: Macmillan, 1947; new edition: n.p.: Da Capo Press, 2000, p. 143.
[7] Hassell 1988, pp. 276–77, 280.

those to the soldiers who depended on what he did in his staff position? Or to the armed forces supreme commander? What if they conflicted? An incredible dilemma.

Early on, Tresckow realised that the regime was forcing the army into complicity with its most appalling crimes. He believed that the entire regime must be overthrown. He could not, of course, do it alone. He needed to find support among both military and civil leaders. These included outright followers of Hitler, opportunists, narrow-thinking specialists in their various métiers, and true opponents of National Socialism. While Hitler was miraculously successful, even diehard enemies of the dictator did not think a coup d'état could be risked, either because too many other leaders would remain loyal to Hitler, or because there would not be 'public support' for it. It was necessary to wait for 'setbacks' that would make the public understand the need for a coup.[8] This amateur psychology was flawed, of course. Support for a disastrous leadership may well decline in adversity, but not to the extent of accepting treason and a 'stab in the back'. At the same time, Hitler had shown that public opinion could be moulded. Moreover, Germany would be unable to negotiate peace terms from a position of weakness. All attempts to 'influence' the personages who were the ones called upon to lead had been in vain.

The dilemma was insoluble and was overcome, in the end, by the strength of character of men like Tresckow, Stauffenberg, Hassell, Beck, Oster, and Goerdeler, who were prepared to sacrifice their lives. As Tresckow put it to Stauffenberg in June 1944: 'We must prove to the world and to future generations that the men of the German Resistance movement dared to take the decisive step and to hazard their lives upon it. Compared with this objective, nothing else matters'.[9] But in 1940 Tresckow considered an assault on Hitler's rule possible only if the offensive operations in France failed, as he said to his special missions officer in his staff.[10] In April 1941 he expressed himself in the same vein, to another interlocutor, saying that the offensive against the Soviet Union ought to fail, for political reasons; that it was a terrible dilemma; and that if the offensive succeeded, neither the generals nor the nation could be convinced of the necessity to resist the regime.[11] He wanted Hitler

[8] Hoffmann, *History*, pp. 134, 148, 166.

[9] Fabian von Schlabrendorff, *Revolt Against Hitler*, London: Eyre and Spottiswoode, 1948, p. 131.

[10] Fabian von Schlabrendorff, *Offiziere gegen Hitler*, Zurich: Europa Verlag, 1946, p. 52.

[11] Bodo Scheurig, Befragung: Wolf Graf von Baudissin (Hamburg, 21.11.1969), Institut für Zeitgeschichte, ZS/A-31, Bd. 2. Cf. Günther Gillessen, 'Tresckow und der Entschluß

removed. At the same time he was committed, to the day of his death, to do his soldierly duty, and to his nation and his fellow soldiers. He was instrumental in helping General Erich von Manstein gain a hearing with Hitler in February 1940 for his 'sickle-cut' plan to defeat France, and he did his best to make German forces succeed in the Soviet Union.

Yet even the conception and preparation of the war against the Soviet Union had been criminal, and its conduct consummated Hitler's criminal designs. By May 1941, Tresckow had learned of Hitler's order that all captured political commissars in the Red Army were to be shot out of hand, that is, officers in uniform in the enemy's fighting troops with the task of upholding the discipline and 'morale' of the troops were to be murdered. Tresckow used an opportunity to bring his objection to this breach of international law to Hitler's attention, through Hitler's army adjutant, Major Gerhard Engel. He also declared that he would do all he could to sabotage the order.[12] Further, he knew from Police- and *SS*-General Arthur Nebe, an *SS* and Security Police Task Force commander, that Himmler had ordered the Task Forces (*Einsatzgruppen*) in July (or August) 1941 to exterminate *all* Jews. Tresckow beseeched his commander-in-chief, his uncle Field Marshal Fedor von Bock, to lodge a formal protest with Hitler against orders that gave soldiers license to kill outside legitimate combat, and to prevent the *SS* and Security Police Task Force B (*Einsatzgruppe B*) that operated in and behind Army Group Centre's frontline from carrying out illegal executions.[13] On a summer evening on the banks of the Beresina, in August, Tresckow told Bock's adjutant, Major (Res.) Carl-Hans Graf von Hardenberg, that all efforts to influence the leadership to remonstrate 'against ordered crime and military madness' had been in vain. They must think about bringing Hitler down. By the end of September, Tresckow had decided to initiate revolutionary action.[14]

zum Hochverrat: Eine Nachschau zur Kontroverse über die Motive', *Vierteljahrshefte für Zeitgeschichte* 58 (2010): 365–86.

12 [Gerhard] Engel, *Heeresadjutant bei Hitler 1938–1943: Aufzeichnungen des Majors Engel*, ed. Hildegard von Kotze, Stuttgart: Deutsche Verlags-Anstalt, 1974, pp. 102–3; Gerhard Engel, Generalleutnant a.D., letter 4 May.1972 to Bodo Scheurig, Institut für Zeitgeschichte, ZS/A-31, Bd. 2:

'Dass Tr. ein Gegner des Kommissar-Befehls war, war weit über den Rahmen seines Stabes hinaus bekannt. Wie er überhaupt in Kameradenkreisen, vor allem im Bereich seines Heeresgruppenkommandos, keinen Hehl aus seiner politischen Auffassung machte'.

13 Bodo Scheurig, *Henning von Tresckow: Ein Preusse gegen Hitler. Biographie*, Berlin: Propyläen, 2004, p. 126; Gillessen, 'Tresckow', pp. 372–73, 380–81.

14 Horst Mühleisen, 'Patrioten im Widerstand: Carl-Hans Graf von Hardenbergs Erlebnisbericht', *Vierteljahrshefte für Zeitgeschichte* 41 (1993): 449–50.

He sent his special-missions officer, Second Lieutenant (Res.) Fabian von Schlabrendorff to Berlin, to see if there were 'useful crystallisation points at home'. Guttenberg put Schlabrendorff in touch with Ulrich von Hassell. Hassell noted: 'He came to me through Guttenberg in order to inform himself on foreign affairs'.[15] The phrase means that Schlabrendorff saw other opponents of the regime, too. In fact, Schlabrendorff had known Guttenberg since the early 1930s, and Oster since 1938. He contacted Oster regularly when in Berlin, and also Ernst Freiherr von Weizsäcker, state secretary in the Foreign Office.[16] He assured Hassell that in Army Group High Command they were 'ready for anything', although they knew that Bock would not support them.[17]

In point of foreign policy, Hassell deprecated Schlabrendorff's suggestion that after the fall of the regime, they must immediately make peace as an illusion; on the contrary, they must declare their predisposition for a useful peace but at the same time proclaim the continuation of the war with all available means in order to secure acceptable terms. He told Schlabrendorff that, after the expected temporary conclusion of offensive operations in the winter months, his principals were to send a higher-ranking person for further consultations. They must also understand that they could not count on popular support – rather, that people would accuse them of having stolen Hitler's victory and of being unable to bring peace, too.

On the whole, Hassell found the episode pleasing in that for the first time there had come 'a kind of initiative from *there*'.[18] A month later, Hassell found Berlin disconsolate at the reversals before Moscow, but he had the impression of an 'increasing "disposition" in the military leadership to no longer go along with the entire outrageous disgrace', the shameless actions 'in the East against Jews and prisoners, in Berlin and other large cities against harmless, respected Jews'.[19]

[15] Hassell 1988, p. 278.

[16] Schlabrendorff, *Offiziere gegen Hitler*, pp. 19, 21, 51–54 (sketch of acquaintance with Hassell, in essence confirming Hassell's account); also in Fabian von Schlabrendorff, *Offiziere gegen Hitler: Neue, durchgesehene und erweiterte Ausgabe*, ed. Walter Bussmann, Berlin: Wolf Jobst Siedler Verlag, 1984, pp. 51–53; Schlabrendorff, *Revolt*, pp. 44–45; there is a brief reference to Schlabrendorff's contact with Hassell in Fabian von Schlabrendorff, *The Secret War Against Hitler*, New York, Toronto, London: Pitman Publishing Corporation, 1965, p. 141, and no references in Fabian von Schlabrendorff, *Begegnungen in fünf Jahrzehnten*, Tübingen: Rainer Wunderlich Verlag Hermann Leins, 1979.

[17] Hassell 1988, p. 278.

[18] Hassell 1988, p. 278.

[19] Hassell 1988, pp. 279–80.

Tresckow's initiative has rightly been called the step from opposition to high treason, and the birth of the plot to kill Hitler.[20] Tresckow was in Berlin and Potsdam in November and continued his efforts. He had reported sick and checked into a Berlin hospital in order to make some contacts. He called his journalist friend Karl Silex, who was a veteran naval officer, editor-in-chief (*Chefredakteur*) of *Deutsche Allgmeine Zeitung*, and on war service in the Naval High Command as a lieutenant-commander (*Korvettenkapitän z.V. im Oberkommando der Marine*).[21] Tresckow told him that since the Battle of Viasma, which ended on 18 October, the war was lost, Hitler was mad and must be removed, and could Silex name a few Englishmen whom 'we' could contact. Silex said he certainly knew some names, but the British would take such a contact as an admission of weakness and would only prosecute the war with redoubled energy. To Tresckow's question, what Silex would now do, Silex said that on the day the conspirators succeeded, he and his newspaper would be at their disposal, whereupon Tresckow replied: 'Just as wimpish as Kluge, Rundstedt and Manstein. Everybody wants to take part only when success is assured'.[22] Tresckow was at home again for the holidays around Christmas, until two or three days before 6 January 1942.[23]

Two things are clear from Hassell's diary entries: First, it took high-level generals to be the arm of an anti-Hitler fronde. Without the aid of military force, the civilians could not hope to dislodge the regime. Second, after a successful coup, the rebels would likely be no more than a liquidation committee.[24]

At that same time, Carl Friedrich Goerdeler was writing his ninety-nine-page memorandum 'Das Ziel'. He was in the centre of the conspiracy.[25]

The meaning of the memorandum depends in part on its intended readership. Neither Goerdeler's biographer, Gerhard Ritter, nor the editors of a large body of Goerdeler's political writings say to whom

[20] Gillessen, p. 381.

[21] Cf. Walter Lohmann and Hans H. Hildebrand, *Die Deutsche Kriegsmarine 1939–1945: Gliederung – Einsatz – Stellenbesetzung*, Bad Nauheim: Verlag Hans-Henning Podzun, 1956–1964, p. 291/363.

[22] Scheurig, *Tresckow*, p. 137, cites Karl Silex, *Mit Kommentar: Lebensbericht eines Journalisten*, Frankfurt: S. Fischer Verlag, 1968, pp. 220–21.

[23] Eta von Tresckow to Tresckow 6 January 1942, Eta von Tresckow Papers.

[24] Hassell 1988, pp. 278, 290–91.

[25] Hauptmann d. R. Hermann Kaiser, Tagebuch 1941–1944, transcribed by Peter M. Kaiser, typed, unpublished, 11 September 1941; 10, 15, 17, 19 October 1941; 18, 30 November 1941.

Goerdeler had directed his memorandum. Only Hans Mommsen saw the link between Goerdeler's writing of it and Hassell's references to his discussions about its issues with Goerdeler, Beck, Popitz, Professor Jens Peter Jessen, the lawyer Helmuth James von Moltke (who worked as a war counsellor/*Kriegsverwaltungsrat* in the Foreign-Countries division within Canaris' Foreign-Countries/Counter-intelligence Bureau in Armed Forces Supreme Command), Peter Graf Yorck von Wartenburg of the *Reich* prices commissioner's office, Adam von Trott zu Solz of the Foreign Office, and Guttenberg.[26] Beck, retired Chief of the General Staff, was under *Gestapo* observation; Goerdeler and Hassell were semi-active in post-retirement positions; the others were in active civil-service or military positions.

Memoranda that mentioned 'inhuman crimes' of the regime in the conquered territories, such as Goerdeler's 1940 memorandum on the 'State of the Economy and Administration' (*Stand von Wirtschaft und Verwaltung*),[27] or the memorandum 'The Aim' (*Das Ziel*),[28] were meant for those who were planning the overthrow of Hitler's dictatorship. General Ludwig Beck ranked foremost among them.

On 1 November 1941, Hassell noted,

> Numerous conversations with Geissler [Popitz]; repeatedly together with him and Nordmann [Jessen], once each with Forster [Beck, Halder?] and Pfaff [Goerdeler]. Four of us (Geissler, Nordmann, Pfaff and I) once talked over the whole situation 'in case of the case'. Pfaff [Goerdeler] was relatively agreeable but evidently held something back so that one had the impression that he would possibly go his own separate route.[29]

The 'whole situation' included difficulties at the eastern front; the 'intolerable conditions' developing in the occupied territories; 'revulsion of all decent human beings at the shameless measures in the East against Jews and prisoners, in Berlin and other large cities against harmless, respected Jews'; and a growing disposition in the military leadership to refuse further participation in 'the entire outrageous disgrace'. On 21 December

[26] Ritter, *Goerdeler*, p. 280; Gillmann and Mommsen, *Politische Schriften*, pp. LXXXIV, 863; cf. Hassell 1946, pp. 243–49; Hans Mommsen, 'Gesellschaftsbild und Verfassungspläne des deutschen Widerstandes', in Walter Schmitthenner and Hans Buchheim, eds., *Der deutsche Widerstand gegen Hitler: Vier historisch-kritische Studien*, Cologne, Berlin: Kiepenheuer and Witsch, 1966, p. 270n109.

[27] Gillmann and Mommsen, *Politische Schriften*, pp. 801–23.

[28] Gillmann and Mommsen, *Politische Schriften*, p. 897.

[29] Hassell 1988, pp. 279–80; Ritter, *Goerdeler*, missed Hassell's references to discussions with Goerdeler.

Hassell noted that 'during the last weeks' he had 'numerous conversations about the fundamental issues of a regime change, very often with Geissler [Popitz], repeatedly with him, Pfaff [Goerdeler], Geibel [Beck], once also with Otto [Planck] and once with Nordmann [Jessen]. A principal difficulty always resides in the sanguine, viewing-things-in-a-desired-light and in some respects really "reactionary" Pfaff [Goerdeler] who has otherwise brilliant qualities'.[30] Hassell also had contacts with Trott, Yorck, Moltke, Guttenberg, and Fritz Dietlof Graf von der Schulenburg and sought to bring about 'a kind of trait d'union with the Younger Ones'. Trott spoke passionately against any appearance of the 'reactionary', 'gentlemen's club' (*Herrenclub*), and militarism. Hassell agreed with this, but contrary to Trott considered English Christian pacifists 'absolutely useless as a reliable political factor', and generally he found it necessary to oppose Trott's 'theoretical-illusionist world view'. The Younger Ones rejected Goerdeler, who for his part 'assumes an almost entirely negative position' toward their ideas.[31] Hassell himself noted at the end of December that he was thinking about 'one or several fanfare-like speeches at the psychologic moment'.[32]

Moltke for his part from January 1940 onward had gathered like-minded persons to try to lay the political, social, and philosophical foundations for a post-Hitler Germany. The group was much concerned with the freedom of the individual and the use of state power.[33] Moltke had written a paper on foreign-policy objectives, for 'the state that is to be created', dated 24 April 1941.[34] If Goerdeler was sanguine and in pursuit of illusory aims, Moltke's outlook was no less idealist; in the memorandum, he said there existed these intellectual trends:

'a. The end of power politics.
b. The end of nationalism.
c. The end of the concept of race.
d. The end of the power of the state over the individual'.[35]

[30] Hassell 1988, p. 289.

[31] Hassell 1988, pp. 289–91.

[32] Hassell 1988, p. 292.

[33] See Ger van Roon, *Neuordnung im Widerstand: Der Kreisauer Kreis innerhalb der deutschen Widerstandsbewegung*, Munich: R. Oldenbourg, 1967, pp. 211–61; Ger van Roon, *German Resistance to Hitler: Count von Moltke and the Kreisau Circle*, trans. Peter Ludlow, London: Van Nostrand Reinhold, 1971, pp. 101–66; Hoffmann, *History*, pp. 49–53.

[34] Moltke papers in the possession of his widow, Freya von Moltke, Norwich, Vermont, and in *Bundesarchiv* Koblenz, N 1750 Bd. 1 (formerly: Kl. Erw. 824–2); printed in Roon, *Neuordnung*, pp. 507–17; Roon, *German Resistance*, pp. 3117–328.

[35] The memorandum continued, 'These four connecting links for actions by communities will be confuted by this war. They will lead themselves ad absurdum, they have partially

The rejection of the 'race concept' is absent from later memoranda, but the last draft for the New Order, headed only 'Draft of 9 August 1943' declares: 'The right to work and property, regardless of race, nationality and religious affiliation is protected by public authority'.[36]

Moltke made similar enquiries as Tresckow, also in September 1941. Also through Guttenberg's good offices, he met with a cousin of (then) Major (General Staff) Claus Graf von Stauffenberg, Hans Christoph Freiherr von Stauffenberg, who, like Moltke, was on war service in the same agency as Moltke. Moltke asked Freiherr von Stauffenberg: 'Don't you have a cousin in the *Führer*'s Headquarters? Couldn't something be done with him?' Moltke's interlocutor relayed the question to Berthold Graf von Stauffenberg, Claus' elder brother, who brought Claus' answer back to Moltke a few weeks afterward. Berthold reported: 'I spoke with Claus. He says we must win the war first. During the war one cannot do that sort of thing, particularly not during a war against the Bolsheviks. But afterwards, when we come home, we shall clear out that brown plague'.[37]

It was a time of feverish discussions and planning, of searching for a way to stop the madness, a time of competing concepts of how to bring about or help along the demise of the regime, and of how to plan for the time afterward.

In Paris, Captain Reinhard Brink in Commander-in-Chief West Field Marshal Erwin von Witzleben's staff in St Germain urged upon the C-in-C West in December 1941, after Brauchitsch had been allowed to resign, that it was 'time', and all were expecting him to act. Brink, and by autumn 1941 Captain Ulrich Wilhelm Graf Schwerin von Schwanenfeld in Witzleben's staff, too, had decided that 'any attempted uprising was without hope of success so long as Hitler was still alive', and they tried to convert Witzleben to their view. But Witzleben maintained, still after 18 December, that one must not begin the restoration of the rule of law with the profoundly unlawful act of an assassination. Brink replied that others would ease this concern for him, meaning that plans for Hitler's

already done so: the greatest expansion of power will not bring peace; nationalism has already proven itself as no longer being an attractive slogan, thus in France, thus in Germany; the race concept is absurd when the country supposedly protecting and upholding the race associates itself with its stated racial enemies, and when on the other hand the racially tolerant country protects race interests; when the greatest power of the state over the individual does not lead to peace, then this will lead to a curtailment of this power'. Roon, *Neuordnung*, p. 511; Roon, *German Resistance*, p.321.

[36] Moltke papers; Roon, *Neuordnung*, pp. 567–71; Roon, *German Resistance*, pp. 347–57, is a partially inaccurate translation.

[37] Peter Hoffmann, *Claus Schenk Graf von Stauffenberg: Die Biographie*, 3rd ed., Munich: Pantheon, 2009, pp. 240–41; Hoffmann, *Stauffenberg* (English), p. 140.

assassination were already in train.[38] Brink himself and Major (General Staff) Alexander von Voss, *Rittmeister d.R.* Alfred Gaf von Waldersee (personnel officer [IIa] in the staff of the commandant of Paris), General Ernst Schaumburg, and Captain Graf Schwerin, were plotting to kill Hitler if he visited one of the headquarters in France.[39] Witzleben, forewarned, nevertheless told another conspirator, Lieutenant-Colonel (General Staff) Helmuth Groscurth, that in case Halder supported a coup, the plan was to invite Hitler to a large parade.[40] The *Gestapo* in Berlin received information near the end of February 1942 'that England had recruited fanatical elements of the Balkan colony in Buenos Aires to carry out terror acts and assassinations against high-level personages' in Europe, and seven of them had proceeded to England.[41]

The fact that in mid-November Voss had written farewell letters to his wife and to his two children, as well as the contents of the letters, are evidence that Voss was involved in coup plans that might cost him his life; he wrote to his wife that he would leave this world with the deepest gratitude and without so much as a ghost of a doubt, and wishing that God might protect her and the children. [42]

Witzleben agreed to send someone to explore any such inclinations on the eastern front. He sent Major von Voss, who began his journey on 22 January, but Voss only got as far as 'Mauerwald', the Army High Command Headquarters in East Prussia. Here he was able to speak with the Chief of the General Staff, General Halder, on 25 January. Halder considered the situation in Russia as militarily promising and excluded any participation in a coup; nothing must be allowed to happen to Hitler, who was the only one who could keep the armed forces and the nation united and strong.[43] At the beginning of March, Hassell recorded that

[38] Gerhard Ringshausen, 'Hans-Alexander von Voss (1907–1944): Offizier im Widerstand', *Vierteljahrshefte für Zeitgeschichte* 52 (2004): 381.

[39] Peter Hoffmann, *Widerstand, Staatsstreich, Attentat: Der Kampf der Opposition gegen Hitler*, 4th ed., Munich: R. Piper and Co., 1985, pp. 325–26; Hoffmann, *History*, p. 260; Detlef Graf von Schwerin, *'Dann sind's die besten Köpfe, die man henkt': Die junge Generation im deutschen Widerstand*, Munich, Zurich: R. Piper and Co., 1991, pp. 231–33; Ringshausen, 'Hans-Alexander von Voss', pp. 381–83; Keilig, *Das deutsche Heer*, p. 211/289.

[40] Helmuth Groscurth, *Tagebücher eines Abwehroffiziers 1938–1940*, Stuttgart: Deutsche Verlags-Anstalt, 1970, p. 46.

[41] RSHA Schnellbrief Amt IV A 4a, Berlin 3 March 1942 to *Gestapo* in Aachen, National Archives, College Park, Maryland, EAP 173-e-10–12/90a, microcopy T-175 Roll 490 frames 9352265–9352267.

[42] Ringshausen, 'Hans-Alexander von Voss', p. 381.

[43] Franz Halder, *Kriegstagebuch*, vol. 3, Stuttgart: W. Kohlhammer Verlag, 1964, p. 390; Ringshausen, 'Hans-Alexander', p. 390; it appears that it was not snow storms that

Beck considered Halder to have buckled or gone soft.[44] Beck knew that Halder, who as Chief of the General Staff in any case had no troops under his command, had proven unhelpful to the conspirators from the moment of his appointment in August 1938.[45]

Voss had planned to continue his journey to the Crimea, presumably to seek out Fieldmarshal von Manstein who commanded 11th Army, with messages from Witzleben. Now he wrote to his wife that he could not get a flight to continue his travels. It seems, however, that this continuation had been contingent upon Halder's support, which had not materialised.[46] Voss returned to St Germain and gave his report to Witzleben on 31 January. By this time Witzleben had contracted pneumonia, and in February he needed an operation. He directed his confidants not to pursue the matter of a coup further.

Both Goerdeler and Moltke also looked for political and physical support for their concepts. Moltke was gathering around him people representing the churches, the trades unions, the foreign service, and the civil administration, and he was also seeking conspirators in the military forces. He tried – unsuccessfully – on 15 November 1941 to win over for his 'plans' the deputy commander II corps and commander of Military District II (Stettin), *General der Artillerie* Max Föhrenbach. On 22 November he was going to see General Beck and met with Dohnanyi to prepare for this, as well as his meeting with Halder, and for a further discussion with Föhrenbach and Beck on 18 December. He hoped 'that it will now be possible to take 2 or 3 big steps forward before Christmas'.[47] Moltke was trying to instigate Hitler's overthrow. This is clear from his letter to his wife Freya of 8 February 1942: People were telling him before Christmas 'it's too early' and now he hears that 'it's too late': 'It is sad to see how right Peter [Count Yorck von Wartenburg] and I were in our diagnosis that the 18th of December 1941 was the "right" day'.[48] The 18th of December was the day after Hitler informed Brauchitsch that his resignation would be accepted, and the day before Hitler's assumption of the position of commander-in-chief of the army.

prevented Voss from proceeding east, as Schwerin, *Dann sind's die besten*, pp. 217, 231–34, has it; rather it was Halder's refusal to support a coup.

44 Hassell 1988, p. 300.

45 Hoffmann, *History*, pp. 81–96.

46 Ringshausen, 'Hans-Alexander von Voss', pp. 382–83.

47 Helmuth James von Moltke, *Letters to Freya 1939–1945*, New York: Alfred A. Knopf, 1990, pp. 184–86; Michael Balfour and Julian Frisby, *Helmuth von Moltke: A Leader Against Hitler*, London: Macmillan, 1972, pp. 166–67; Keilig, *Das deutsche Heer*, p. 211/86.

48 Moltke, *Letters*, p. 208.

Goerdeler showed or read the first part of his memorandum to the Social-Democrat trades-union leader Wilhelm Leuschner after New Year's Day 1942.[49] He also thoroughly discussed his memorandum, in the days before 15 January 1942, with Johannes Popitz, General Ludwig Beck, Ulrich von Hassell, Colonel Hans Oster, and Oster's coworker Hans von Dohnanyi.[50]

[49] Mommsen, *Gesellschaftsbild*, p. 270n109, cites 'Lipgens a.a.O.'; Walter Lipgens, ed., *Europa-Föderationspläne der Widerstandsbewegungen 1940–1945: Eine Dokumentation*, Munich: R. Oldenbourg Verlag, 1968, pp. 146–49, reproduces notes by Leuschner entitled 'Arbeiterfrage'. Lipgens cites J.G. Leithäuser, *Wilhelm Leuschner: Ein Leben für die Republik*, Cologne: Bund-Verlag, 1962, pp. 208–10, as evidence, but there is nothing relevant there. But Lipgens, pp. 147–48n3, quotes from the original notes in Wilhelm Leuschner Jr.'s 'Archiv Leuschner', on the occasion of Leuschner's reading of J. Huizinga, *Im Schatten von Morgen*: '"Die Betonung des Nationalen ist an und für sich schon eine Krisenerscheinung; zeigt Macht darüber hinausgewachsen". – Notiz über ein (oder anhand eines) Gespräch [*sic*] mit Gleichgesinnten (notiert auf der Rückseite eines Kalenderblatts "53. Woche, 28.-31. Dezember 1941"): "Wo. ist über Mangel an Voraussicht und Entschlossenheit, über die falsche Einschätzung der in dieser Zeit wirksamen Kräfte, über Unmaß an Illusionen und Vertrauensseligkeit aufs tiefste erschüttert. Revolution 1933 künstlich gemacht und technisch organisiert, keine organische Fortsetzung [sondern] Überspanntheit, aber auch Reaktion längst überwundener Epoche unserer Geschichte. Ein Zurück gibt es in Geschichte [*sic*] niemals, auch wertlos, da kurzlebig ... [*sic*] [Es gilt] Kraftproben um Vorherrschaft [des] einen oder andern Volkes ablösen [*sic*]. 1914/18 nicht geklärt, muß jetzt erfolgen, wenn nicht Europa, auch Deutschland in Verelendung versinken soll. Technische Entwicklung zwingt zu großen Wirtschaftsräumen. [NS-Regime ist] mit unredlichen Mitteln in Besitz [der] Macht ". – Diese Sätze, angefangen von "Revolution 1933 künstlich gemacht und technisch organisiert ", sind wörtliche oder fast wörtliche Zitate aus Goerdelers Denkschrift "Das Ziel", aus dem Ende des ersten und dem Anfang des zweiten Abschnitts (vgl. *Schramm*, Beck und Goerdeler, a.a.O., S. 88–92!); jedes Bruchstück findet sich dort. So ist fast sicher, daß " Wo" als „Goerdeler" zu lesen ist und daß Goerdeler Dezember 1941 oder Januar 1942 (der Angabe von *Hassell*, Tagebücher S. 244, entsprechend) unter Anwesenheit Leuschners das erste Viertel seiner Denkschrift "Das Ziel" vorgelesen haben muß (auch ein Beitrag zu deren Datierung, vgl. oben Nr. 34, Anm.1)'. [*sic*] are mine, all other [] are Lipgens'.

[50] Hassell 1988, pp. 293–94: Hassell wrote about his conversations with Popitz, Goerdeler, Beck, 'etc.', as well as Oster and Dohnanyi, before travelling on 15/16 January 1942 to Brussels to see Falkenhausen and Paris to see Witzleben, his conversations 'über die Lage, die zu befolgende Taktik und vor allem die in den Gesprächen mit Spielberg [Falkenhausen] und Scherz [Witzleben] zu befolgenden Richtlinien', that Beck and Goerdeler were astonishingly optimistic 'concerning the possibilities for both'; 'both' must mean Falkenhausen and Witzleben. Hassell continues that Goerdeler 'verfasste für diesen Fall ein Dokument, das wir durchsprachen. Nordmann [Jessen] und ich bestanden auf der Änderung in dem Sinne keine Reaktion" und kein untauglicher Versuch, eine tatsächliche Entwicklung einfach streichen zu wollen. Das Ganze gefiel mir nicht restlos, ich nahm es aber mit und gab es nachher zweifach Scherz [Witzleben]'. 'Diesen Fall' in the context must mean the talks with Falkenhausen and Witzleben because Goerdeler had prepared guidelines (*Richtlinien*) for this case. This was not Goerdeler's 'The Aim' but a *Proklamation* to be issued on the occasion of the coup; Schwerin, *Dann*

Hassell travelled to Brussels to see Falkenhausen on 16 January 1942, and on to Paris to lecture before Witzleben's and the military governor in France, General Joachim von Stülpnagel's officers about '*Lebensraum* and Imperialism', as a cover for conspiratorial contacts with Falkenhausen, Witzleben's personal aide Captain (Res.) Graf Schwerin, Witzleben, and Colonel (General Staff) Hans Crome, intelligence officer (*Ic*) in Stülpnagel's staff.[51] Beck and Goerdeler wanted the coup against the regime to be started through a separate armistice in the west, in Belgium and France. Both Falkenhausen and Witzleben regarded this as utopian, and Hassell apparently concurred.[52] Schlabrendorff recalled in his 1946 memoir that the Army Group Centre conspirators could not be sufficiently reassuring about Field Marshal von Bock to encourage Witzleben to take an initiative; Tresckow could only say he hoped to carry Bock along.[53] Thus cohered Tresckow's eastern network and the western Beck-Goerdeler-Hassell-Witzleben plot.

Hassell's visit to Paris had been prepared by Professor Jessen through Crome.[54] In August 1944, Crome was in Soviet captivity, when he wrote, for Stalin's eyes, an account of what he knew of the background of the 20 July 1944 plot. The account, which recently turned up in a Russian archive, confirms and complements Hassell's diary entries of 1942. The People's Commissariat for Internal Affairs of the Union of Soviet Socialist Republics (NKVD) and the Main Administration of Military

sind's die besten Köpfe, pp. 231–32; Ludwig Beck, *Studien*, Stuttgart: K.F. Koehler Verlag, 1955, pp. 227–58.

51 Hassell 1988, pp. 294–97; see note 54 below.

52 Hassell 1988, p. 297.

53 Schlabrendorff, *Offiziere* (1946), p 54.

54 Crome personnel file, Bundesarchiv-Militärarchiv Pers 1/12423. For this and the following two paragraphs: Копия, Совершенно секретно, Первод с немецкого, СОВСТВЕННОРУЧННЕ ПОКАЗАНИЯ военнопленного полковника Генштаба немецкой армии КРОМЭ ГАНСА. 4 сентября 1944 года, State Archive of the Russian Federation (GARF), Fond 9401, Opis' 2, Akte 66, Bl. 293–323; translated by Yulia Tunina as: Copy, Top Secret, Translation from German, HOLOGRAPHIC TESTIMONY of a prisoner of war colonel of the General Staff of the German Army CROME Hans, 4 September year 1944; translated from Russian into German by Kristin von Tschilschke as: K O P I E, Absolut geheim, Übersetzung aus dem Deutschen, HANDSCHRIFTLICHE ZEUGENAUSSAGEN des gefangenen Oberst im Generalstab der deutschen Armee CROME, Hans. 4. September 1944 (Staatsarchiv der Russischen Föderation [GARF]); henceforth cited as Crome 1944; Crome was in General Joachim von Stülpnagel's and subsequently in the staff of General Carl Heinrich von Stülpnagel who succeeded his cousin in March 1942; Bundesarchiv-Militärarchiv Pers 1/12423; Hassell 1988, p. 295. Witzleben, Commander-in-Chief West, had been in the conspiracy as early as 1938; Hoffmann, *History*, pp. 66–96.

Counter-intelligence/SMERSH routinely interrogated captured German General Staff officers. After the failed uprising of 20 July 1944, the interrogators sought to learn all they could about the background and the aims of the conspirators, with a view to Soviet–Russian post-war policy.[55]

Jessen had met Crome on several previous occasions and knew of his opposition to Hitler. He had come to Paris in October 1941 and told Crome that a secret organisation had been formed in Berlin with the aim of removing Hitler and his regime, and of ending the war. Jessen said the inner circle consisted of General Beck, Admiral Canaris, General Olbricht, Field Marshal von Witzleben, Colonel Oster, Goerdeler, and himself, Jessen. He asked Crome to build up a liaison between the Paris group and the Berlin central organisation. In December 1941 Crome informed Witzleben of his, Crome's, role.

When Witzleben retired effective 15 March 1942, Crome was posted as chief of staff to XLII Army Corps on the Crimea in May 1942; in December 1942 he became chief of staff of IV Army Corps at Stalingrad, where he was taken prisoner on 31 January 1943.[56] After reading press reports about the 20 July 1944 insurrection, he came forward to testify and to write down in German what he knew of the new formation of the conspiracy in 1941. Lawrenti Pawlowitsch Berija, people's commissar for internal affairs (state security) of the USSR, had the deposition translated and edited into the standard form for such submissions to 'State Defence Committee – Comrade Stalin I.V.', to Vyacheslav Mikhailovich Molotov (foreign minister), Georgiy Maximilyanovich Malenkov (Politbureau candidate, member of Defence Committee), Ivanovich Ilyichev (head of Main Intelligence Directorate), Vsevolod Nikolayevich Merkulov (head of NKGB), and Viktor Semyonovich Abakoumov (chief of Main Administration Counter-intelligence SMERSH). In his account given in captivity, Crome claims for himself a rather more central role in the

[55] Stalin worried about Germany recovering rapidly after the war and aligning herself with the 'West'. The Soviet leaders wished to maintain the alliance with the Western powers, to have a strong role in the control of Germany and its industrial heartland, and to prevent a German re-armament and integration into the Western orbit. Hans-Peter Schwarz, *Vom Reich zur Bundesrepublik: Deutschland im Widerstreit der aussenpolitischen Konzeptionen in den Jahren der Besatzungsherrschaft 1945–1949*, 2nd ed., Stuttgart: Deutsche Verlags-Anstalt, 1980, p. 223; Milovan Djilas, *Gespräche mit Stalin*, Frankfurt: S. Fischer Verlag, 1962, p. 147.

[56] Bundesarchiv-Militärarchiv Pers 1/12423; Witzleben reported sick on 8 March 1941; his successor, Field Marshal Gerd von Rundstedt, was appointed Supreme Commander West and Army Group D on 15 March 1941; Keilig, *Heer*, pp. 211/368.

conspiracy than other evidence would support.[57] He wrote that there had been enthusiasm in Germany about the German–Russian 'friendship pact' in 1939, and that military men were much inclined to cooperation with Russia. Crome described the conspiracy as consisting mainly of General Beck, Field Marshal von Witzleben, General von Falkenhausen, Admiral Canaris, General Olbricht, and Brigadier Oster, and, on the civil side, Goerdeler, Popitz, Hassell, and Jessen. He said he knew all of them, and that he had recruited, while on the Crimean Peninsula in the summer of 1942, then Brigadier (*Generalmajor*) Fritz Lindemann, who at the time commanded 132nd Infantry Division; *Generalleutnant* Erwin Jaenecke, then commanding 389th Infantry Division and later general commanding IV Army Corps at Stalingrad; *Generalleutnant* [Friedrich] Schmidt, on the Crimea in the summer of 1942, when Schmidt commanded 50th Infantry Division[58]; *Generalmajor* Hans Freiherr von Boineburg-Lengsfeld, commander of 23rd Panzer Division, in Paris in January 1942; Colonel (General Staff) Hans Speidel, on General Joachim von Stülpnagel's staff, in France at the end of 1941[59]; Lieutenant-Colonel (General Staff) Schuchardt, intelligence officer on the staff of Army Group A command (*Ic/AO*) in South Russia in the summer of 1942[60]; Major (General Staff) Hans-Alexander von Voss, intelligence staff officer on Witzleben's staff in St Germain in autumn 1941[61]; and Captain (Res.) Ulrich Graf Schwerin von Schwanenfeld, on Witzleben's staff as special missions officer in 1941. While most of these are unlikely to have been Crome's recruits, he does differentiate between conspirators he knew personally and others about whom he had learned by hearsay. He dates

[57] See an analysis of this process in Peter Hoffmann, *Stauffenbergs Freund: Die tragische Geschichte des Widerstandskämpfers Joachim Kuhn*, Munich: C.H. Beck, 2007, pp. 183–85.

[58] 15th ID must be a mistake, it was at Juchnow and Gshatsk during January–April 1942 and in France from May to December 1942, and never commanded by a Generalleutnant Schmidt; 50th ID was in Sebastopol and on Kertch from January to August 1942 and on the Crimea during September–October 1942; Georg Tessin, *Verbände und Truppen der deutschen Wehrmacht und Waffen SS im Zweiten Weltkrieg 1939–1945*, vols. 3 and 5, Frankfurt: E.S. Mittler and Sohn, n.d.

[59] Hans Speidel, *Aus unserer Zeit: Erinnerungen*, Frankfurt, Vienna: Propyläen Verlag, 1977, p. 101.

[60] Crome does not give a first name; Oberstleutnant i.G. Karl Schuchardt, from No. 15 I.R., colonel from 1 January 1943, seems the only likely match; cf. Christian Zweng, *Die Dienstlaufbahnen der Offiziere des Generalstabes des deutschen Heeres 1935–1945*, vol. 2, Osnabrück: Biblio Verlag, 1998, p. 268; Tessin, *Verbände und Truppen*, vol. 5, pp. 62–63; Tessin, *Verbände und Truppen*, vol. 8, p. 122.

[61] Ringshausen, 'Hans-Alexander von Voss', p. 376.

Hassell's January 1942 visit to Paris for 'spring' but otherwise reports essentially the same events as Hassell, including those involving Carl Burckhardt's journey to England. He describes himself as having opposed any peace negotiations with Britain and as having spoken of the necessity of orientation to the East 'in spring 1942' in Paris; Jessen and Hassell had taken a position directly but had not supported Crome's point of view. Also 'in spring 1942', Hassell told him of efforts by Burckhardt to bring about peace talks between Britain and Germany in Geneva in May 1942. Hassell, he said, was clearly an adherent of Western orientation. Then he elaborated by saying 'that England has considerable connections and influence in the social circles of Germany, especially in its western part'. The interrogators' – and Stalin's – interests are addressed in further comments: 'That is why there is no doubt that the English use widely all possible channels in order to provide their influence on the course of the internal development in Germany, with the purpose in this regard to outrun the Soviet Union'.[62] Crome's account does lend colour to the drama at the turn of 1941/1942.

From Paris Hassell travelled on to Geneva on 20 January and talked with Burckhardt for two and a half hours. Burckhardt had returned two weeks earlier from a trip to England and informed Hassell that the willingness prevailed in government circles to come to an arrangement with 'a decent Germany', and that he had always been asked about 'the generals'. He stressed that a 'new Germany' must be strong and determined and able to continue fighting, under no circumstances must it 'run after the English', but must meet them with cool self-confidence. At the beginning of February, Hassell was back in Berlin.[63] At a meeting in Professor Jessen's flat in Berlin at the end of January, Beck, Olbricht, Oster, Jessen, and Crome agreed, in Hassell's absence, on a list for a new government consisting of Witzleben as *Reich* president, and a cabinet with Falkenhausen as chancellor, Konstantin Freiherr von Neurath or Weizsäcker as foreign minister, Beck as war minister, Schacht as economics minister, Goerdeler as interior minister, and Popitz as finance minister.[64] On 28 March 1942, Hassell noted intensive conversations at Jessen's with Beck and Goerdeler, and he recorded, 'Few prospects. Geibel [=Beck] constituted as centre'.[65] Hassell did not record whether

[62] Crome 1944; Hassell 1988, pp. 297–98.
[63] Hassell 1988, pp. 297–98.
[64] Crome 1944.
[65] Hassell 1988, p. 307; Hassell used 'Geibel' as code for Beck.

the cabinet list was discussed and what Goerdeler thought of it. Beck as centre meant that the Witzleben-Falkenhausen list was not realistic.

It was a time of reversals for the conspiracy. The German front in Russia had stabilised and begun to advance again, the Japanese achieved victories in the Far East, Witzleben was gravely ill, Hassell and Popitz were under *Gestapo* surveillance, and in Beck's circle 'everything was running strongly asunder'.[66] There was now, in March 1942, no immediate prospect for Goerdeler's plan to be put into effect. In August 1942, Hassell noted that the National Socialists in the Foreign Office and the *Gestapo* were doing their best with threats, close surveillance, and occasional arrests to intimidate and disperse persons who had realistic views about the war and its course and who looked for alternatives to its rapid progress to the abyss.[67]

The evidence for timing the composition of Goerdeler's memorandum is in part also internal: Goerdeler twice mentions the attack upon the Soviet Union (22 June 1941) as a fact.[68] Further, he often refers to the totality of politics as explicitly opposed to General Erich Ludendorff's doctrine of 'Total War'; General Ludwig Beck delivered a lecture about this doctrine at the Wednesday Society (*Mittwochgesellschaft*) meeting in his house on 17 June 1942.[69] Ludendorff's doctrine may be assumed to have been a topic in the numerous discussions between Hassell, Goerdeler, and Beck during the months from October 1941 to July 1942. Discussion in January 1942 on a future government may have been occasioned by Goerdeler's memorandum. It appears to have brought military–civil rivalry to the surface, briefly put Beck's authority in doubt, and then left Beck's and Goerdeler's positions strengthened.

The evidence as a whole dates the memorandum's completion for a time during the months of December 1941 and January 1942.[70]

[66] Hassell 1988, pp. 300, 305, 316–19.

[67] Hassell 1988, pp. 318–19.

[68] Gillmann and Mommsen, *Politische Schriften*, pp. 886–87.

[69] Klaus Scholder, ed., *Die Mittwochs-Gesellschaft: Protokolle aus dem geistigen Deutschland 1932 bis 1944*, Berlin: Severin und Siedler, 1982, pp. 292–94; Gillmann and Mommsen, *Politische Schriften*, pp. 875–944, e.g., 876–77; General [Erich] Ludendorff, *Der totale Krieg*, Munich: Ludendorffs Verlag, 1935.

[70] Kieffer, 'Goerdelers Vorschlag', pp. 475–76, cites Hermann Graml, 'Die aussenpolitischen Vorstellungen des deutschen Widerstandes', in Walter Schmitthenner und Hans Buchheim, eds., *Der deutsche Widerstand gegen Hitler: Vier historisch-kritische Studien*, Cologne, Berlin: Kiepenheuer and Witsch, 1966, p. 43 and note 85; Mommsen, Gesellschaftsbild, p. 133 and note 109; Gillmann and Mommsen, *Politische Schriften*, p. 873.

Deportations of Jews from Vienna, Prague, and Moravska Ostrava to the *Generalgouvernement*, the German-occupied part of Poland that had not been annexed to Germany, began early in 1940; the first deportations from Germany were deportations of 6,500 Jews from Baden and the Saar to Gurs in unoccupied France in October 1940. Concurrently, emigration and settlement plans were still being pursued, mainly the Madagascar plan.[71] Major deportations began only in autumn 1941, first from the *Reichsprotektorat Böhmen und Mähren*, formerly Czechia, and shortly later, in October and November from Germany and from German-occupied and associated territories – from Romania, Bulgaria and Hungary, Norway, Denmark, the Netherlands, Belgium, Luxembourg, France, Italy, and the Balkans through the years almost to the end of 1944. The Jews were deported to ghettos and from there to extermination camps, or directly to death camps and killing fields.[72] Of the six camps for systematic exterminations of mostly Jews, Sinti and Roma, political prisoners, and prisoners of war – Chełmno (Poland), Belzec (Poland), Sobibór (Ukraine), Treblinka (Poland), Auschwitz (German-annexed), Majdanek (Poland) – Auschwitz and Majdanek operated from 1 October 1941, mainly as 'work camps', Majdanek in the first place as a prisoner-of-war camp; in each of them many hundreds died in the construction stage, and Sobibor functioned as a station for gas vans that began killing operations in December 1941. All six death camps operated systematically as killing centres from about the middle of 1942.[73]

On 28 October 1941 Goebbels ordered intensified propaganda about the 'Jewish Question' (*Judenfrage*).[74] Two days later Goebbels realised that the campaign in Russia would not achieve its goals by the end of the year.[75] Although Goebbels believed that the Japanese attack on the United States on 7 December would significantly reduce American supplies to Britain, he was too realistic not to recognise that this thought was mainly a welcome distraction from the dire situation at the front

[71] Hilberg, *Destruction*, p. 397.

[72] Hilberg, *Destruction*, pp. 398–860.

[73] Ino Arndt, Wolfgang Scheffler, 'Organisierter Massenmord an Juden in nationalsozialistischen Vernichtungslagern', *Vierteljahrshefte für Zeitgeschichte* 24 (1976): 105–35; Wolfgang Scheffler, 'Chelmno, Sobibór, Belzec und Majdanek', in Eberhard Jäckel und Jürgen Rohwer, eds., *Der Mord an den Juden im Zweiten Weltkrieg: Entschlussbildung und Verwirklichung*, Stuttgart: Deutsche Verlags-Anstalt, 1985, pp. 145–60; Wolfgang Benz, ed., *Dimension des Völkermords: Die Zahl der jüdischen Opfer des Nationalsozialismus*, Munich: R.Oldenbourg Verlag, 1991, pp. 23–65.

[74] Goebbels, *Tagebücher II Band* 2, pp. 194–95.

[75] Goebbels, *Tagebücher II Band* 2, pp. 204, 208.

in Russia.[76] Goebbels allowed himself temporarily to be influenced by Hitler's optimism, which was itself a little forced. On 12 December he recorded in his diary that army 'officers who were inward opponents of the *SS* now had the best opportunity to win their soldiers for this view'.[77] On the following day, he was more explicit and referred to the mass murder of the Jews when he wrote that he and Hitler understood that they 'must be victorious if only because otherwise they as individuals, and as a nation, would be liquidated', as Hitler had said in his speech on 13 December before the regional Nazi Party leaders (*Gauleiters*). In regard to the Jewish Question, Hitler wanted a clean slate. He predicted to the Jews that, if they brought about another world war, they would be annihilated. The world war is here, Goebbels remarked, 'the annihilation of Jewry must be the necessary consequence', and, '[w]hen the German people again now in the Eastern Campaign have sacrificed close to 160,000 dead, so the authors of this bloody conflict must pay for it with their lives'.[78]

By 13 December Goebbels hoped only 'to stabilize half a peace in Europe' in 1942, and to take notice of the others' war making only through appropriate armaments. General Alfred Jodl, chief of *Wehrmacht* leadership staff, and Colonel Rudolf Schmundt, chief *Wehrmacht* adjutant to the *Führer*, 'now' admitted that the military men had underestimated the potential of the Bolsheviks, and they agreed that it was time to strike some hard notes vis-à-vis the home front. To begin with, Goebbels called in State Secretary Wilhelm Kleinmann of the Ministry of Transport to deliver to him stern reproaches regarding the mismanagement of transport capacities.[79] Although Goebbels, in his character as propaganda minister, did his best to keep a stiff upper lip, many passages in his diaries in these days sound like whistling in the dark.[80] Goebbels was also aware that 'Moscow' expected a bloody showdown between the NSDAP and the *Wehrmacht*.[81]

At that time the insidiously cynical 'Eleventh Decree to the *Reich* Citizen Law' (*Elfte Verordnung zum Reichsbürgergesetz*) of 25 November

[76] Goebbels, *Tagebücher II Band* 2, pp. 455, 467, 471.
[77] Goebbels, *Tagebücher II Band* 2, p. 485.
[78] Goebbels, *Tagebücher II Band* 2, pp. 494, 498–99.
[79] Goebbels, *Tagebücher II Band* 2, pp. 527–42 (see Goebbels on Jews pp. 533–34).
[80] [Joseph Goebbels], *Die Tagebücher von Joseph Goebbels. Teil II. Diktate 1941–1945. Band 3. Januar-März 1942*, Munich, New Providence, London, Paris: K.G. Saur, 1994, pp. 33, 35, 43, 45, 48, 57–58.
[81] Goebbels, *Tagebücher II Band* 3, p. 79.

1941 was issued.[82] It declared that Jews who took their permanent residence beyond the German frontiers lost their German citizenship (*Staatsangehörigkeit*): 'The habitual residence abroad is a given if a Jew resides abroad in circumstances which indicate that he is not merely temporarily residing there'. Jews who were deported to an extermination camp in Poland fell under the decree, although, in a bizarre twist, not those who were deported to Kulmhof (Chełmno) and Auschwitz, because these had been annexed to Germany. Further: The property of Jews who lost their German *Staatsangehörigkeit* on the basis of this decree became *Reich* property, and this applied also to the property of Jews without citizenship (stateless, *staatenlos*) if they had or took up their habitual residence abroad; such property, the decree said, was to be used 'for purposes connected with the solution of the Jewish Question'.

Hassell recorded Goebbels' anti-Jewish propaganda in November, which accused the Jews of war guilt, linked the persecution of the Jews with the prospects for victory, and declared all who cultivated any private contacts with Jews national traitors.[83] In Berlin the police forced Jews, at 2 A.M., to sign papers that they voluntarily vacated their apartments and transferred their property to the state.[84]

At that time *SS* and police *Einsatzgruppen* in the Soviet Union were killing tens of thousands of Jewish men, women, and children. Mass murders on the territory of the Soviet Union were in progress: from 27 to 29 August 1941, the *HSSPF Russland-Süd* (higher *SS* and police leader Russia South), *SS-Obergruppenführer* Friedrich Jeckeln, had his own staff company and bodyguard (*Stabskompanie*) together with Police Batallion 320 shoot 23,600 Jews, including women and children.[85] *Sonderkommando 4a*, which was attached to 6th Army Command, reported more than 57,000 Jews killed by November 1941. *Einsatzgruppe D* advanced with

[82] 'Elfte Verordnung zum Reichsbürgergesetz. Vom 25. November 1941', *RGBl. 1941 I*, pp. 722–24. Nota bene: *Reichsbürger*, literally '*Reich* citizen', or '*Reich* burgher', was explicitly not an equivalent of *Staatsangehöriger*, literally 'member of the state'. It marginalised Jews who were German *Staatsangehörige*, or state citizens, by depriving them of the right to vote in *Reichstag* elections and to hold public office. But it did not infringe upon their German state citizenship. It explicity differentiated between *Staatsangehöriger* and *Reichsbürger*.

[83] Longerich, *Davon*, p. 191.

[84] Hassell 1988, pp. 281–82.

[85] Klaus-Michael Mallmann, 'Der qualitative Sprung im Vernichtungsprozess: Das Massaker von Kamenez-Podolsk Ende August 1941', *Jahrbuch für Antisemitismusforschung* 10 (2001): 240–42.

Manstein's 11th Army and killed approximately 55,000 persons by the beginning of December 1941.[86] A minimum total of 6,329 Jews were killed by *Sonderkommando 4b* by mid-1943.[87]

Deportations of Jews from occupied France had begun in July 1941; Jews were being killed with gas in killing centres in Poland and in Auschwitz from the beginning of September 1941; and about 6,000 German Jews from Breslau, Munich, Frankfurt/Main, Vienna, and Berlin were deported to Kowno and Riga and shot upon their arrival on 25 and 29 November 1941.[88]

This was what Goerdeler was discussing with Hassell, Popitz, Jessen, and Beck. Goerdeler and his interlocutors were well aware of what was happening on the eastern front. As early as September 1940, in his memorandum *Stand von Wirtschaft und Verwaltung*, Goerdeler wrote about the abominations of the German administration 'in the conquered eastern territories' (*in den eroberten Ostgebieten*): 'What conditions prevail there, is known. The inhuman crimes which are being committed there must and shall horribly mar German honour for a long time'.[89] In a memorandum of November 1940, Goerdeler stated how appalled he was at 'the killing of the so-called incurable mental patients' (*die Tötung der sogenannten unheilbar Geisteskranken*).[90] And in 'The Aim', he referred to the 'expropriation, destruction etc. of Jewish property and life in Germany'; a new order must await the assessment of the entire extent of the events.[91] At the beginning of 1942, Goerdeler also recorded his outrage at the deportations of Leipzig Jews on 19 and 27 January 1942.

[86] Christian Streit, 'Angehörige des militärischen Widerstands und der Genozid an den Juden im Südabschnitt der Ostfront', in Gert R. Ueberschär, ed., *NS-Verbrechen und der militärische Widerstand gegen Hitler*, Darmstadt: Primus Verlag, 2000, pp. 90–103, cites Ereignismeldung UdSSSR Nr. 143 of 8 December 1941 and Nr. 145 of 12 December 1941, in BA Berlin-Lichterfelde R 58/219.

[87] Ronald Headland, *Messages of Murder: A Study of the Reports of the Einsatzgruppen of the Security Police and the Security Service, 1941–1943*, London and Toronto: Associated University Presses, 1992, p. 101.

[88] Eugen Kogon, Hermann Langbein, Adalbert Rückerl, et al., eds., *Nationalsozialistische Massentötungen durch Giftgas: Eine Dokumentation*, Frankfurt: S. Fischer Verlag, 1983, pp. 81–212 (killings with gas began in Auschwitz on 3 September 1941); Peter Longerich, *Politik der Vernichtung: Eine Gesamtdarstellung der nationalsozialistischen Judenverfolgung*, Munich, Zurich: Piper, 1998, pp. 434–44, 452–58, 464; Hilberg, *Destruction*, p. 353.

[89] Gillmann and Mommsen, *Politische Schriften*, p. 821.

[90] Gillmann and Mommsen, *Politische Schriften*, p. 826.

[91] Gillmann and Mommsen, *Politische Schriften*, p. 897.

While expressing sympathy and commiseration, he predicted that the German nation would experience horrific retribution.[92]

At this moment in history, in autumn 1941, when the German Army nearly collapsed before Moscow, and Japan and the United States entered the war, the enormous tensions are palpable in Hassell's diary entries in December 1941 and January 1942. Hassell described Goerdeler as sanguine, but even the sceptic Hassell viewed the situation as promising for a coup against the regime. The ramifications of the birth of the plot against Hitler, however, extend further.

Goerdeler also had discussions with Leo Baeck, the president of the National Association of German Jews (*Reichsvereinigung der deutschen Juden*), before and during the war. Recently discovered documents show that on 5 March 1942, the *Gestapo* ordered Leo Baeck to prepare, together with other scholars, a 'scholarly work about the history of the Jews in Europe'.[93] The fourth installment of the typescript of over 1,600 pages was submitted to the *Gestapo* on 2 October 1942.[94]

After the war, Leo Baeck never mentioned that the *Gestapo* had ordered him and other scholars to produce the work. Baeck and his coworkers had been faced with the chance of extending their lives, if only by a few months. In view of the length of the work and Leo Baeck's contacts with Robert Bosch and Carl Goerdeler, his own recollection in 1955 that he had begun working on it in 1938, and that a Resistance circle originally had asked him to do this, is nevertheless plausible.[95]

Leo Baeck recalled, in conversation with Robert Weltsch and Hans Reichmann at his house in London on 6 August 1955, that he had been asked by persons belonging to the German Resistance, through the mediation of a Robert Bosch Company executive who was closely

[92] Helmut Krausnick, ed., 'Goerdeler und die Deportation der Leipziger Juden', *Vierteljahrshefte für Zeitgeschichte* 13 (1965): 338–39.

[93] Fritz Backhaus, Martin Liepach, 'Leo Baecks Manuskript über die "Rechtsstellung der Juden in Europa": Neue Funde und ungeklärte Fragen', *Zeitschrift für Geschichtswissenschaft* 50/1 (2001): 57, 61; Hermann Simon, 'Bislang unbekannte Quellen zur Entstehungsgeschichte des Werkes "Die Entwicklung der Rechtsstellung der Juden in Europa, vornehmlich in Deutschland"', in Georg Heuberger und Fritz Backhaus, eds., *Leo Baeck 1873–1956: Aus dem Stamme von Rabbinern*, Frankfurt: Jüdischer Verlag im Suhrkamp Verlag, 2001, pp. 103–10.

[94] Backhaus and Liepach, 'Leo Baecks Manuskript', p. 62, record that part 4, of 5, was submitted at the beginning of October 1942.

[95] Hans Reichmann, 'Excerpts from Leo Baeck's Writings: Foreword: The Fate of A Manuscript', *Leo Baeck Institute Year Book* 3 (1958): 361–63; Scholtyseck, *Robert Bosch*, p. 278; Arnold Paucker, *Deutsche Juden im Kampf um Recht und Freiheit*, Teetz: Hentrich und Hentrich, 2003, pp. 247–50.

associated with Goerdeler and his conspiratorial activities, Hans Walz, whom Baeck did not mention by name, to write 'a book on the development of the status of the Jews in Europe'.[96] Baeck also recalled that his 'industrialist contact' in Stuttgart asked him – he did not say when – to draft a 'manifesto to the German people' for the time when the underground opposition would assume power.[97]

Among the few pieces of evidence of Baeck's contacts with the German Resistance is a conversation Baeck had with Arthur Primrose Young in Oxford in the summer of 1946. In 1938 and 1939, Young had been Goerdeler's interlocutor as an emissary of the former head of the British Foreign Office, Sir Robert Vansittart. Baeck told Young in 1946 'that he had seen a great deal of Goerdeler in Berlin during the early part of the war, and had attended some of the meetings of the resistance movement'.[98] Since Baeck recalled in 1955 that he had then already been at work on his book on the legal status of the Jews, it is likely that he discussed the matter with Goerdeler.[99]

Baeck's work is founded upon, and embraced, the same principles of the legal equality of all Germans including Jews, the same principles of human dignity and rights that govern the passage in Goerdeler's 1941/42 memorandum on 'a new order of the status of the Jews' in the world, and the same principles that Goerdeler cited as his chief motivation in his writings in prison in January 1945.[100] In a letter of 4 January 1955 to Baurat Albrecht Fischer, an executive of the Robert Bosch Company, Baeck wrote:

> When after decades our time shall have attained its proportions, he [Carl Goerdeler] and the men who joined themselves with him shall stand as the great ones in their [land?] and that for which they staked their lives will be recognized in its full dramatic greatness. For Germany, much depends on this being recognized with full gratitude.[101]

No doubt, Goerdeler's relationship with Leo Baeck was also on his mind when he composed his memorandum, 'The Aim'.

[96] Reichmann, 'Excerpts', p. 362. A typescript copy of Leo Baeck's 'Die Rechtsstellung der Juden in Europa' is in Leo Baeck Collection, Leo Baeck-LBI London, Nachlass, AR 7161, of which a microfilm is in Leo Baeck Institute, New York, Archives MF 538.

[97] Scholtyseck, *Robert Bosch*, p. 278; Paucker, *Deutsche Juden*, pp. 246–50; Reichmann, *Excerpts*, pp. 361–63.

[98] Young, *The 'X' Documents*, p. 210; see also Young's papers at http://www.warwick.ac.uk/services/library/mrc/ead/242.htm.

[99] Backhaus and Liepach, 'Leo Baecks', p. 65.

[100] Gillmann and Mommsen, *Politische Schriften*, p. 1250.

[101] Leo Baeck to Albrecht Fischer 4 January 1955, Fischer Papers in Bosch Archive and Bundesarchiv Koblenz N Goerdeler, Carl/35.

5

Document

Years of efforts to temper or change the discrimination and persecution policies of Hitler's government, and times of confusion about whether it was the *Führer* himself or extremist elements that directed the outrages, went by before the multitude of laws and decrees, almost all of them published, left no more doubt about who was responsible. Failed attempts to enlist the British government in endeavours to bring Hitler down or at least force him to give the Jews better terms of emigration; failed plots against Hitler; and a string of Hitler's successes, seemingly unbroken until about November 1941: All this was discouraging yet also confirmed that the military arm was indispensable for regime change, and that military support for a coup d'état was not forthcoming in the face of success. At the end of 1941, however, the regime's situation seemed desperate and more promising for the conspirators. The British Empire, the Soviet Union, and the United States of America were at war with Germany, Italy, and Japan. Neither Japan nor Germany was a match for the resources of America and Russia. Hitler's strategy of waging war on one front at a time had collapsed; reality belied his predictions of victory over the Soviet Union, and his attempt to keep the United States out of the war by holding large numbers of Jews hostage had failed; it could look as though the days of his regime were already numbered. Hitler sensed the danger; when he had to accept the resignation of the commander-in-chief of the army, Field Marshal von Brauchitsch, who had a serious cardiac condition, he did not appoint a successor but took over direct command of the army himself on 19 December 1941. In these weeks of instability, the conspirators against Hitler saw an opportunity. In these weeks, Goerdeler composed his ninety-nine-page memorandum called 'The Aim' (*Das Ziel*) to lay the foundations for the post-Hitler state.[1]

The following extract from Goerdeler's memorandum 'The Aim' will be analysed below:

11. A new order for the status of the Jews seems required in the entire world; because everywhere there are movements in progress which, without an organic order in place, cannot be halted, and which, without such order, will lead only to injustices, atrocities[2] and if to nothing else to an unsatisfactory disorder. It is a commonplace that the Jewish nation[3] belongs to another race. Opinion is divided in the Jewish nation on whether it ought to seek independence in the form of a state or not. The Zionists have always been demanding and preparing for their own state. Until 1933 they have not played a significant role. Yet the world will come to rest only if the Jewish nation receive a truly practicable opportunity to

[1] [Carl Goerdeler], 'Das Ziel', typed, ninety-nine pages, Bundesarchiv, Koblenz, Goerdeler Papers, N 1113/54.

The passage is taken from the copy in the German Federal Archives (*Bundesarchiv*), although there are printed publications of the memorandum. The first of these, published in 1965, was altered stylistically by the editor: Wilhelm Ritter von Schramm, ed., *Beck und Goerdeler: Gemeinschaftsdokumente für den Frieden 1941–1944*, Munich: Gotthold Müller Verlag, 1965, pp. 81–166. The second one, published in 2003 by Susanne Gillmann and Hans Mommsen in their edition of Goerdeler's *Politische Schriften und Briefe*, pp. 875–944, is based on another copy that was in the possession of the Goerdeler family at the time ('*Original im Privatbesitz der Familie Goerdeler*'; Gillmann and Mommsen, *Politische Schriften*, p. 873n1). Gillmann and Mommsen say that the copy they used is not entirely identical to the first copy in the *Bundesarchiv*, from which Schramm produced his edition, and that Schramm made 'stylistic and text-forming changes of his own' ('*eigene stilistische und textgestalterische Korrekturen*'), which he did not indicate and which raise 'source-critical concerns' about his edition; the version that Gillmann and Mommsen used became part of the Bundesarchiv, Koblenz, Goerdeler Papers, as N 1113/54 in 2004; its pp. 28–30 are the source of the quotations in this book, the passage on the status of the Jews. This version bears an inscription in Gerhard Ritter's hand: '*Mir von Dr. Goerdeler persönlich gegeben für Eigengebrauch, insbes[ondere] nach Kriegsende. Vorbereiten! Ritter*'. Gillmann and Mommsen implicitly also criticise Bodo Scheurig, ed., *Deutscher Widerstand 1938–1944: Fortschritt oder Reaktion?* Munich: Deutscher Taschenbuch Verlag, 1969, pp. 53–129 ('*Scheurig hat die Version von Schramm ohne Änderungen übernommen*').

[2] Goerdeler's term is '*Unmenschlichkeiten*', literally 'inhumanities'; in the context of the time in which he wrote, the word means atrocities. Goerdeler used almost the same language as President Wilson had done at the Paris Peace Conference; see above, Chapter 3 at note 6.

[3] Goerdeler's word is '*Volk*', which may be translated 'people' or 'nation'; 'nation' is the translation used throughout here for '*Volk*', as it approximates more closely what Goerdeler was advocating: a Jewish national state. Today, many find the contention that the Jews belonged to another race may be unacceptable, but in Goerdeler's time, it was a commonplace, everywhere, not merely in Germany.

found their own state and to maintain it. Such a territory with conditions quite worth living in can be found either in parts of Canada or South America. Once this question has been resolved through the powers' concerted action, there will result the following natural settlement[4] for German conditions: the Jew is a citizen of his Jewish state, like every other foreign citizen in Germany he has the right to carry on a trade[5] within the laws that apply to everyone else. But he is excluded as is every Englishman, Frenchman etc. from becoming a public official, electing people's representatives or being elected. On the other hand he enjoys exactly the same rights as every other foreigner who lives in Germany and who has or has not property. As far as the so-called Nuremberg race laws are concerned, they will be entirely disposed of through this settlement. The question of racial mixing must always be left to the wholesome sense of the people. A marriage between a Jew and a non-Jewish woman forces her to assume the nationality of the husband, just as if she intended to become a Frenchwoman or an Englishwoman. Conversely the same legal consequence occurs, but only if the marriage was concluded before the Nuremberg Laws,[6] otherwise only the grandchildren will receive German citizenship. No rule without exception! Jews are[7] German citizens

a) who had served in the war as German soldiers, and their direct descendants,
b) who, or whose direct ancestors possessed German citizenship on 1 July 1871,

[4] Goerdeler's term is '*Regelung*'.

[5] Goerdelers's term is '*Recht der gewerblichen Betätigung*'; *Reich* law included in the term 'Gewerbe', all occupations including those of physicians, pharmacists, advocates, and lawyers; see 'Gewerbeordnung für den Norddeutschen Bund. Vom 21. Juni 1869', Bundesgesetzblatt 1869, Berlin: Redigirt im Büreau des Bundeskanzlers, gedruckt in der Königlichen Geheimen Ober-Hofdruckerei (R.v. Decker), 1869, pp. 245–82.

[6] Reichsbürgergesetz, 15. September 1935, *RGBl. I 1935*, p. 1146; 'Gesetz zum Schutze des deutschen Blutes und der deutschen Ehre. Vom 15. September 1935', *RGBl. I 1935*, pp. 1146–47; 'Erste Verordnung zum Reichsbürgergesetz. Vom 14. November 1935', *RGBl. I 1935*, pp. 1333–34; 'Erste Verordnung zur Ausführung des Gesetzes zum Schutze des deutschen Blutes und der deutschen Ehre. Vom 14. November 1935', *RGBl. I 1935*, pp. 1334–36; 'Zweite Verordnung zum Reichsbürgergesetz. Vom 21. Dezember 1935', *RGBl. I 1935*, p. 1524–25; cf. Lothar Gruchmann, '"Blutschutzgesetz" und Justiz: Zur Entstehung und Auswirkung des Nürnberger Gesetzes vom 15. September 1935', *Vierteljahrshefte für Zeitgeschichte* 31 (1983): 418–42; Jeremy Noakes and Geoffrey Pridham, *Documents on Nazism, 1919–1945*, New York: Viking Press, 1974, pp. 463–67. Goerdeler apparently referred to the 'Erste Verordnung zum Reichsbürgergesetz', *RGBl. I 1935*, pp. 1333–34, § 5 Abs. 2c but he erred; the Nuremberg Race Laws had no bearing upon citizenship; the *Reichsbürgergesetz* stated in § 1 (2) that acquisition of state citizenship/*Staatsangehörigkeit* was governed by the *Reichs- und Staatsangehörigkeitsgesetz* (*Die Staatsangehörigkeit wird nach den Vorschriften des Reichs- und Staatsangehörigkeitsgesetzes erworben.*); Kieffer, *Goerdelers Vorschlag*, p. 491; the *RuStAG* did not stipulate that a husband's citizenship followed that of his wife, but the opposite.

[7] Goerdeler uses legal language in which laws were phrased, for example, the 21 November 1938 law declaring the Sudetenland a part of the German *Reich*: '*Durch die Wiedervereinigung sind die alteingesessenen Bewohner der sudetendeutschen Gebiete deutsche Staatsbürger nach Massgabe näherer Bestimmung*', *RGBl. I 1938*, p. 1641.

c) who, and whose direct descendants possessed German citizenship on 1 August 1914 and belonged to Christian religious denominations[8],
d) who are descendants of a mixed marriage which was concluded before 1 February 1933 if they belong to a Christian religious denomination.

In the past years undoubtedly an injustice has been bred through expropriation, destruction etc. of Jewish property and life in Germany, which we cannot answer for before our consciences and before history. Here the possibilities for a new settlement can be examined and resolved only when the whole dimension of the events[9] has been determined. It will then emerge that we, with a view to our standing in the world and to our own conscience must on our own initiative take the path to healing. Beside the pursuit of this aim, those immediate measures must be taken which are necessary for reasons of foreign policy for the de-toxification of public opinion, and which are indispensable for the restoration of German self-esteem and which are required out of a clear sense of justice of which we are fully conscious:

a) the restrictions upon the Jews in the access to food supplies, housing and telephone service, in their cultural activities, health care, adoption of names[10] are to be abolished;
b) the ghettos in the occupied territories are to be arranged humanely; the relevant indigenous authorities will decide upon their further destiny with the approval of the military governors since for example the Poles have a different attitude toward the question than the Dutch.[11]

[8] Goerdeler's term is '*christlichen Religionsgemeinschaften*'.

[9] The reference '*des Geschehens*' = 'events' can only be to what preceded the phrase: 'expropriation, destruction etc. of Jewish property and life in Germany', thus including mass murder.

[10] 'Gesetz über die Änderung von Familiennamen und Vornamen. Vom 5. Januar 1938', *RGBl. 1938 I*, pp. 9–10; 'Zweite Verordnung zur Durchführung des Gesetzes über die Änderung von Familiennamen und Vornamen. Vom 17. August 1938', *RGBl. 1938 I*, p. 1044.

[11] German: 11. *Eine Neuordnung der Stellung der J u d e n erscheint in der ganzen Welt erforderlich; denn überall sind Bewegungen im Gange, die sich ohne organische Ordnung nicht aufhalten lassen und die ohne eine solche Ordnung nur zu Ungerechtigkeiten, Unmenschlichkeiten und mindestens zur unbefriedigenden Unordnung führen. Daß das jüdische Volk einer anderen Rasse angehört, ist eine Binsenweisheit. Im jüdischen Volke selbst sind die Meinungen geteilt, ob es eine staatliche Selbständigkeit erstreben soll oder nicht. Die Zionisten haben schon seit jeher einen eigenen jüdischen Staat verlangt und vorbereitet. Eine bedeutende Rolle haben sie bis 1933 nicht gespielt. Zur Ruhe wird die Welt aber doch nur kommen, wenn das jüdische Volk eine wirklich ausnützbare Möglichkeit erhält, einen eigenen Staat zu gründen und zu erhalten. Ein solches Gebiet läßt sich auf*

jeden Fall unter durchaus lebenswerten Umständen entweder in Teilen Canadas oder Südamerikas finden. Ist diese Frage durch Zusammenwirken der Mächte gelöst, so ergibt sich für die deutschen Verhältnisse folgende natürliche Regelung: Der Jude ist Staatsbürger seines jüdischen Staates, er hat, wie jeder andere Fremdbürger in Deutschland, nach den für jeden anderen geltenden Gesetzen das Recht der gewerblichen Betätigung. Dagegen scheidet, wie für jeden Engländer, Franzosen usw. aus, öffentlicher Beamter zu werden, in die Volksvertretungen zu wählen oder gewählt zu werden. Auf der anderen Seite genießt er genau die gleichen Rechte wie jeder andere Ausländer, der in Deutschland wohnt und Vermögen hat oder nicht. Was die sogenannten Nürnberger Rassegesetze betrifft, so erledigen sie sich durch diese Regelung auch vollkommen. Die Frage der Rassenvermischung muß stets dem gesunden Sinn des Volkes überlassen bleiben. Eine Ehe zwischen einem Juden und einer Nichtjüdin zwingt diese, der Staatsangehörigkeit des Mannes zu folgen, wie wenn sie Französin oder Engländerin werden wollte! Auch umgekehrt tritt diese Rechtsfolge ein, aber nur wenn die Ehe vor den Nürnberger Gesetzen geschlossen war; andernfalls erhalten erst die Enkel deutsche Staatsangehörigkeit. Keine Regel ohne Ausnahme! Deutsche Staatsangehörige sind Juden

a) die als deutsche Soldaten am Kriege teilgenommen haben und ihre direkten Nachkommen,
b) die oder deren direkte Vorfahren am 1.7.1871 deutsche Reichsangehörigkeit besaßen und ihre direkten Nachkommen,
c) die am 1.8.1914 die deutsche Staatsangehörigkeit besaßen und christlichen Religionsgemeinschaften angehörten und noch angehören, sowie ihre direkten Nachkommen,
d) Abkömmlinge einer Mischehe, die vor dem 1.2.1933 geschlossen ist, sofern sie einer christlichen Religionsgemeinschaft angehören.

In den vergangenen Jahren ist zweifellos ein Unrecht durch Enteignung, Zerstörung usw. jüdischen Besitzes und Lebens in Deutschland großgezogen, das wir vor unserem Gewissen und der Geschichte nicht verantworten können. Hier werden die Möglichkeiten einer Neuordnung erst dann geprüft und gelöst werden können, wenn der ganze Umfang des Geschehens feststeht. Es wird sich dann ergeben, daß wir im Hinblick auf unsere Stellung in der Welt und auf unser eigenes Gewissen aus eigenem Antrieb den Weg zur Heilung beschreiten müssen. Neben der Verfolgung dieses Zieles müssen diejenigen S o f o r t maßnahmen ergriffen werden, die aus außenpolitischen Gründen zur Entgiftung der öffentlichen Meinung notwendig, zur Wiederherstellung der deutschen Selbstachtung unerläßlich und aus klaren [sic] und uns vollkommen bewusstem Gerechtigkeitsgefühl geboten sind:

a) die Beschränkungen der Juden auf dem Gebiete des Ernährungs-, des Wohnungs- und des Fernsprechwesens, der kulturellen Betätigung, der Gesundheitspflege, der Namensgestaltung sind aufzuheben;
b) die Ghettos in den besetzten Gebieten sind menschenwürdig zu gestalten; über ihr weiteres Schicksal bestimmen die zuständigen einheimischen Behörden mit Genehmigung der Militärgouverneure, da z.B. die Polen zu der Frage anders stehen wie die Holländer.

6

Analysis 1: Meanings

Section I in Goerdeler's memorandum 'The Aim' is headed 'The Totality of Policy' (*Die Totalität der Politik*) in reference to General Erich Ludendorff's doctrine of Total War.

Much like Moltke's 1940–1941 drafts, but in rich and emotional language unlike Moltke's dry, legal idiom, the memorandum addresses the fundamental issues facing human society and the state – the natural environment; provision for material and spiritual needs; freedom of scientific enquiry; freedom of religion, law, and justice; patriotism[1]; human virtues; and the grand principle of subordination to divine guidance. Policy (*Politik*) must encompass *all* of these premises, and it must seek a balance of interests instead of an unscrupulous use of power. Policy must also remain in control during war: 'There is not a totality of war as such, there is only a totality of policy in war as in peace'. The discourse about Total War in the sense that in war any means were legitimate had been possible in the last fifty years only because policy had failed. The aim was the balance of peace.

These principles are followed by a first historical *tour d'horizon*, describing the policies of Bismarck's successors as having abandoned the comprehensive meaning of policy, of having become 'naïve, superficial and frivolous', and generally describing human affairs as characterised by gains in intellectual liberty on the one hand and loss of humility leading to hubris on the other hand. Divine and natural laws must be acknowledged and honoured. Foreign-policy and domestic-policy aims must be based upon them.

[1] See J.J. Rousseau, 'Considérations sur le gouvernement de Pologne, et sur sa réformation projetée en avril, 1772', in *Oeuvres: Nouvelle Édition: Politique*, Paris: Werdet et Lequien Fils, 1876, pp. 271–303.

The section headed 'II. The Foreign Policy Aim' consists of a series of comments and proposals on international issues such as free trade; the Far East, where Japan was engaged in a campaign to conquer the Philippines, Indochina, Thailand, and the Netherlands East Indies, in what it called its 'Greater East Asia Co-prosperity Sphere'; Africa and colonies; Hitler's appalling foreign-policy bungling and bullying; and conditions for peace and European cooperation. The section heaps scorn and ridicule upon the National Socialist 'ideology': 'Eternal battle means permanent waste of resources' (*Ewiger Kampf bedeutet dauernde Kräftevergeudung*).[2] Although there had been illegitimate regimes who had gained power by dishonest means, Goerdeler predicted that the more ruthlessly the 'superior' power exploited subjected peoples, the more rapidly it would itself collapse; in the process the conquering and overpowering people lost its intellectual, psychological, and physical resources (*Kräfte*), but the subjected people gained them. With global sweep, he compared the growth of the British Empire to the slower and currently interrupted growth of a pan-European development (*Großraumentwicklung*). He ridiculed Hitler's 'superior statecraft', which found the 'highest values' in the Nordic races only to rape them in 1940 and to abandon 'white' interests in East Asia to the 'yellow' ones. Goerdeler subjected the National Socialist 'race' ideology to scornful sarcasm. He distinguished between 'white' and 'yellow' races, and the 'English race' and the German and Scandinavian 'races', the Jewish race, using 'race' in the ethnic sense as interchangeable with 'people' or 'nation' (*Volk*), not in a biological sense.[3] On 12 November 1933, Chaim Weizmann told James G. McDonald, recognising the 'evident dangers' facing the Jews: 'The Jews had always survived through the remnants of the race, and they might have to do so again'.[4] Using *Volk* (twice in Goerdeler's proposal) in referring to the Jewish nation is analogous to using *Volk* for the German or French nation.

[2] Gillmann and Mommsen, *Politische Schriften*, p. 876.

[3] Goerdeler's word is '*Volk*', which may be translated 'people' or 'nation'; 'nation' is the translation used throughout here for '*Volk*', as it approximates more closely what Goerdeler was advocating: a Jewish national state. Today, the contention that the Jews belonged to another 'race' may not be acceptable, but in Goerdeler's time, it was a commonplace, everywhere, not merely in Germany. See Goerdeler's references to 'race' in Gillmann and Mommsen, *Politische Schriften*, pp. 880–81 ('englische Rasse'), 886, 889; Kieffer, 'Goerdelers Vorschlag', pp. 478–81. Kieffer, p. 494, points out that Goerdeler could not have been concerned with 'race' because he exempted, in his categories (c) and (d), certain baptised (therefore former) Jews from the loss of citizenship, and baptism did not change race; but Goerdeler refers to these former Jews collectively as 'Jews' – no doubt a sign of poor draftsmanship.

[4] McDonald, *Advocate*, pp. 152.

Goerdeler's, like Weizmann's, use of the term 'race' does not carry the biological sense of 'race' that the National Socialists postulated. They tried to apply it through the determination of Jewish ancestry, which in fact could establish only descent from religious Jews (*Glaubensjuden*), or cultural or ethnic Jews. In the twenty-first century, 'race' and 'racist' have become pejoratives. In Weizmann's and Goerdeler's time, it was not so. At the time, there were extremists, fanatics, and misguided people who believed there were physically distinguishable 'races' within the general framework of the Caucasian, Negroid, and Asiatic 'races'. The National Socialists did not refer to the 'Nordic', 'Germanic', and 'Jewish' 'races' as subdivisions, but as discrete 'races'. In Goerdeler's reference to 'racial mixing' in cases of marriages between Jews and non-Jews, he wants this to be 'left invariably to the wholesome sense of the people'. 'The people' here has no ethnic meaning.[5] Goerdeler followed an analysis of European developments in the twentieth century with a comprehensive condemnation of 'the totalitarian assertion of unreason and immorality'.[6] 'It is stupid and arrogant to speak of a German master human.'[7]

The proposal for 'a new order for the status of the Jews' in the entire world concludes Section II on 'The Foreign Policy Aim'. The 'status of the Jews in the entire world' was an international issue, not a German internal one, and it is therefore placed in the foreign-policy part of the memorandum.[8]

Section III, 'Internal Policy', deals with law and justice: 'First of all, law and decency are to be restored'.[9]

After German mass killings of Jews, priests, and university professors, in Poland in 1939 and 1940, and in Russia since 1941, Goerdeler sought to set out in his memorandum comprehensive measures not only for the Jews 'in the entire world', but also for international relations and national renewal.

In reading the considerations below, it may be helpful to keep a copy of the text of Goerdeler's proposals in Section II/11 at hand.

Goerdeler's proposals on behalf of the Jews 'in the entire world' were proposals for a global arrangement to protect all Jews. In Goerdeler's view, the comprehensive answer was that Jews everywhere became citizens of

[5] Gillmann and Mommsen, *Politische Schriften*, p. 896.
[6] Gillmann and Mommsen, *Politische Schriften*, p. 888.
[7] Gillmann and Mommsen, *Politische Schriften*, p. 889.
[8] Kieffer, 'Goerdelers Vorschlag', pp. 476–77.
[9] Gillmann and Mommsen, *Politische Schriften*, p. 897. Goerdeler uses the term '*Recht und Anstand*'; *Recht*, literally right, in German also has the meaning of law and justice.

a Jewish state. Goerdeler here writes about matters of international and national law. His intention to save the Jews is clear, although what he wrote is not a legal document. In his appeal to all humans, written in prison on 27 January 1945, he deplored in the strongest terms the crimes against the Jews, he cited his own commitment to the protection of the Jews, beginning in Leipzig in April 1933, and he declared his intensive preoccupation with any and all measures that might have helped to save the Jews.[10]

Goerdeler began by demanding 'a new order for the status of the Jews' in the entire world, 'because everywhere there are movements in progress which, without an organic order in place, cannot be halted, and which, without such order, will lead only to injustices, atrocities'. Those movements, injustices, and atrocities included the pogroms in Russia and Eastern Europe, the Arabs' opposition to Jewish settlement in the British Mandate territory of Palestine, the persecution of the Jews in Germany, and, since the start of the war in September 1939, the beginning of mass murders in Poland, when several thousand Jews were killed along with intellectuals, priests, and members of the upper class.[11] In 1941 killing Jews had become a systematically executed programme particularly in the Soviet Union, where the *Einsatzgruppen* killed hundreds of thousands. Unspeakable atrocities and hundreds of the most brutal murders of Jews were perpetrated in Romania in January 1941. The American minister in Romania, Franklin Mott Gunther, attributed them to German instigation and in his reports spoke of 'the forces now at work in Europe'. In July 1941 he reported on six months of appalling persecutions of Jews and systematic mass shootings of hundreds of Jews by Romanian Army units. Later in the year, Gunther reported that 20,000–30,000 Jews were being deported from Romania and likely murdered in Transnistria; the American Department of State reacted by contemplating the settlement of 300,000 Jews from Romania in Syria or Palestine, without seeing requirements such as transport and acceptance at the presumed destinations realisable.[12] Gunther suggested in a letter to the president on 5 August 1941 that much of the 'diabolical' measures taken by the

[10] Gillmann and Mommsen, *Politische Schriften*, p. 1239.

[11] Helmut Krausnick, 'Die Einsatzgruppen vom Anschluss Österreichs bis zum Feldzug gegen die Sowjetunion: Entwicklung und Verhältnis zur Wehrmacht', in Helmut Krausnick and Hans-Heinrich Wilhelm, *Die Truppe des Weltanschauungskrieges: Die Einsatzgruppen der Sicherheitspolizei und des SD 1938–1942*, Stuttgart: Deutsche Verlags-Anstalt, 1981, pp. 32–106, esp. pp. 63, 77, 89, 93, 95, 97–101.

[12] *Foreign Relations of the United States. Diplomatic Papers: 1941* (*FRUS 1941*), vol. II, Washington: United States Government Printing Office, 1959, pp. 860–68, 875.

Romanian government against Jews could be discouraged if the British government were in a position to announce 'the definite allocation now of a large territory in Africa available immediately as a homeland for the unwanted Jews of Europe'. He repeated his suggestion in a telegram to the secretary of state on 1 November 1941.[13]

Such 'movements' against Jews in many parts of the world, Goerdeler maintained, needed to be 'halted'. This was only possible through the removal of Hitler and his regime. The ultimate solution, in Goerdeler's view, was a Jewish state, and citizenship of that state for the Jews of the entire world.

Goerdeler referred to 'Jews' as citizens of the Jewish state, and to those 'Jews' who were German citizens at the same time, as German citizens. He defined them as persons with dual citizenship, as holding German citizenship *beside* Jewish citizenship, without any need for individual decisions, *ipso facto*, automatically.

On the one hand, he was discoursing about the 'new order for the status of the Jews [...] in the entire world'. They would be Jewish citizens in the framework of international law. Based on the German national legal system, the German internal 'natural settlement'[14] would be that the Jew is a citizen of his Jewish state, like every other foreign citizen in Germany was a citizen of his or her state. In both instances of Goerdeler's use of the term 'Jew', Goerdeler is referring to Jews as citizens of their Jewish state, not as members of an ethnic or cultural, much less a racial, group. He places them in the category of citizens of a foreign state in the same sense as he does in his reference to 'every Englishman, Frenchman etc.'[15]

Goerdeler goes on to explain that in Germany the Jew (as a citizen of the Jewish state) would be 'excluded as is every Englishman, Frenchman etc. from becoming a public official, electing people's representatives or being elected'. Although these were the political rights from which the '*Reich* Citizen Law' excluded Jews who were otherwise German citizens, Goerdeler's explanation makes clear that in his projected Germany, the Jew with non-German citizenship is excluded from political rights not as an ethnic Jew but as a citizen of a foreign country.

Under the German citizenship law of 1913, anyone who acquired another citizenship lost his or her German citizenship, unless they met

[13] *FRUS 1941*, vol. II, p. 870.

[14] Goerdeler's term is '*Regelung*'.

[15] The author thanks Fritz Kieffer (letter to the author 21 September 2009) for his assistance in clarifying these terms.

certain conditions (including residence in Germany and the authorities' permission to hold dual citizenship).[16] On the other hand, the passage in Goerdeler's memorandum continues, he enjoys 'exactly the same rights as every other foreigner who lives in Germany and who has or has not property. As far as the so-called Nuremberg race laws are concerned, they will be entirely disposed of through this settlement'.[17] Goerdeler appears not to have remembered the doctrine that new law replaced or nullified old law if the new was in conflict with the old (*lex posterior derogat priori*), although he implicitly applies the doctrine here.[18]

Throughout his memorandum, Goerdeler makes clear his rejection of 'the so-called Nuremberg race laws', directly and indirectly. He seeks by his proposal to render them invalid and moot; his proposal will deprive 'the so-called Nuremberg race laws' of their object; they become null and void. It has been shown that Goerdeler generally rejected, scorned, and satirised the National Socialist 'race' ideology.[19]

'The so-called Nuremberg race laws' and their implementation decrees defined 'Jews' and, particularly through the '*Reich* Citizen Law' (*Reichsbürgergesetz*), curtailed political rights for German 'Jews' (now defined), to wit, the right to vote and to hold public office, but they explicitly

[16] 'Reichs- und Staatsangehörigkeitsgesetz. Vom 22. Juli 1913', *Reichs-Gesetzblatt. 1913.* Enthält die Gesetze, Verordnungen usw. vom 7. Januar bis 20. Dezember 1913 nebst einem Vertrage vom Jahre 1909, drei Übereinkommen vom Jahre 1910, einer Übereinkunft und drei Verträgen vom Jahre 1911 und zwei Allerhöchsten Verordnungen, vier Gesetzen, einem Vertrage, zwei Abkommen und zwei Bekanntmachungen vom Jahre 1912. (Von Nr. 4156 bis einschl. Nr. 4326.) Nr. 1 bis einschl. Nr. 75, Berlin: Herausgegeben im Reichsamte des Innern. Zu beziehen durch alle Postanstalten. [O.J. Impressum auf dem letzten Blatt: 'Den Bezug des Reichs-Gesetzblatts vermitteln nur die Postanstalten. Herausgegeben im Reichsamt des Innern. – Berlin, gedruckt in der Reichsdruckerei'. Ohne Jahr], pp. 583–93; § 6 (p. 584): '*Durch Eheschließung mit einem Deutschen erwirbt die Frau die Staatsangehörigkeit des Mannes.*' *§ 9 (p. 585): 'Die Einbürgerung in einen Bundesstaat darf erst erfolgen, nachdem durch den Reichskanzler festgestellt worden ist, daß keiner der übrigen Bundesstaaten Bedenken dagegen erhoben hat; erhebt ein Bundesstaat Bedenken, so entscheidet der Bundesrat*'. Dual citizenship with permission: §25 (p. 589). Kieffer, 'Goerdelers Vorschlag', p. 491n107, cites Bernhard Lösener and Friedrich A. Knost, *Die Nürnberger Gesetze über das Reichsbürgerrecht und den Schutz des deutschen Blutes und der deutschen Ehre nebst den Durchführungsverordnungen, dem Ehegesundheitsgesetz sowie sämtlichen einschlägigen Bestimmungen (insbesondere über den Abstammungsnachweis) und den Gebührenvorschriften*, Berlin: Verlag Franz Vahlen, 1936, p. 8 (in 2. neubearbeitete und erweiterte Auflage, 1937, p. 10).

[17] Gillmann and Mommsen, *Politische Schriften*, p. 896.

[18] I thank Fritz Kieffer for pointing out this principle; see Ludwig Enneccerus and Hans Carl Nipperdey, *Enneccerus-Kipp-Wolff, Allgemeiner Teil des Bürgerlichen Rechts: Ein Lehrbuch*, Tübingen: J.C.B. Mohr (Paul Siebeck), 1959, p. 287.

[19] See Goerdeler's references to 'race' in Gillmann and Mommsen, *Politische Schriften*, pp. 880–81 ('englische Rasse'), 886, 889; Kieffer, 'Goerdelers Vorschlag', pp. 478–81. See also note 3 above.

had no bearing upon German state citizenship (*Staatsangehörigkeit*).[20] Nota bene: *Reichsbürger*, literally '*Reich* citizen', or '*Reich* burgher', was explicitly not an equivalent of *Staatsangehöriger*, literally 'member of the state', or 'subject of the state'.

Reichsbürger was a new term intended to distinguish between persons of 'German and ethnically-kindred[21] blood' and others, the intention being to separate 'Jews' from 'Germans'. As far as German law was concerned, German religious Jews, therefore, did not lose their German state citizenship (*Staatsangehörigkeit*) through the 1935 Nuremberg Race Laws or any other laws before November 1941. The '*Reich* Citizen Law' states explicitly that German state citizenship, or being a German subject, 'is acquired according to the terms of the *Reich* Citizenship Law [*Reichs- und Staatsangehörigkeitsgesetz*]', which was by birth, legitimisation, marriage, acceptance, or naturalisation.[22] The '*Reich* Citizen Law' and its first implementation decree (*Erste Verordnung zum Reichsbürgergesetz*) provided that only a *Reichsbürger* could vote or hold public office, and that Jews could not be *Reichsbürger*. It marginalised Jews who were German *Staatsangehörige*, or state citizens, by depriving them of the right to 'vote in political matters' and to hold public office, but it did not infringe upon their German state citizenship. It explicitly differentiated between *Staatsangehöriger* and *Reichsbürger*. Declaring 'the so-called Nuremberg race laws' moot, however, did not mean that German Jews as defined by 'the so-called Nuremberg race laws' who had become citizens of the Jewish state had their political rights as Germans restored, only that they could not be deprived of the civil rights they did not have in Germany as citizens of a Jewish state and that no foreigner in Germany had.

[20] Gillmann and Mommsen, *Politische Schriften*, p. 896; 'Reichsbürgergesetz', 15. September 1935, *RGBl. I 1935*, p. 1146; 'Gesetz zum Schutze des deutschen Blutes und der deutschen Ehre. Vom 15. September 1935', *RGBl. I 1935*, pp. 1146–47; 'Erste Verordnung zum Reichsbürgergesetz. Vom 14. November 1935', *RGBl. I 1935*, pp. 1333–34; 'Erste Verordnung zur Ausführung des Gesetzes zum Schutze des deutschen Blutes und der deutschen Ehre. Vom 14. November 1935', *RGBl. I 1935*, pp. 1334–36; 'Zweite Verordung zum Reichsbürgergesetz. Vom 21. Dezember 1935', *RGBl. I 1935*, p. 1524–25; cf. Gruchmann, *Blutschutzgesetz und Justiz*, pp. 418–42; Noakes and Pridham, *Documents on Nazism*, pp. 463–67. Goerdeler apparently referred to the 'Erste Verordnung zum Reichsbürgergesetz', *RGBl. I 1935*, pp. 1333–34, § 5 Abs. 2c, but he erred; the Nuremberg Race Laws had no bearing upon citizenship. Contemporary commentary declared that the principles of the *Reichs- und Staatsangehörigkeitsgesetz* about acquisition and loss of German citizenship were in no way affected; Kieffer, 'Goerdelers Vorschlag', p. 491; the *RuStAG* did not stipulate that a husband's citizenship followed that of his wife but the opposite; cf. Kieffer, 'Goerdelers Vorschlag', p. 491.

[21] German: *artverwandt* can also be translated as congeneric.

[22] 'Reichs- und Staatsangehörigkeitsgesetz', *Reichs-Gesetzblatt. 1913*, §§ 3–16.

A few lines down, however, it occurred to Goerdeler that many, perhaps most, German 'Jews' as defined by 'the so-called Nuremberg race laws' might wish to retain their German citizenship if becoming citizens of a Jewish state meant, barring the exceptions allowed in the *Reich* Citizen Law of 1913 (*Reichs- und Staatsangehörigkeitsgesetz, RuStAG*), losing their German citizenship.

The haste in which Goerdeler composed his memorandum is evident generally in its rambling and expansive style. Here, in Section II/11 on the status of the Jews, the untidy and poorly thought-out nature of the document reveals itself in the incoherent consideration of the issue of citizenship. The consideration is first sidetracked into the 'question of racial mixing'. Then it returns tangentially to the citizenship issue in cases of non-Jewish women marrying Jewish citizens, and it says that in such cases the woman is forced to 'assume the nationality of the husband'. This was true under *RuStAG* § 6 if the 'Jew' in the 'marriage between a Jew and a non-Jewish woman' was a German citizen and the non-Jewish woman was not, or if a Jewish woman was not a German citizen. It applied only to cases of non-German women marrying a male German citizen. The *RuStAG*, of course, could say nothing about the wives of foreign citizens. But Goerdeler had just assigned Jewish citizenship to all Jews, without exempting German Jews as defined by 'the so-called Nuremberg race laws', and the Jewish state's citizenship law might not allow dual citizenship, and so a 'Jew' who was a citizen of the Jewish state and also a German citizen would not exist.

The sentence following this contains another error.

Goerdeler wrote that a woman of non-Jewish citizenship who married a 'Jew' who was a Jewish citizen became a Jewish citizen. This Jewish state did not yet exist, so that any such rule had yet to be codified by the (future) Jewish state. It is certainly correct that under German law a woman of German citizenship lost her German citizenship if she married a Jewish citizen. Then Goerdeler continued that 'conversely the same legal consequence occurs, but only if the marriage was concluded before the Nuremberg Laws, otherwise only the grandchildren will receive German citizenship'. This is nonsense. The German law (*RuStAG* § 17) determined that a woman who was a German citizen lost her German citizenship through marriage to a foreigner. Goerdeler could not know what the law of the future Jewish state would say. Furthermore, the grandchildren of Jewish citizens were not entitled to German citizenship. If 'conversely' (*umgekehrt*) means that if a Jewish woman who was a citizen of the Jewish state married a non-Jew, she lost her Jewish citizenship and acquired German citizenship according to German law (*RuStAG* § 6), then Goerdeler misread German law on this point. Neither the 'Law for the Protection of German Blood and German Honour' (*Gesetz zum Schutze des deutschen Blutes und der deutschen Ehre*) nor the '*Reich* Citizen Law' (*Reichsbürgergesetz*), 'the so-called Nuremberg race laws', changed the terms of the 1913 citizenship law.[23] To the contrary, the '*Reich* Citizen Law' explicitly affirmed that state citizenship was subject to the terms of the *RuStAG* of 22 July 1913. This meant that persons born in Germany whose fathers were not German citizens were not German citizens by birth (although they could acquire German citizenship under the terms of the *RuStAG* §§ 3, 8–16). Under the German *RuStAG* § 4, the father's citizenship determined that of his children (*ius sanguinis*).[24] According to the 1933 census, 41,312 of the foreign religious Jews in Germany had been born in Germany or in parts of Germany lost through the Treaty of Versailles.[25] They were not therefore entitled to German citizenship but could only apply for it under existing rules. But the '*Reich* Citizen Law' and its first ordinance did not affect German 'citizenship' as defined by the *RuStAG*. A German citizen as defined by the *RuStAG*, whether Jewish or not, could, for example, hold a German passport.

What follows further makes clear that Goerdeler did not want 'the so-called Nuremberg race laws' to turn German Jews into second-class citizens without political rights. The restrictions in these laws were humiliating and marginalising. Voting rights in the dictatorship were meaningless, and holding public office had already been restricted. But the humiliation, the effect of being pilloried, and other consequences of being legally defined, declared, and described a 'Jew' were insupportable. The aim of Goerdeler's entire memorandum was the restoration of law and justice after Hitler's removal, after which political rights, too, would again have meaning.

Goerdeler's proposal, after his surprising error about the effect of the Nuremberg Race Laws upon citizenship (*Staatsangehörigkeit*), suddenly erupts into this exclamation:

> No rule without exception! Jews are German citizens
>
> a) who had served in the war as German soldiers, and their direct descendants,
> b) who, or whose direct ancestors possessed German citizenship on 1 July 1871,
> c) who, and whose direct descendants possessed German citizenship on 1 August 1914 and belonged to Christian religious denominations,[26]

[23] See pp. 15–16, 124; note 20 above.

[24] *RuStAG* 22 July 1913, §§ 3–4.

[25] *Statistik des Deutschen Reichs*. Band 451, 5, p.14.

[26] Goerdeler's term is '*christlichen Religionsgemeinschaften*'.

d) who are descendants of a mixed marriage which was concluded before 1 February 1933 if they belong to a Christian religious denomination.

Category (a) includes wives because under German law (*RuStAG* § 6) they automatically had the husband's citizenship, and they could not be excluded from it regardless of their premarital status (recent immigrant, foreign citizen, etc.); their children's citizenship was determined by that of the father (*RuStAG* § 4). No doubt Goerdeler's best argument was that in favour of war veterans. The *RuStAG* already included, in § 12, a bias in favour of persons who had served in the German military forces. It stipulated that upon application, a foreigner who had done active military service for at least one year 'like a German in the Army or in the Navy' must be naturalised.

Category (b) includes parts of the other three categories. According to the North German Confederation's citizenship law of 1 June 1870, all Jews resident within the borders of the German *Reich* that was founded in November 1870 and proclaimed on 18 January 1871 were German citizens *ipso facto* as citizens of the North German Confederation (*Bundesangehörige*) if in 1867 or thereafter they were 'subjects, citizens' in a state now part of the German *Reich*.[27] Goerdeler's date of 1 July

[27] 'Publikandum. Vom 26. Juli 1867 [...] Verfassung des Norddeutschen Bundes', in *Bundes-Gesetzblatt des Norddeutschen Bundes 1867*, Berlin: Königliche Geheime Ober-Hofbuchdruckerei (R.v. Decker), 1867, pp. 1–23, esp. 2–3.

The Constitution of the North German Confederation said: Federal laws supersede state (land) laws; every subject of the Confederation has equal rights as every permanent inhabitant of every federal state. 'Bundesgesetzgebung. Artikel 2. Innerhalb des Bundesgebietes übt der Bund das Recht der Gesetzgebung nach Maaßgabe des Inhalts dieser Verfassung und mit der Wirkung aus, daß die Bundesgesetze den Landesgesetzen vorgehen [. . .] Artikel 3. Für den ganzen Umfang des Bundesgebietes besteht ein gemeinsames Indigenat mit der Wirkung, das der Angehörige (Unterthan, Staatsbüger) eines jeden Bundesstaates in jedem anderen Bundesstaate als Inläder zu behandeln und demgemäß zum festen Wohnsitz, zum Gewerbebetriebe, zu öffentlichen Ämtern, zur Erwerbung von Grundstücken, zur Erlangung des Staatsbürgerrechts und zum Genusse aller sonstigen bürgerlichen Rechte unter denselben Voraussetzungen wie der Einheimische zuzulassen, auch in Betreff der Rechtsverfolgung und des Rechtsschutzes demselben gleich zu behandeln ist. In der Ausübung dieser Befugnis darf der Bundesangehörige weder durch die Obrigkeit seiner Heimath, noch durch die Obrigkeit eines anderen Bundesstaates beschränkt werden [. . .] Dem Auslande gegenüber haben alle Bundesangehörigen gleichmäßig Anspruch auf den Bundesschutz' 'Publikandum. Vom 26. Juli 1867 [. . .] Verfassung des Norddeutschen Bundes', in *Bundes-Gesetzblatt des Norddeutschen Bundes 1867*, Berlin: Redigirt im Büreau des Bundeskanzlers. Berlin, gedruckt in der Königlichen Geheimen Ober-Hofbuchdruckerei (R.v. Decker), pp. 1–23, esp. 2–3.

'Gesetz über die Freizügigkeit. Vom 1. November 1867', in *Bundes-Gesetzblatt des Norddeutschen Bundes 1867*, Berlin: Redigirt im Büreau des Bundeskanzlers. Berlin, gedruckt in der Königlichen Geheimen Ober-Hofbuchdruckerei (R.v. Decker), pp. 55–58: § 1 Jeder Bundesangehöorige hat das Recht, innerhalb des Bundesgebietes:

1871 is an error and legally irrelevant; 1 January 1871 is the date when the North German Confederation's 'Law about acquisition and loss of

1) *an jedem Orte sich aufzuhalten oder niederzulassen, wo er eine eigene Wohnung oder ein Unterkommen sich zu verschaffen imstande ist;*
2) *an jedem Orte Grundeigenthum aller Art zu erwerben;*
3) *umherziehend oder an dem Orte des Aufenthalts, beziehungsweise der Niederlassung, Gewerbe aller Art zu betreiben, unter den für Einheimische geltenden gesetzlichen Bestimmungen.' (still § 1:) 'Keinem Bundesangehörigen darf um des Glaubensbekenntnisses willen oder wegen fehlender Landes- oder Gemeindezugehörigkeit der Aufenthalt, die Niederlassung, der Gewerbebetrieb oder der Erwerb von Grundeigenthum verweigert werden'.*

'Gewerbeordnung für den Norddeutschen Bund. Vom 21. Juni 1869', in *Bundesgesetzblatt 1869*, pp. 245–82: '*§ 1. Der Betrieb eines Gewerbes ist Jedermann gestattet, soweit nicht durch dieses Gesetz Ausnahme oder Beschränkungen vorgeschrieben oder zugelassen sind. Wer gegenwärtig zum Betriebe eines Gewerbes berechtigt ist, kann von demselben nicht deshalb ausgeschlossen werden, weil er den Erfordernissen dieses Gesetzes nicht genügt*'.

Exempt from the application of the present law are *Fischerei*, '*die Ausübung der Heilkunde*', *Apotheken, Unterrichtswesen, advokatorische u. Notariatspraxis*, '*Gewerbebetrieb der Auswanderungs-Unternehmer und Auswanderungs-Agenten*', *Versicherungen, Eisenbahnen, Lotterie, öffentliche Fahren, Rechtsverhältnisse von Schiffsmannschaften auf Seeschiffen*. The Trade Regulation Act (*Gewerbeordnung*) was *Reich* law.

Result: 'Trade' ('*Gewerbe*') includes lawyers, advocates, notaries, physicians, and so on.

'Gesetz betreffend die Gleichberechtigung der Konfessionen in bürgerlicher und staatsbürgerlicher Beziehung. Vom 3. Juli 1869', in *Bundes-Gesetzblatt 1869*, p. 292:

'*Einziger Artikel*

Alle noch bestehenden, aus der Verschiedenheit des religiösen Bekenntnisses hergeleiteten Beschränkungen der bürgerlichen und staatsbürgerlichen Rechte werden hierdurch aufgehoben. Insbesondere soll die Befähigung zur Theilnahme an der Gemeinde- und Landesvertretung und zur Bekleidung öffentlicher Ämter vom religiösen Bekenntis unabhängig sein'.

'Gesetz über die Erwerbung und den Verlust der Bundes- und Staatsangehörigkeit. Vom 1. Juni 1870', in *Bundes-Gesetzblatt des Norddeutschen Bundes. 1870*, Redigirt im Büreau des Bundeskanzlers. Berlin: gedruckt in der Königlichen Geheimen Ober-Hofbuchdruckerei (R.v. Decker), [1871], pp. 355–60, defined: *§. 1. Die Bundesangehörigkeit wird durch die Staatsangehörigkeit in einem Bundesstaat erworben und erlischt mit deren Verlust.*' '*§. 2. Die Staatsangehörigkeit in einem Bundesstaate wird fortan nur begründet*:

1) *durch Abstammung (§. 3.),*
2) *durch Legitimation (§. 4.),*
3) *durch Verheirathung (§. 5.),*
4) *für einen Norddeutschen durch Aufnahme, und*
5) *für einen Ausländer durch Naturalisation* (§§. 6. ff.).
   Die Adoption hat für sich allein diese Wirkung nicht.'

§ 3: Children of a North German (after 1 June 1871: of a German) born in wedlock acquire by birth the father's citizenship (*Staatsangehörigkeit*); children of a North German (after 1 June 1871: of a German) born out of wedlock acquire by birth the mother's citizenship (*Staatsangehörigkeit*).

§ 4: Legitimisation of illegitimate children.

§ 5: Marriage.

§ 6: Acceptance through certificate, etc.

the Federal and State citizenship' of 1 June 1870 was promulgated; this became the law in all of Germany on 1 June 1871.[28] German citizenship in the German *Reich* was based on the North German Confederation's citizenship law of 1 June 1870.[29] This law became a law of the *Reich* that was founded in November 1870 and proclaimed on 18 January 1871.[30] Inhabitants of Alsace-Lorraine and Heligoland became *Reich* citizens (*Reichsangehörige*) by the laws of 8 January 1873 and 1 April 1891, respectively.[31] German citizenship (*Reichsangehörigkeit*) could be acquired by birth, legitimisation, marriage (for women), admission, or naturalisation (for foreigners).

Categories (c) and (d) expand category (b) by suspending the requirement of citizenship on 1 July 1871 (see above) on condition of adherence to a Christian religious community. This included immigrants and their wives (*RuStAG* § 6) of the years 1871 to 1914 if they had become German citizens and Christians before 1 August 1914; it also included a substantial though unverifiable number of children who were baptised immediately after birth and therefore not registered in any category connected with Jewishness. It did not include immigrants of the years 1871 to 1914 if they were religious Jews, unless they were also in category (a),

[28] 'Gesetz über die Erwerbung und den Verlust der Bundes- und Staatsangehörigkeit. Vom 1. Juni 1870', in *Bundes-Gesetzblatt des Norddeutschen Bundes. 1870*, Redigirt im Büreau des Bundeskanzlers. Berlin: gedruckt in der Königlichen Geheimen Ober-Hofbuchdruckerei (R.v. Decker), [1871], pp. 355–60.

[29] 'Gesetz über die Erwerbung und den Verlust der Bundes- und Staatsangehörigkeit [*sic*]. Vom 1. Juni 1870', in *Bundes-Gesetzblatt des Norddeutschen Bundes. 1870*, Berlin: Gesetz-Sammlungs-Debits- und Zeitungs-Komtoir, 1870, pp. 355–60.

[30] 'Vertrag, betreffend den Beitritt Bayerns zur Verfassung des Deutschen Bundes [*sic*]. Vom 23. November 1870; nebst Schlussprotokoll von demselben Tage', in *Bundes-Gesetzblatt des Deutschen Bundes* [*sic*]. *1870*, Berlin: Gesetz-Sammlungs-Debits- und Zeitungs-Komtoir, 1870. In: *Reichs-Gesetzblatt. 1871*, Berlin: Kaiserliches Post-Zeitungsamt, 1871, pp. 9–26; 'Vertrag zwischen dem Norddeutschen Bunde, Baden und Hessen einerseits und Württemberg andererseits, betreffend den Beitritt Württembergs zur Verfassung des Deutschen Bundes [*sic*], nebst dazu gehörigem Protokoll. Vom 25. November 1870', in *Bundes-Gesetzblatt des Norddeutschen Bundes. 1870*, Berlin: Gesetz-Sammlungs-Debits- und Zeitungs-Komtoir, 1870, pp. 654–57; 'Gesetz, betreffend die Einführung Norddeutscher Bundesgesetze in Bayern. Vom 22. April 1871', in *Bundes-Gesetzblatt des Deutschen Bundes* [*sic*]. *1870*. In: *Reichs-Gesetzblatt. 1871*, Berlin: Kaiserliches Post-Zeitungsamt, 1871, pp. 87–90.

[31] 'Gesetz, betreffend die Einführung des Reichsgesetzes über die Freizügigkeit vom 1. November 1867 und des Reichsgesetzes über die Erwerbung und den Verlust der Bundes- und Staatsangehörigkeit [*sic*] vom 1. Juni 1870. Vom 8. Januar 1873', in *Reichs-Gesetzblatt. 1873*, Berlin: Kaiserliches Post-Zeitungsamt, 1873, pp. 51–52; 'Verordnung, betreffend die Einführung von Reichsgesetzen in Helgoland. Vom 22. März 1891', in *Reichs-Gesetzblatt. 1891*, Berlin: Kaiserliches Post-Zeitungsamt, 1891, pp. 21–24.

and it did not include the small number of immigrants naturalised after 1 August 1914 unless they were also in category (a)[32]; those here excluded from *ipso facto* German citizenship could apply for German citizenship or for reinstatement – in any case, they had the protection of being citizens of the Jewish state.

The reference in category (c) to Jews 'who, and whose direct descendants possessed German citizenship on 1 August 1914 and belonged to Christian religious denominations' – persons, that is, who were no longer religious Jews – raises the question of whether this was an error in drafting. Persons belonging to Christian religious associations were Christians, not Jews. Since Goerdeler repeatedly had made clear his rejection of racial categorisations in these matters – nay, his contempt for the National Socialist antisemitic ideology – Goerdeler included converted Jews because the National Socialists regarded them as Jews. The attacker – the National Socialists – chose his targets, and the defender had to respond accordingly. Goerdeler included the category as one of the targeted ones, although after Hitler's overthrow and the creation of a Resistance government, all discrimination of Jews would be ended. Nevertheless, the racial attack had been made, and Goerdeler's intention was that Jewish citizenship would protect all potential targets. Goerdeler included the category as one of potential targets. He might have made that explicitly clear. One must keep in mind, however, that Goerdeler's document was never examined and discussed by any other experts or committees of experts in the way draft bills were treated in ministerial bureaucracies and in parliamentary committees. Goerdeler might have written his own analysis and commentary for the document, but the pressure of events and time had no doubt limited the time and care Goerdeler had been able to give to drafting this memorandum.

The same considerations apply to category (d), descendants of mixed Jewish-Christian marriages.

German Jews (as defined by 'the so-called Nuremberg race laws') in the four categories were to be granted *ipso facto* dual citizenship, as the following considerations will show. Goerdeler's 'exception' was to cover almost all German Jews, as the analysis of the numbers below will show; his 'exception' negates any theoretical effect of the 'the so-called Nuremberg race laws'. According to legal doctrine, 'new' law replaces 'old' law if the former contradicts the latter: *lex posterior derogat priori.*

[32] See Chapter 7.

The *ipso facto* exceptions are new law – they contradict and therefore nullify the old law ('the so-called Nuremberg race laws').[33]

But what is the 'rule', and what is the 'exception'? The rule is not the one Goerdeler established: Jews become citizens of the Jewish state. The rule

[33] Enneccerus and Nipperdey, *Enneccerus-Kipp-Wolff*, p. 287.

Cf. Dipper, 'Widerstand', pp. 364–65; Dipper, 'Resistance', p. 72. Dipper changed what Goerdeler had written, and Dipper's English version, in addition to Dipper's changes of Goerdeler's language in the German original, *added* 'frontline'. Goerdeler's words are 'who served in the war as German soldiers, and their direct descendants' ('*die als deutsche Soldaten am Kriege teilgenommen haben und ihre direkten Nachkommen*'); Goerdeler did not mention, contrary to what Dipper says, 'assimilative efforts'; Goerdeler did not refer to 'naturalization before 1871', as Dipper says; and he did not mention 'baptism', as Dipper says (Dipper's original German article says Goerdeler wanted to exempt from loss of German citizenship only those '*die ihr Assimilationsbestreben durch Teilnahme am Ersten Weltkrieg, Einbürgerung vor 1871 oder Taufe dokumentieren können*'; none of these terms or phrases is in Goerdeler's memorandum).

Hans Mommsen wrote that Goerdeler 'wanted to treat all Jews living in Germany as registered aliens and to deprive them of citizenship, the right to vote and access to public office'. Mommsen, *Widerstand*, pp. 388–91; Mommsen, *Alternatives*, pp. 258–62, esp. 259.

Theodore Hamerow wrote that Goerdeler wanted to 'place most German Jews in the category of resident aliens'. Theodore S. Hamerow, *On the Road*, p. 296. Hamerow also points out a passage in a memorandum Goerdeler had written on internal policy, which the editors of his principal political works date 'August/September 1934'. Hamerow, *On the Road*, p. 128; Gillmann and Mommsen, *Politische Schriften*, p. 342. Hamerow, apparently following Gerhard Ritter, *Goerdeler* 1956 (1st ed. 1954), p. 75 (Hamerow cites the 1st ed., p. 64; Gillmann and Mommsen also cite the 1st ed., p. 68), describes the memorandum as addressed to Hitler, which is what Ritter may have read on a copy at his disposal since he quotes in quotation marks 'An den Reichskanzler', but Ritter does not cite any evidence; Gillmann and Mommsen, *Politische Schriften*, p. 342, consider unconfirmed that Goerdeler had addressed the memorandum to Hitler, since they could not find any copy with this heading or notation. Goerdeler's biographer Gerhard Ritter describes this memorandum as 'a first, still quite openly prosecuted attack against the party regime in the "Third Reich"'. Ritter, *Goerdeler*, p. 72. Hamerow acknowledges: 'That Goerdeler was indeed opposed to the violent persecution of Jews is clear'. Hamerow, *On the Road*, p. 128. But Hamerow seems to have missed Goerdeler's point when he cites his opposition in the 1934 memorandum to 'excessive measures against the Jews'. Goerdeler advocated a 'consolidation' of German racial policies and argued: 'What the law has put in place will be understood as self-protection and barely questioned abroad, if in this framework everything now transacts itself with iron discipline, avoiding excesses and pedantism' (Gillmann and Mommsen, *Politische Schriften*, p. 368).

These and a number of other commentators refer to two passages in Goerdeler's proposal that, on closer examination, turn out to contradict one another. Friedrich Tomberg, *Weltordnungsvisionen im deutschen Widerstand*, Berlin: Frank and Thimme, 2005, p. 72; Reich, *Goerdeler*, p. 160; Christoph Markschies, 'Carl und Friedrich Goerdeler', in Joachim Mehlhausen, ed., *Zeugen des Widerstands*, Tübingen: J.C.B. Mohr (Paul Siebeck), 1996, pp. 142, 161–62; Steffen Held, 'Carl Goerdeler in Leipzig – Antisemitismus und Kommunalverwaltung 1933–1936', in Dan Diner, ed., *Leipziger Beiträge zur jüdischen Geschichte und Kultur*, vol. 1, Munich: K.G. Saur, 2003, pp. 307–8; H.W. Koch, *In the Name of the Volk: Political Justice in Hitler's Germany*, New York: St. Martin's Press, 1989, p. 180, says Goerdeler wanted to deport the German Jews, for which there exists no evidence.

is the rule of the *RuStAG* that German Jews who became citizens of the Jewish state lost their German citizenship. The basis for Jewish state citizenship is international law. German domestic law could not change this. However, Goerdeler did not want German Jews to become foreigners, and thus residents with lesser rights. Therefore he declared the 'exception' of the four categories, (a) to (d), from the rule that Jews become citizens of the Jewish state and that German Jews (as defined by 'the so-called Nuremberg race laws') thereby, according to the *RuStAG*, would lose their German citizenship. The 'exception' is made *not* from the 'rule' that Jews become citizens of the Jewish state. The 'exception', a spontaneous exclamation, is one from the rule of the German citizenship law of 1913 that Germans who acquired another citizenship lost their German citizenship unless they resided in Germany and had the German authorities' permission to hold dual citizenship. Under Goerdeler's 'exception', Jews who became citizens of the Jewish state *ipso facto* would regain German citizenship (*Wiedereinbürgerung*, re-naturalisation), so that they held dual Jewish and German citizenship. As Jewish and German citizens, they would not be affected by any special laws or ordinances. The 'so-called Nuremberg race laws [...] will be entirely disposed of through this settlement' – doubly so: The new law nullified the old if the new law contradicted the old.[34]

The *Reichsbürgergesetz* could not deprive Jewish state citizens of 'full political rights as determined by law', namely, as the First Implementation Decree (*Erste Verordnung zum Reichsbürgergesetz*) explained, 'the right to vote in political matters' and 'to hold public office'.[35] Jews who held Jewish-state citizenship would lack political rights as foreigners, not as German citizens subject to a special, discriminatory law, but merely like Goerdeler's examples of 'any Englishman, Frenchman etc.'. Those whom Goerdeler declared German citizens in his four defined categories, (a) to (d), of 'Jews' who were 'exceptions' were not affected by the *Reichsbürgergesetz* either: Farther down in his memorandum, Goerdeler declared that every citizen from the age of twenty-four had the right to vote.[36] This included all Germans and therefore the Jews whom Goerdeler had declared Germans. Whether this was a patch-up solution or a comprehensive one depended on the numbers, which will be addressed below.

Goerdeler wrote as a jurist. His drafting, however, was not careful. In his proposal in 'The Aim', he removed restrictions here and there but

[34] Enneccerus and Nipperdey, *Enneccerus-Kipp-Wolff*, p. 287.

[35] 'Erste Verordnung zum Reichsbürgergesetz. Vom 14. November 1935', *RGBl. I 1935*, pp. 1333–34.

[36] Gillmann and Mommsen, *Politische Schriften*, p. 931.

not in a systematic manner. He declared that Jews with the new Jewish state citizenship would be equal to other foreigners in their freedom to follow a trade or business (*Gewerbe*). Goerdeler did not explicitly say so, but this had to imply that Jews with German citizenship (of this more below) would not have lesser rights than foreigners. It also protected them against 'Aryanisation' – confiscation of their property and penal sanctions. Trades and businesses included all the occupations from which Jews were barred by laws and decrees issued since 30 January 1933, and by the Nuremberg Race Laws and their implementation decrees – notaries, lawyers,[37] physicians,[38] veterinarians, dentists, pharmacists,[39] and teachers.[40] Numerous further restrictions followed, mostly elaborations of a total of about 350 existing laws and ordinances.[41] The most important ones are referred to in Chapter 1.[42] Readers of Goerdeler's memorandum who knew the contents of the two Nuremberg Race Laws and of the two dozen implementation decrees issued from November 1935 to November 1941 knew what Goerdeler was referring to when he asserted the right of citizens of a Jewish state to follow a trade,[43] and when he specified that 'the restrictions upon the Jews in the access to food supplies, housing and telephone service, in their cultural activities, health care,[44] adoption of names[45] were to be abolished'. Jews were subject to

[37] 'Fünfte Verordnung zum Reichsbürgergesetz. Vom 27. September 1938', *RGBl. 1938 I*, pp. 1403–6; 'Sechste Verordnung zum Reichsbürgergesetz. Vom 31. Oktober 1938', *RGBl. 1938 I*, pp. 1545–46.

[38] 'Vierte Verordnung zum Reichsbürgergesetz. Vom 25. Juli 1938', *RGBl. 1938 I*, pp. 969–70; 'Verordnung über die Teilnahme von Juden an der kassenärztlichen Versorgung. Vom 6. Oktober 1938', *RGBl. 1938 I*, p. 1391; 'Dritte Verordnung zum Reichsbürgergesetz. Vom 14. Juni 1938', *RGBl. 1938 I*, pp. 627–28.

[39] 'Dritte Verordnung zum Reichsbürgergesetz. Vom 14. Juni 1938', *RGBl. 1938 I*, pp. 627–28; 'Achte Verordnung zum Reichsbürgergesetz. Vom 17. Januar 1939', *RGBl. 1939 I*, pp. 47–48.

[40] 'Zehnte Verordnung zum Reichsbürgergesetz. Vom 4. Juli 1939', *RGBl. 1939 I*, pp. 1097–99.

[41] Kieffer, 'Goerdelers Vorschlag', p. 490n102.

[42] See Chapter 1, pp. 12–16.

[43] '*Recht der gewerblichen Betätigung*' includes trades, commercial and professional occupations; in the cases of physicians and lawyers, practitioners had to meet the same standards as other Germans, or other foreigners.

[44] 'Vierte Verordnung zum Reichsbürgergesetz. Vom 25. Juli 1938', *RGBl. 1938 I*, pp. 969–70; 'Verordnung über die Teilnahme von Juden an der kassenärztlichen Versorgung. Vom 6. Oktober 1938', *RGBl. 1938 I*, p. 1391;.

[45] 'Gesetz über die Änderung von Familiennamen und Vornamen. Vom 5. Januar 1938', *RGBl. 1938 I*, pp. 9–10; 'Zweite Verordnung zur Durchführung des Gesetzes über die Änderung von Familiennamen und Vornamen. Vom 17. August 1938', *RGBl. 1938 I*, p. 1044.

reduced rations and to restrictions in hours and places for shopping, and they could be banned from parks, public places, and benches. There was quasi Ghettoisation in constricted and cramped housing with one room to a family in 'Jewish Houses' (*Judenhäuser*); from 1 September 1941 Jews had to wear a yellow Star of David visibly upon their clothing.[46]

What he was declaring abolished were the most serious discriminating measures in the Nuremberg Race Laws and their implementation decrees.[47]

[46] *RGBl. 1938 I*, p. 1676; *RGBl. 1939 I*, pp. 864–65; *RGBl. 1941 I*, Berlin: Reichsverlagsamt, 1941, p. 547; cf. Angela Schwarz, 'Von den Wohnstiften zu den "Judenhäusern"', in Angelika Ebbinghaus and Karsten Linne, eds., *Kein abgeschlossenes Kapitel: Hamburg im 'Dritten Reich'*, Hamburg: Europäische Verlagsanstalt, 1997, pp. 232–47.

[47] 'Reichsbürgergesetz. Vom 15. September 1935', *RGBl. 1935 I*, p. 1146; 'Gesetz zum Schutze des deutschen Blutes und der deutschen Ehre. Vom 15. September 1935', *RGBl. 1935 I*, pp. 1146–47; 'Erste Verordnung zum Reichsbürgergesetz. Vom 14. November 1935', *RGBl. 1935 I*, p. 1333–34; 'Erste Verordnung zur Ausführung des Gesetzes zum Schutze des deutschen Blutes und der deutschen Ehre. Vom 14. November 1935', *RGBl. 1935 I*, pp. 1334–36; 'Zweite Verordnung zum Reichsbürgergesetz. Vom 21. Dezember 1935', *RGBl. 1935 I*, pp. 1524–25; 'Erste Verordnung zur Durchführung des Gesetzes über die Änderung von Familiennamen und Vornamen. Vom 7. Januar 1938', *RGBl. 1938 I*, p. 12; 'Zweite Verordnung zur Durchführung des Gesetzes über die Änderung von Familiennamen und Vornamen. Vom 17. August 1938', *RGBl. 1938 I*, p. 1044; 'Viertes Gesetz zur Änderung des Gesetzes über das Versteigerergewerbe. Vom 5. Februar 1938', *RGBl. 1938 I*, p. 115; 'Verordnung gegen die Unterstützung der Tarnung jüdischer Gewerbebetriebe. Vom 22. April 1938', *RGBl. 1938 I*, p. 404; 'Verordnung über die Anmeldung des Vermögens von Juden. Vom 26. April 1938', *RGBl. 1938 I*, pp. 414–15; 'Dritte Verordnung zum Reichsbürgergesetz. Vom 14. Juni 1938', *RGBl. 1938 I*, pp. 627–28; 'Gesetz zur Änderung der Gewerbeordnung für das Deutsche Reich. Vom 6. Juli 1938', *RGBl. 1938 I*, pp. 823–24; 'Vierte Verordnung zum Reichsbürgergesetz. Vom 25. Juli 1938', *RGBl. 1938 I*, pp. 969–70; 'Verordnung über die Teilnahme von Juden an der kassenärztlichen Versorgung. Vom 6. Oktober 1938', *RGBl. 1938 I*, p. 1391; 'Fünfte Verordnung zum Reichsbürgergesetz. Vom 27. September 1938', *RGBl. 1938 I*, pp. 1403–6; 'Erste Verordnung über die berufsmässige Ausübung der Krankenpflege und die Errichtung von Krankenpflegeschulen (Krankenpflegeverordnung – KPflV -). Vom 28. September 1938', *RGBl. 1938 I*, p. 1310; 'Verordnung über Reisepässe von Juden. Vom 5. Oktober 1938', *RGBl. 1938 I*, p. 1342 (all passports were invalid, but valid again if 'the passport authority provided them [the passports] with a notation, determined by the Reich Minister of the Interior, that designated the bearer as a Jew' (*wenn sie von der Passbehörde mit einem vom Reichsminister des Innern bestimmten Merkmal versehen werden, das den Inhaber als Juden kennzeichnet*); 'Sechste Verordnung zum Reichsbürgergesetz. Vom 31. Oktober 1938', *RGBl. 1938 I*, pp. 1545–46; 'Verordnung gegen den Waffenbesitz der Juden. Vom 11. November 1938', *RGBl. 1938 I*, p. 1573; 'Verordnung zur Ausschaltung der Juden aus dem deutschen Wirtschaftsleben. Vom 12. November 1938', *RGBl. 1938 I*, p. 1580; 'Verordnung zur Wiederherstellung des Strassenbildes bei jüdischen Gewerbebetrieben. Vom 12. November 1938', *RGBl. 1938 I*, p. 1581 ('§ 1 Alle Schäden, welche durch die Empörung des Volkes über die Hetze des internationalen Judentums gegen das nationalsozialistische Deutschland am 8., 9. und 10. November 1938 an jüdischen Gewerbebetrieben und Wohnungen entstanden sind,

The implementation decrees *were* the laws. The '*Reich* Citizen Law' (*Reichsbürgergesetz*) stated that state citizenship (*Staatsangehörigkeit*) was regulated by the '*Reich* and State Membership Law' (*Reichs- und Staatsangehörigkeitsgesetz*) of 1913; and that exclusively persons of 'German or congeneric blood' could be *Reichsbürger* with the right to vote and to hold public office. The right to vote was meaningless in Hitler's dictatorship. The right to be a *Reichsbürger* was to be granted in a '*Reich* Citizen Letter' (*Reichsbürgerbrief*).[48] The term *Reichsbürger* does not appear in the '*Reich* and State Membership Law' (*RuStAG*). *Reichsbürgerbriefe* were never issued. The legal consequences of the *Reichsbürgergesetz* were limited. Its effects lay in social marginalisation and exclusion, and in insult and humiliation.

The Nuremberg 'Law for the Protection of German Blood' (*Gesetz zum Schutze des deutschen Blutes und der deutschen Ehre*)[49] also became moot in Goerdeler's memorandum, as he left it to individual Jews and non-Jews whether they decided to marry a partner in the other category.

sind von dem jüdischen Inhaber oder jüdischen Gewerbetreibenden sofort zu beseitigen'.); 'Verordnung über eine Sühneleistung der Juden deutscher Staatsangehörigkeit. Vom 12. November 1938', *RGBl. 1938 I*, p. 1579 ('*Juden deutscher Staatsangehörigkeit in ihrer Gesamtheit wird die Zahlung einer Kontribution von 1 000 000 000 Reichsmark an das Deutsche Reich auferlegt*'.); 'Erlass des Führers und Reichskanzlers über die Entziehung des Rechts zum Tragen einer Uniform. Vom 16. November 1938', *RGBl. 1938 I*, p. 1611; 'Verordnung über die öffentliche Fürsorge für Juden. Vom 19. November 1938', *RGBl. 1938 I*, p. 1649; 'Verordnung zur Durchführung der Verordnung zur Ausschaltung der Juden aus dem deutschen Wirtschaftsleben. Vom 23. November 1938', *RGBl. 1938 I*, p. 1642; 'Polizeiverordnung über das Auftreten der Juden in der Öffentlichkeit. Vom 28. November 1938', *RGBl. 1938 I*, p. 1676; 'Verordnung über den Einsatz des jüdischen Vermögens. Vom 3. Dezember 1938', *RGBl. 1938 I*, pp. 1709–12; 'Siebente Verordnung zum Reichsbürgergesetz. Vom 5. Dezember 1938', *RGBl. 1938 I*, p. 1751; 'Zweite Verordnung zur Durchführung der Verordnung zur Ausschaltung der Juden aus dem deutschen Wirtschaftsleben. Vom 14. Dezember 1938', *RGBl. 1938 I*, p. 1902; 'Hebammengesetz. Vom 21. Dezember 1938', *RGBl. 1938 I*, pp. 1893–94; 'Zweite Verordnung über Mietbeihilfen. Vom 31. Dezember 1938', *RGBl. 1938 I*, p. 2017; 'Achte Verordnung zum Reichsbürgergesetz. Vom 17. Januar 1939', *RGBl. 1939 I*, pp. 47–48; 'Neunte Verordnung zum Reichsbürgergesetz. Vom 5. Mai 1939', *RGBl. 1939 I*, p. 891; 'Zehnte Verordnung zum Reichsbürgergesetz. Vom 4. Juli 1939', *RGBl. 1939 I*, pp. 1097–99; 'Polizeiverordnung über die Kennzeichnung der Juden. Vom 1. September 1941', *RGBl. 1941 I*, p. 547 (yellow Star of David inscribed 'Jude' for Jews over six years of age); 'Elfte Verordnung zum Reichsbürgergesetz. Vom 25. November 1941', *RGBl. 1941 I*, pp. 722–24; 'Zwölfte Verordnung zum Reichsbürgergesetz. Vom 25. April 1943', *RGBl. 1943 I*, pp. 268–69; 'Dreizehnte Verordnung zum Reichsbürgergesetz. Vom 1. Juli 1943', *RGBl. 1943 I*, p. 372.

[48] 'Reichsbürgergesetz. Vom 15. September 1935', *RGBl. 1935 I*, p. 1146.

[49] 'Gesetz zum Schutze des deutschen Blutes und der deutschen Ehre. Vom 15. September 1935', *RGBl. 1935 I*, pp. 1146–47.

From Goerdeler's comment that 'the so-called Nuremberg race laws' would be 'entirely disposed of through this settlement', it is clear that Goerdeler deprecated these laws and wanted them to become invalid. An understanding of what he wrote must take his intention into account.

At the same time, he declared that certain categories of Jews 'are German citizens'. The expression (*Deutsche Staatsangehörige sind Juden* ...) is a now-archaic form of legal language, with the meaning 'it is decreed that ...'.[50]

In order to determine what the author of the memorandum 'The Aim' wanted, German law requires in legal cases of the jurist, prosecutor, judge, lawyer, or the historian – that the interpreter search for the author's 'true will' as opposed to a purely literal interpretation.[51]

At this point, one may ask: Why did Goerdeler not declare that all Jews who held German citizenship on 30 January 1933 retained it regardless of whether they acquired another citizenship?

It may have occurred to him. Strong reasons against such a proposal must have been immediately obvious to him. He was, one must remind oneself, a municipal administrator trained in administrative law, with much experience at both the municipal and national government level. The principal obstacles were the following.

Such a proposal would have required the suspension of § 25 Section 2 of the *RuStAG* of 1913. This section, speaking of German citizens, stated that a person does not lose his citizenship if, before acquiring a foreign citizenship, he had applied to retain his German citizenship and his application had been approved by the relevant authority in his home state after it had consulted 'the German consul'.[52] Thus § 25 Section 2 assumed that the person seeking permission to hold both German and a foreign citizenship resided mainly or much of the time abroad, and this section is the only reference to the possibility of dual citizenship. To accommodate in German law the proposal that all Jews who held German citizenship on 30 January 1933 retained it regardless of whether they acquired another citizenship, this section would have had to be

[50] Cf. the 21 November 1938 law declaring the Sudetenland a part of the German *Reich*: 'Durch die Wiedervereinigung sind die alteingesessenen Bewohner der sudetendeutschen Gebiete deutsche Staatsbürger nach Massgabe näherer Bestimmung', *RGBl. I 1938*, p. 1641.

[51] *Bürgerliches Gesetzbuch* '*§ 133 Auslegung einer Willenserklärung*:
Bei der Auslegung einer Willenserklärung ist der wirkliche Wille zu erforschen und nicht an dem buchstäblichen Sinne des Ausdrucks zu haften', in *Reichs-Gesetzblatt. 1896*, Berlin: zu haben im Kaiserlichen Post-Zeitungsamt, [1896], Nr. 21, p. 217.

[52] *RuStAG* § 25, 2.

changed so that it allowed Jews with Jewish citizenship to retain German citizenship at the same time.

Such a change either would have had to allow the holding of dual citizenship generally, or would have had to single out a religious or ethnic minority for special treatment (*Sonderrecht*). This would have contravened the constitutional equality principle.[53] It would have created an arbitrary precedent for discrimination in favour of or against minorities. By a general permission for Germans to hold dual citizenship, however, the state would have abrogated its sovereign right to define its citizens. This was not an option in German legal thought. If states did not determine who their citizens were, the ultimate consequence would have been that all inhabitants of the earth held the same citizenship. The world was not and is not ready for this. Besides, a country allowing dual citizenship generally would have faced unwanted consequences, such as evasion of military service, capital flight, and tax flight.

Goerdeler evidently was prepared to accept these unwanted effects as far as possible. At the same time, he understood that 'exceptions' had to be limited to have legitimacy. His categories (a) to (d) would have met, although they hardly would have satisfied, this requirement, as the analysis of the numbers in Chapter 7 will show.

Persons in Goerdeler's categories (c) and (d) might not have become Jewish citizens automatically. The retention of German citizenship would be of the greatest importance to them. Concerning dependants, Goerdeler (1) believed that women and children received the citizenship of the (Jewish) father or husband; he (2) knew that the National Socialists regarded Christian (converted) former Jews or Christians descended from Jews as Jews; he (3) knew that conversions of Jews to Christianity had been adopted by many since the rise of National Socialism, since the years 1928/1930, in the hope of protecting themselves and their families against persecution; and he (4) knew that the position taken by the churches and especially the Catholic Church represented a protection for Jews in interfaith marriages and their children.[54]

Goerdeler's proposal for a Jewish state and its citizenship for all Jews was utopian, almost in the strict sense of the word. At the time Goerdeler casually suggested 'parts of Canada or South America' as possible regions for the foundation of a Jewish state; the British Mandate territory of

[53] 'Die Verfassung des Deutschen Reichs. Vom 11. August 1919', in *Reichs-Gesetzblatt. Jahrgang 1919*, art. 109–18.

[54] See Beate Meyer, *'Jüdische Mischlinge': Rassenpolitik und Verfolgungserfahrung 1933–1945*, 2nd ed., Hamburg, Munich: Dölling und Galitz Verlag, 2002, p. 24.

Palestine was no longer the viable option that Goerdeler had considered it in 1937 and 1939.[55] In his 'Thoughts of One Condemned to Death', written in prison in September 1944, however, Goerdeler suggested 'Palestine or South America'.[56] How likely was it that Jewish citizens of states that did not allow dual citizenship would give up their existing citizenship in order to hold Jewish citizenship, or hold German citizenship? Would Jewish citizens of states that did allow dual citizenship accept Jewish citizenship if they did not intend to reside in the Jewish state? One answer can be that states who insist that their nationals do not lose their citizenship in this, their home state, disregard requirements in other states to renounce their old citizenship upon acquiring their new one.

Goerdeler sought a global 'new order for the status of the Jews'. He had only the vague hope that international consultation would lead to an agreement, but he could not speak for Jews in foreign countries. His memorandum was designed above all as the basis for German government policy after Hitler had been overthrown.

The seeming references in Goerdeler's proposal to the Nuremberg Race Laws as operative conditions are the product of poor draftsmanship. The memorandum was written in desperate haste under pressure of time, and in face of formidable competition from the left led by Moltke. Goerdeler was aware of competing proposals being prepared.[57] Goerdeler's aim to protect Jews in general and German Jews in particular is nevertheless evident, not merely in his deprecation of the Nuremberg Race Laws (for Jews with Jewish-state citizenship they would be 'completely disposed of'). By giving German Jews dual citizenship, this was to doubly protect them. But he also declared abolished, without differentiating between German and non-German Jews, the restrictions against Jews that he had enumerated, and that were contained in the decrees implementing the Nuremberg Race Laws.

[55] Gillmann and Mommsen, *Politische Schriften*, pp. 578–79: '*Wenn aber Deutschland die Entwicklung der Judenfrage in Osteuropa zum Anlass nimmt, eine positive Lösung des Judenproblems – Palästina reicht nicht aus – unter allen beteiligten und interessierten Staaten anzuregen, so würde sofort jede Hemmung, die mit dieser Frage in Verbindung steht, auch in den Vereinigten Staaten beseitigt sein, da sich dann das grösste Interesse aller an einer positiven Lösung offenbaren müsste*'. *Palestine. Statement of Policy: Presented by the Secretary of State for the Colonies to Parliament by Command of His Majesty, May, 1939 Accounts and Papers: (12.) State Papers: Session 8 November 1938–23 November 1939*, vol. 27, London: HMSO, 1939. See pp. 63, 89–90 above.

[56] Gillmann and Mommsen, *Politische Schriften*, pp. 1184–85.

[57] Hassell 1988, p. 290; see pp. 97–99 above.

7

Analysis 2: Numbers

The chapters on background (2) and context (4) showed Goerdeler personally defending and protecting Jews, where he could, against mistreatment and discrimination from the moment Hitler had become chancellor, and how he had progressed to opposition, conspiracy, and treason from attempts to influence German policy from 'within', based on his status as *Reich* prices commissioner until July 1935 and afterwards as an economic adviser to the government. At a turning point in the war, in the latter months of 1941, Goerdeler composed a ninety-nine-page memorandum for fellow conspirators designed as a basis for the renewal of German government and society after Hitler's fall. The context included efforts by a number of conspirators even then to bring about Hitler's downfall. They were motivated by the regime's crimes against Jews, prisoners of war, and civil populations in occupied territories; by the unjust war and its blundering conduct and the destruction of German and non-German lives and physical assets; and by morality and common decency. In the face of the mass murder of Jews in the Soviet Union and the beginning of deportations of the German Jews, Goerdeler wrote into his memorandum a proposal by which he intended to protect the Jews in the entire world, an arrangement that would place the Jews out of the reach of persecution by providing them, through international agreement, with the citizenship of a Jewish state and the international-law protection of the Jewish state's government and diplomatic representatives. Goerdeler presumed that, analogous to the rules of German citizenship law, German Jews by acquiring another citizenship would lose their German citizenship

(*Staatsangehörigkeit*).[1] At the same time, Goerdeler did not want the German Jews to lose their German citizenship. In his memorandum, he defined categories of German Jews who were to be exempt from the loss of their German citizenship that, according to the German citizenship law of 1913 (*Reichs- und Staatsangehörigkeitsgesetz, RuStAG*), would have been the automatic consequence of their acquisition of another citizenship.

Goerdeler did not just express his intention unequivocally; the further analysis of his proposals (VI/1) confirmed his intention to protect all Jews, and to keep German Jews secure in the possession or recovery of their German citizenship. The analysis also revealed contradictions and legal complications. Goerdeler did not elaborate upon the numbers of Jews whom his proposals sought to protect against the loss of their German citizenship. He could not have had at his disposal precise numbers of German Jews in question; he could only use the census numbers up to and including those of 1933. It may not have occurred to him that half a century later a historian would suggest that he proposed to protect only 'those who could prove their assimilative efforts through front-line duty during World War I, naturalization before 1871, or baptism'. Not only had this critic changed Goerdeler's words from 'who had participated in the war as German soldiers' (*die als deutsche Soldaten am Kriege teilgenommen haben*) to 'through front-line duty during World War I', thus echoing complaints during the war of 1914–1918 that had resulted in a survey of Jews in military service, but he also asserted that, according to Goerdeler, 'baptized Christians, "descendants of a mixed marriage" contracted before the Nazi takeover, would also be recognized. A parallel to the Nuremberg Laws suggests itself for obvious reasons'. The historian who wrote this did so in face of Goerdeler's expressed deprecation of 'the so-called Nuremberg race laws' and Goerdeler's statement that by his plan they would 'be entirely disposed of'. The critics disregard the fact that Goerdeler used race neither as a value judgement nor as a biological term, but as the English speak of the 'English race', in the sense of 'nation'. Goerdeler did not consider any race of higher or lower value than others. Indeed, he ridiculed Hitler's policies of 'praising the highest values in the Nordic race, in order in 1940 to rape them and at the same time to abandon white interests in East Asia to the yellow ones'. And:

> it is stupid and presumptuous to speak of Germans as a master race. It is foolish to demand respect for one's national honour and independence and deny it to

[1] Gillmann and Mommsen, *Politische Schriften*, pp. 1184–85.

others. The nation that will naturally take over the leadership of Europe is one that respects smaller nations and tries to guide their destiny with wisdom and skill, not with brute force.[2]

A critic wrote that Goerdeler 'wanted to treat all Jews living in Germany as registered aliens and to deprive them of citizenship, the right to vote and access to public office', the last two points being stipulated in the *Reich* Citizen Law (*Reichsbürgergesetz*). Again, in the face of Goerdeler's express intention and expectation that 'the so-called Nuremberg race laws' would 'be entirely disposed of', a third critic states that Goerdeler wanted to 'place most German Jews in the category of resident aliens'.[3] All of them imported into their reading of Goerdeler's proposal an assumption for which there is no support in the record. A

[2] Walter Lipgens, *Documents on the History of European Integration*, vol. 1, New York: Walter de Gruyter, 1985, p. 399; Gillmann/Mommsen, *Politische Schriften*, p. 889.

[3] Gillmann and Mommsen, *Politische Schriften*, pp. 863, 896. Sabine Gillmann and Hans Mommsen, the editors of a selection of Goerdeler's political writings, did not address the issue of numbers. Dipper in his poorly researched 1983 article convicts Goerdeler of antisemitism on the basis of this statement: 'It is a commonplace that the Jewish nation belongs to another race'. Dipper, Widerstand, p. 365; Dipper, Resistance, pp. 51–93, here pp. 66–67, 71–73 (p. 72, commenting on Goerdeler's proposals regarding the Jews in the entire world: 'The discriminating nature of these immediate measures could be explained by Goerdeler's long-term goal – a result of the "commonplace" that the "Jewish people belong to a different race" – to establish a Jewish state "under livable conditions in parts of Canada or South America" through international cooperation. As soon as this was achieved, Goerdeler proposed to deprive all Jews automatically of their German citizenship, except for those who could prove their assimilative efforts through front-line duty during World War I, naturalization before 1871, or baptism. Baptized Christians, "descendants of a mixed marriage" contracted before the Nazi takeover, would also be recognized. A parallel to the Nuremberg Laws suggests itself for obvious reasons'.); Mommsen, 'Widerstand gegen Hitler und die nationalsozialistische Judenverfolgung', in Mommsen, ed., *Alternative*, pp. 388–91; Mommsen, *Alternatives*, pp. 258–62, here – p. 259 – Mommsen writes that Goerdeler 'wanted to treat all Jews living in Germany as registered aliens and to deprive them of citizenship, the right to vote and access to public office'; Theodore S. Hamerow, *On the Road*, p. 296, makes the same sweeping statement that Goerdeler wanted to 'place most German Jews in the category of resident aliens'; Kieffer, 'Goerdelers Vorschlag', p. 480n44 cites Ulrich Heinemann and Michael Krüger-Charlé, 'Arbeit am Mythos: Der 20. Juli 1944 in Publizistik und wissenschaftlicher Literatur des Jubiläumsjahres 1994 (Teil II)', *Geschichte und Gesellschaft* 23 (1997): 475–501 esp. p. 490n 62.

See Gillmann and Mommsen, *Politische Schriften*, p. 886.. Hamerow, *On the Road*, p. 296, and Theodore S. Hamerow, *Die Attentäter: Der 20. Juli – von der Kollaboration zum Widerstand*, Munich: C.H. Beck, 1999, p. 319, writes as though Goerdeler had intended that *in consequence of* the 'truism' that the Jews belonged to a different race, most German Jews should be placed 'in the category of resident aliens'. Walter Lipgens, *Documents on the History of European Integration*, p. 399; Gillmann and Mommsen, *Politische Schriften*, p. 889.

simple consideration makes plain that if the accusation against Goerdeler that he proposed to deprive the great majority of German Jews of their German state citizenship were true, then it would mean that more than 50 percent of the 400,935 German Jews counted in the 1933 census had been naturalised after 1871.

Another consideration leads to a similar result. Of the population of 550,000 Jewish German citizens as on 1 August 1914, approximately 100,000 or 18 percent of the total German Jewish population during the war served in the army, navy, and colonial forces (*Schutztruppe*), and approximately 80,000 of them or four-fifths had served at the front; 12,000 of them had fallen, 35,000 received medals, 23,000 were promoted, over 2,000 received officer's commissions, and 1,159 were made medical officers and higher-level officials.[4] If only 60,000 of the surviving 88,000 veterans married German Jews and produced an average of one child, then their total would have been 208,000, more than half the Jews with German citizenship resident in Germany in 1933.[5] If the average was two children, then their total would have been 268,000. The 100,000 Jews who performed military service during the war must have included immigrants who were able to improve their status in Germany through military service.

The statistics cited thus far mean that the overwhelming majority of German Jews fell into Goerdeler's categories (a) and (b).[6]

[4] See Egmont Zechlin, *Die deutsche Politik und die Juden im Ersten Weltkrieg*, Göttingen: Vandenhoeck and Ruprecht, 1969, pp. 516–67 = chapter 'Juden und Antisemitismus im Weltkrieg'. *Prüfung der Klagen, dass 'eine grosse Zahl im Heeresdienst stehender Juden verstanden haben, eine Verwendung ausserhalb der vordersten Front, als in dem Etappen- und Heimatgebiet und in Beamten- und Schreibstellen zu finden'* (Zechlin, p. 527). On 30 October 1916, the Prussian War Ministry ordered the statistical analysis of the Jews' part in the war as at 1 November 1916. See also Jacob Segall, *Die deutschen Juden als Soldaten im Kriege 1914–1918*, Berlin: Philo-Verlag, 1921; *Statistik der Juden* (Vorwort vom 1. Mai 1917), Berlin, 1918, pp. 152 et seq. Results: Segall, *Die deutschen Juden als Soldaten*, esp. p. 38; Reichsbund jüdischer Frontsoldaten, ed., *Die jüdischen Gefallenen des deutschen Heeres, der deutschen Marine und der deutschen Schutztruppen 1914–1918*, Berlin, 1932, esp. p. 419. See also Werner T. Angress, 'The German Army's "Judenzählung" of 1916: Genesis – Consequences – Significance', *Leo Baeck Institute Year Book* 23 (1978): 117–37. The number of those in military service during the First World War for the entire population in Germany (67,790,000) is 13,250,00, or 19.5 percent.

[5] *Statistik des Deutschen Reichs 451, 5*, p. 13: Of the 499,682 religious Jews counted in Germany on 16 June 1933 (without Saarland), 400,935 were German citizens, and 98,747 were foreign citizens or without citizenship. *Statistik des Deutschen Reichs* 470, p. 5, has 502,799 as the total; p. 7 lists 403,432 with German citizenship and 99,367 foreigners of the Jewish religion (*Glaubensjuden*).

[6] There are no national statistics available for naturalisations after 1 July 1871. They could be researched in the archives of the individual states (*Länder*). Fritz Kieffer, 'Auszug aus

The number of marriages in Germany generally reached high numbers in the years 1919 to 1921: 894,978 in 1920 compared to 352,543 in 1918 and 731,157 in 1921. The greatest numbers of marriage partners in 1920 were those aged twenty-one to twenty-six years, ranging between 68,225 and 68,505 (twenty-six and twenty-one years old) and 84,861 (twenty-three years old). The number of births increased, too, but not nearly to the same extent: 939,938 in 1917, 956,251 in 1918, 1,299,404 in 1919, 1,651,593 in 1920, and 1,611,420 in 1921.[7]

Between 1901 and 1932, 113,548 Jewish men married Jewish women. In the same period, 40,679 Jewish persons married a non-Jewish partner.[8] In 1920, 894,978 women entered into marriage, and among them 8,393 were Jewish women. Also in 1920, 7,497 of these Jewish women married Jewish men; 1,315 Jewish men married non-Jewish women (927 Lutheran/Reformed, 294 Roman Catholic, 19 'other' Christians, 75 with undetermined religious affiliation). A total of 896 Jewish women married non-Jewish partners in 1920.[9] In the war years, the numbers had been less than half those of 1920: In 1917, for example, of 2,033 Jewish men who married, 1,402 married Jewish women, and 631 married non-Jewish partners.[10] In the same year, of 1,806 Jewish women who married, 1,402 married Jewish men, and 404 married non-Jewish men.[11]

At the time of the 1933 census, the 40,836 Jewish women who had married in the years 1918 to 1928 had given birth to 55,208 children from 1919 to 1929. The exact number is greater because the statistic lists

dem Entwurf vom Dezember 2005: Carl Friedrich Goerdelers Vorschlag zur Gründung eines jüdischen Staates', typescript, Mainz, 2009, p. 4, based on Salomon Adler-Rudel, *Ostjuden in Deutschland 1889–1940*, Tübingen: J.C.B. Mohr (Paul Siebeck), 1959, pp. 20–21, 149.

7 *Statistisches Jahrbuch für das Deutsche Reich. Herausgegeben vom Statistischen Reichsamt. Vierzigster Jahrgang 1919*, Berlin: Verlag des Statistischen Reichsamts, 1919, pp. 40–41, 44–45; *Statistisches Jahrbuch für das Deutsche Reich. Herausgegeben vom Statistischen Reichsamt. Einundvierzigster Jahrgang 1920*, Berlin: Verlag des Statistischen Reichsamts, 1920, pp. 26–36; *Statistisches Jahrbuch für das Deutsche Reich. Herausgegeben vom Statistischen Reichsamt. Zweiundvierzigster Jahrgang 1921/22*, Berlin: Verlag des Statistischen Reichsamts, 1922, pp. 28–45; *Statistisches Jahrbuch für das Deutsche Reich. Herausgegeben vom Statistischen Reichsamt. Dreiundvierzigster Jahrgang 1923*, Berlin: Verlag für Politik und Wirtschaft, 1923, pp. 22–37.

8 *Statistik des Deutschen Reichs. Band 451, 5*, p. 8.

9 *Statistisches Jahrbuch für das Deutsche Reich. Herausgegeben vom Statistischen Reichsamt. Dreiundvierzigster Jahrgang 1923*, Berlin: Verlag für Politik und Wirtschaft, 1923, p. 31.

10 *Statistisches Jahrbuch 1920*, p. 32.

11 *Statistisches Jahrbuch 1920*, p. 32.

women with more than five children only as women with 'five and more' children.[12] This means that Jewish women gave birth to a minimum average of 1.35 children.

The numbers of baptisms and intermarriages increased steadily from the 1870s to 1933. Seventy-five percent of children from mixed marriages between Jews and members of other religious denominations (mainly Christians) were raised in the non-Jewish religion, and only 25 percent were raised to become religious Jews.[13] Between 1901 and 1932, the numbers of intermarriages increased to 40,679, 2.46 percent of all German marriages. For the years 1926 to 1930, they were counted as 7,729 – 2.8 percent of all marriages in Germany.[14] In the years 1931–1932, the Jewish–non-Jewish intermarriages accounted for 2.72 percent of all German marriages.[15]

Conversions are incompletely recorded. In the years 1911 to 1932, 5,620 Jews converted to Lutheran/Reformed confessions.[16]

Goerdeler's categories (c) and (d) addressed the National Socialists' persecution of 'racial' Jews. The categories were not negligible, as Goerdeler was evidently aware, because of the growing numbers of baptisms and intermarriages, and the 75 percent of children of mixed marriages being raised as Christians.[17]

The first question arising from the criticisms is whether Goerdeler proposed to protect most or all German Jews against National Socialist persecution. A close reading of Goerdeler's terms disclosed his clear, unequivocal, and overriding intention to protect all Jews: Jews throughout the world in general, and German Jews in particular.

The next question is: Would Goerdeler's means to his stated end have achieved it had they been put into practice? Did Goerdeler's categories of Jews who were to be considered German citizens include the majority of German Jews? There are subsidiary questions: Would Goerdeler's categories restore German citizenship to Jews who had lost it through the acquisition of another citizenship? Would Goerdeler's categories restore German citizenship to Jews whose German citizenship had been lost through revocation of naturalisation or withdrawal of citizenship under the National Socialist regime?

[12] *Statistik des Deutschen Reichs. Band 470, 1*, p. 7.
[13] *Statistik des Deutschen Reichs 451, 5*, p. 8.
[14] *Statistik des Deutschen Reichs, Band 451, 5*, pp. 8–9.
[15] *Statistik des Deutschen Reichs, Band 451, 5*, pp. 8–9.
[16] *Statistik des Deutschen Reichs 451, 5*, p. 8.
[17] *Statistik des Deutschen Reichs 451, 5*, p. 8.

The 'Law concerning the Revocation of Naturalisations and Withdrawal of Citizenship' of 14 July 1933 provided in § 1 that naturalisations from the time between 9 November 1918 and 30 January 1933 could be revoked 'if the naturalisation is to be seen as not desirable'.[18] Although no doubt this law was deplorable in its application and may have contravened existing German citizenship and constitutional law, it did not conflict with international law, and the international community considered the law an 'internal matter' of Germany. Similar legal instruments were in place in other Western states, based on such criteria as the common good, or race.[19] According to the German citizenship law of 1913, however, persons who had lost their German citizenship could apply for reinstatement.

While the German 'Law concerning the Revocation of Naturalisations and Withdrawal of Citizenship' of 14 July 1933 might be repealed by a post–National Socialist German government, it would have been more difficult to undo its effects. Victims of the law might have emigrated and acquired another citizenship, thereby losing the option to

[18] 'Gesetz über den Widerruf von Einbürgerungen und die Aberkennung der deutschen Staatsangehörigkeit. Vom 14. Juli 1933', *RGBl. I 1933*, pp. 480, 538–39; see also *RuStAG* in *RGBl. 1913*, pp. 583–93. Hans Georg Lehmann, 'Acht und Ächtung politischer Gegner im Dritten Reich. Die Ausbürgerung deutscher Emigranten 1933–45', in Michael Hepp, ed., *Die Ausbürgerung deutscher Staatsangehöriger 1933–45 nach den im Reichsanzeiger veröffentlichten Listen*, vol. 1, Munich, New York, London, Paris: K.G. Saur, 1985, p. XIII, states that the Bundesverwaltungsamt in Cologne had a list of 10,487 revocations based on the Law on Revocation of Naturalisation and Withdrawal of Citizenship, that 6,943 revocations applied to Jews, that they also applied to spouses and children, and that the total was to be calculated as between 14,000 and 21,000 persons who were thus de-naturalised. According to information from Bundesverwaltungsamt dated 6 March 2009, this information is erroneous. The BVA has a list of 19,291 de-naturalisations, which, however, is incomplete and includes non-Jews as well as Jews. Hepp's error has found mention in scholarly literature, most recently in Joachim Neander, 'Das Staatsangehörigkeitsrecht des "Dritten Reiches" und seine Auswirkungen auf das Verfolgungsschicksal deutscher Staatsangehöriger', *theologie.geschichte* 3 (2008): 1–2, http://aps.sulb.uni-saarland.de/theologie.geschichte.

[19] See Stauffenberg, 'Entziehung', pp. 261–76; *Covenant of the League of Nations*, Art. 15, pp. 6–7. Fritz Kieffer, *Judenverfolgung in Deutschland – eine innere Angelegenheit? Internationale Reaktionen auf die Flüchtlingsproblematik 1933–1939*, Stuttgart: Franz Steiner Verlag, 2002, pp. 305–8, cites U.S. secretary of state to U.S. ambassador in Germany 15 October 1936 [*sic*] in *FRUS 1938, I*, pp. 799–800, and Embassy of the United States of America, Berlin (Wilson) to secretary of state 18 October 1938 [*sic*], enclosures 1 and 2, in National Archives (Washington DC) RG 9 340.48 Refugees/879 and Aufzeichnung des Staatssekretärs 18 October 1938 in *ADAP D V* doc. no. 645 pp. 758–59 and Ambassade de France à Berlin to l'Office des Affaires Étrangères du Reich 24 October 1938 in Auswärtiges Amt/Politisches Archiv, Unterstaatssekretär, Judenfrage R 29989; Kieffer, 'Goerdelers Vorschlag', p. 486.

regain their German citizenship.[20] The acquisition of the proposed Jewish citizenship by German Jews would have made the loss of their German citizenship automatic, unless they had obtained permission to hold dual citizenship. Such permissions were rare exceptions and therefore could not be granted to hundreds of thousands of German Jews.

Goerdeler proposed to short-circuit this complication and declared, 'No rule without exception!' He listed four categories of Jews who were to be considered German citizens despite the general rule of Jewish citizenship for all Jews.

Exceptions from laws must be supported by reasons. They must also be limited to avoid the exceptions becoming the rule.[21] Goerdeler provided reasons by citing the disadvantages to Jews if they were not treated as full German citizens. He achieved a quasi limitation through his categories (a) to (d). In the global context, the number of the exceptions was so insignificant that it could not become the rule; not so, however, within the German context. If the limitation within the German legal system was only ostensible, the legal concept of 'exception' broke down.

What Goerdeler constructed indicates a high degree of desperation in someone trained and experienced in law and public administration. Furthermore, the fact that Goerdeler singled out the *German* Jews for this exception, contradicting his own determination of the 'natural settlement[22] for German conditions: the Jew is a citizen of his Jewish state', puts an even greater emphasis on Goerdeler's desperation in trying to protect all Jews and as many German Jews as possible against persecution, but at the same time against loss of German citizenship.

Goerdeler probably did not know that an estimated eleven million Jews in territories under German control were to be murdered, as Heydrich informed a group of state-secretary–level government and *SS*

[20] *RuStAG* 22 July 1913, §§ 25–27, pp. 583–93; 'Gesetz zur Abänderung des Gesetzes über das Paßwesen, des Gebührengesetzes für die Auslandsbehörden und des Reichs- und Staatsangehörigkeitsgesetzes. Vom 5. November 1923', *Reichsgesetzblatt Teil I Jahrgang 1923*. Herausgegeben vom Reichsministerium des Innern, Berlin 1923, Verlag des Gesetzsammlungsamts (*RGBl. I 1923*), p. 1077–78; fee-ordinance of 27 June 1924 (*RGBl. I. 1924*, p. 659); 'Gesetz über den Widerruf von Einbürgerungen und die Aberkennung der deutschen Staatsangehörigkeit. Vom 14. Juli 1933' (*RGBl. I. 1933*, p. 480); ordinance of 5 February 1934 (*RGBl. I. 1934*, p. 85); 'Gesetz zur Änderung des Reichs- und Staatsangehörigkeitsgesetzes. Vom 15. Mai 1935' (*RGBl. I 1935*, p. 593); 'Wehrgesetz. Vom 21. Mai 1935' (*RGBl. I 1935*, pp. 609–14); 'Verordnung zur Regelung von Staatsangehörigkeitsfragen. Vom 20. Januar 1942', *RGBl. I 1942*, p. 40.

[21] Kieffer, 'Goerdelers Vorschlag', p. 492.

[22] Goerdeler's term is '*Regelung*'.

representatives at the 'Wannsee Conference' in Berlin on 20 January 1942.[23] He did know at that time that they were being killed by the hundreds of thousands. He believed that providing them with an internationally recognised Jewish citizenship would protect them – if they could be rescued from Hitler's murder squads. Hitler's removal was a precondition.

Goerdeler could not have known precisely how many German Jews were likely to be affected by what he proposed, but the 1871–1933 census results provided a reasonably accurate notion of the numbers involved. Goerdeler had been the administrator of one of the largest German municipalities, a member in national municipal-administration bodies, and *Reich* prices commissioner (1931–1932, 1934–1935). He was professionally acquainted with matters of the census and statistics.

How effective might Goerdeler's plan might have been: Would the definitions in his categories (a) to (d) have secured German citizenship for a majority of German Jews, or for a minority? Or for all of them?

The term 'German Jews' refers to German citizens (*Staatsangehörige*) who were described in the censuses of the years 1871 to 1933 as adhering to the Jewish faith, or as 'Israelites'. In the 16 June 1933 census, they were called 'religious Jews' (*Glaubensjuden*). The numbers of 'German Jews' in Germany declined overall from 1871 to 1933.[24]

Goerdeler referred in his category (b) to those German Jews and their descendants who had been German citizens on 1 July 1871. This date is an error and legally irrelevant; 1 January 1871 is the date when the North German Confederation's 'Law about acquisition and loss of the Federal

[23] Besprechungsprotokoll, Berlin, Am Großen Wannsee Nr. 56/58, 20 Jan. 1942, Auswärtiges Amt, Politisches Archiv Inland II g 177 Bll. 165–88 (facsimile in Peter Longerich, *Die Wannsee-Konferenz vom 20. Januar 1942: Planung und Beginn des Genozids an den europäischen Juden*, [Berlin]: Edition Hentrich, 1998, pp. 67 et seq.); English in Yitzhak Arad, Israel Gutman, and Abraham Margaliot, eds., *Documents on the Holocaust: Selected Sources on the Destruction of the Jews in Germany and Austria, Poland and the Soviet Union*, 8th ed., Lincoln and London: University of Nebraska Press, Jerusalem: Yad Vashem, 1999, pp. 249–61, esp. 253/255. It is unclear whether the Jews in the Sudetenland were counted; the law declaring the Sudetenland a part of Germany declared its 'inhabitants of long standing German citizens [*Staatsangehörige*] pending detailed regulation': 'Gesetz über die Wiedervereinigung der sudetendeutschen Gebiete mit dem Deutschen Reich. Vom 21. November 1938', *RGBl. I 1938*, p. 1641.

[24] See table at end of the chapter. There are no national statistics available for naturalisations after 1 July 1871. Some of them could be researched in the archives of the individual states (*Länder*). Fritz Kieffer, 'Auszug aus dem Entwurf vom Dezember 2005: Carl Friedrich Goerdelers Vorschlag zur Gründung eines jüdischen Staates', p. 4, based on Adler-Rudel, *Ostjuden*, pp. 20–21 (citing *Allgemeine Zeitung des Judentums* 22 and 29 September 1885), p. 149.

and State citizenship' of 1 June 1870 was promulgated, and this became the law in all of Germany on 1 June 1871[25]. In the 1 December 1871 census, the number of Jews who were German citizens was recorded as 512,158.[26]

In 1910 the number of Jews with German citizenship in Germany reached its highest level at 538,637 (there were in Germany also 76,387 non-German Jews), and so did that of foreigners living in Germany, at 1,129,873.[27] But the growth of the Jewish population did not keep pace with that of the rest of the German population. In the entire period from 1871 to 1933, the numbers of German religious Jews rose only temporarily in absolute terms. Over the decades, emigration exceeded immigration, and other population losses further reduced the numbers.[28] In 1933 there were 111,223 fewer German Jews than in 1871.

The relevant distinctions in the government census results were the following: total population present on census day; German citizens and foreigners; and German population according to their religious affiliations – Protestant, Catholic, other Christian and non-Christian groups, and 'Israelites'. The same distinctions were made within the group of foreigners in the census results of 1910 and afterward. The censuses up to and including that of 1933 counted only religious Jews (*Glaubensjuden*). In the national census of 16 June 1933 for Germany in the borders of 1919, without the *Saarland*, which became part of Germany again only in 1934, respondents had to answer a question about their religious association (*Religionsgesellschaft*) or membership in a 'world-view community',

[25] 'Gesetz über die Erwerbung und den Verlust der Bundes- und Staatsangehörigkeit. Vom 1. Juni 1870', *Bundes-Gesetzblatt des Norddeutschen Bundes. 1870*, Redigirt im Büreau des Bundeskanzlers. Berlin, gedruckt in der Königlichen Geheimen Ober-Hofbuchdruckerei (R. v. Decker), 1871, pp. 355–60.

[26] *Vierteljahreshefte zur Statistik des Deutschen Reichs für das Jahr 1873. Zweites Heft, erste Abtheilung*. Herausgegeben vom Kaiserlichen Statistischen Amt. [Erster Jahrgang.] *Band II. Heft II. Abtheil. 1 der Statistik des Deutschen Reichs*. Berlin, 1873 [*sic*, although the title page of the comprehensive vol. 2 has 1874]. Verlag des Königlich Statistischen Bureaus. (Dr. Engel.), pp. 122, 144.

[27] *Statistik des Deutschen Reichs*, Band 240, pp. 27, 204, 210; *Statistik des Deutschen Reichs. Band 451, 4. Volks-, Berufs- und Betriebszählung vom 16. Juni 1933. Volkszählung. Die Bevölkerung des Deutschen Reichs nach den Ergebnissen der Volkszählung 1933. Heft 4. Die Ausländer im Deutschen Reich. Die Bevölkerung einiger Gebiete des Deutschen Reichs nach der Muttersprache*. Bearbeitet im Statistischen Reichsamt. Berlin: Verlag für Sozialpolitik, Wirtschaft und Statistik, Paul Schmidt, 1936; *Statistik des Deutschen Reichs*, Band 451, 4, p. 9, gives the number of 1,129,951 foreigners for 1910.

[28] Dieter Gosewinkel, '"Unerwünschte Elemente" – Einwanderung und Ausbürgerung der Juden in Deutschland 1848–1933', *Tel Aviver Jahrbuch für deutsche Geschichte* 27 (1998): 74, 83.

as had been the case in the previous censuses.[29] This question required respondents who did not belong to a church or religious association to enter 'none'.[30] Only self-declared Jews affiliated with a religious association or a 'world-view community' were thus counted as Jews.

The 1939 census counted persons defined as Jews under the Nuremberg race laws. 'Jews' so defined were persons who had four or three religious Jews (*Glaubensjuden*) as grandparents; persons with two religious Jewish (*Glaubensjuden*) grandparents were *Mischlinge 1. Grades*; grandchildren of two *Mischlinge 1. Grades* were considered Jews; persons with one religious Jewish (*Glaubensjude*) grandparent were considered *Mischlinge 2. Grades*; their children were considered 'German' (*deutschblütig*); a *Mischling 1. Grades* descended from a pair of religious Jewish (*Glaubensjuden*) grandparents and a pair of nonreligious-Jewish grandparents, thus someone from one religious Jewish (*Glaubensjude*) and one nonreligious-Jewish parent was considered a Jew if he or she was born out of wedlock after 31 July 1936; a *Mischling 1. Grades* was considered a Jew if he or she belonged to a Jewish religious community; a *Mischling 1. Grades* was considered a Jew if he or she was married to a Jew; a *Mischling 1. Grades* descended from a couple consisting of one *Mischling 1. Grades* and a descendant of three religious Jewish (*Glaubensjuden*) grandparents was considered a Jew if the marriage was concluded after 17 September 1935.[31]

In the 1933 census, the total number of Jews in Germany was 499,682. A total of 400,935 (80.2 percent) of the Jews in Germany (without the *Saarland*) were German citizens, and 98,747 Jews in Germany (19.8 percent) were foreigners. These 98,747 foreign Jews included 78,787 citizens of foreign states, 19,746 stateless persons, and 214 persons whose citizenship could not be determined. The proportion of foreigners among Jews in Germany rose from 1910 to 1933 from 14 percent to 19.8 percent.[32] The great majority of foreign religious Jews came from

[29] 'Die Ausländer im Deutschen Reich. A. Die Ausländer insgesamt. I. Die Gesamtzahl der Ausländer im Deutschen Reich und ihre Entwicklung; Vergleich mit dem Ausland [...] II. Die Ausländer nach der Staatsangehörigkeit', *Statistik des Deutschen Reichs. Band 451*, 4, pp. 5, 7–9; *Statistik des Deutschen Reichs. Band 451, 5*, pp. 5–8.

[30] *Statistik des Deutschen Reichs. Band 451, 5*, p. 5.

[31] 'Reichsbürgergesetz. Vom 15. September 1935', *RGBl. I 1935*, p. 1146; 'Gesetz zum Schutze des deutschen Blutes und der deutschen Ehre. Vom 15. September 1935', *RGBl. I 1935*, pp. 1146–47; 'Erste Verordnung zum Reichsbürgergesetz. Vom 14. November 1935', *RGBl. I 1935*, pp. 1333–34; 'Erste Verordnung zur Ausführung des Gesetzes zum Schutze des deutschen Blutes und der deutschen Ehre. Vom 14. November 1935', *RGBl. I 1935*, pp. 1334–36.

[32] *Statistik des Deutschen Reichs. Band 451, 5*, p. 13: Of the 499,682 religious Jews counted in Germany on 16 June 1933 (without Saarland), 400,935 were German citizens, and

Eastern and Southeastern European states. Among the 98,747 foreign Jews, there were in 1933 around 56,000 Polish Jews (57.2 percent of all foreign Jews; they were 38.1 percent of all persons with Polish citizenship in Germany). A total of 19,746 Jews in Germany had no citizenship; they were 'stateless'.[33]

After six years of massive emigration, the census of 17 May 1939 counted 330,539 'Jews' in the territory of Germany including Austria and Sudetenland.[34]

The 22 March 1934 census in Austria counted a total population of 6,760,233, of which 289,305 were foreigners (270,543 with foreign citizenship, 18,762 stateless). In the total population of 6,760,233, there were 6,112,658 Roman Catholics, 295,452 Protestants, and 191,481 'Israelites' (176,034 in Vienna). A total of 106,080 persons were counted as being 'without confession' (*konfessionslos*), meaning without religious affiliation or without self-declared religious identity. These numbers potentially included 'Jews' by post-1935 National Socialist standards.[35] The foreigners and stateless were not listed by religious affiliation, so that it is not possible to say, for example, how many of the 289,305 foreigners,

98,747 were foreign citizens or without citizenship. *Statistik des Deutschen Reichs. Band* 470, p. 5, has 502,799 as the total; p. 7 lists 403,432 with German citizenship and 99,367 foreigners of the Jewish religion (*Glaubensjuden*). See also table at the end of the chapter.

[33] *Statistik des Deutschen Reichs. Band 451, 5*, pp. 13–14. The Central Welfare Agency of German Jews (*Zentralwohlfahrtsstelle der deutschen Juden*) recorded greater numbers of Jews in Germany than the 1933 census. The Agency counted 403,969 Jews in Prussia alone in 1932, in Anhalt 1,140, Baden 24,064, in Bavaria 49,145, Braunschweig 1,753, Bremen 1,328, Hamburg 19,904, Hesse 20,401, Lippe 607, Lübeck 650, Mecklenburg-Schwerin 1,225, Mecklenburg-Strelitz 182, Oldenburg 1,513, Saxony 23,252, Schaumburg-Lippe 180, Thüringen 3,603, and Württemberg 10,827, in sum, 563,743. The Central Welfare Agency of German Jews did not state their criteria. They record only numbers of 'Jews' without distinguishing between German citizens and others. Criteria and/or differing counting methods may be responsible for the deviations from the government census. The present investigation will, however, use the official German census figures. Bella Schlesinger, *Führer durch die jüdische Gemeindeverwaltung und Wohlfahrtspflege in Deutschland 1932–33*, Berlin: Zentralwohlfahrtsstelle der deutschen Juden, 1932, pp. 13, 262, 320, 330, 343, 371, 376, 408, 410, 414, 417, 419, 421, 427, 429.

[34] *Statistik des Deutschen Reichs. Band 552, 4. Volks-, Berufs- und Betriebszählung vom 17. Mai 1939. Volkszählung. Die Bevölkerung des Deutschen Reichs nach den Ergebnissen der Volkszählung 1939. Heft 4. Die Juden und jüdischen Mischlinge im Deutschen Reich.* Bearbeitet im Statistischen Reichsamt. Berlin: Verlag für Sozialpolitik, Wirtschaft und Statistik, Paul Schmidt, Berlin SW 68, 1944, pp. 6–9.

[35] *Statistik des Bundesstaates Österreich. Heft 2. Die Ergebnisse der österreichischen Volkszählung vom 22. März 1934.* Bearbeitet vom Bundesamt für Statistik. Bundesstaat. Textheft, Vienna: Österreichische Staatsdruckerei, 1935, pp. 44–45, 60–61; *Statistik des Bundesstaates Österreich* [...] *Tabellenheft*, Vienna: Österreichische Staatsdruckerei, 1935, pp. 2–3, 16, 20–21.

or how many of the 24,727 Poles among them, were Jews. The largest numbers of foreigners in Austria in 1934 were 115,780 Czechoslovakian citizens, 43,751 Germans, 30,940 Yugoslavs, 24,727 Poles, 18,762 stateless persons, and 16,200 Italians.[36]

In the 1939 German census, 71,126 were counted as *Mischlinge 1. Grades*, and 41,456 as *Mischlinge 2. Grades*. Of the 330,539 'Jews', 33,132 were religious non-Jews: 13,126 'Jews' belonged to Lutheran or Reformed or Free Churches, 10,403 belonged to the Roman Catholic Church, 634 belonged to other religious communities, 3,501 were 'believing-in-God' nonaffiliated, 4,547 declared themselves as nonbelievers (*Glaubenslose*), and 921 made no declaration in this category.[37] Of the *Mischlinge 1. Grades*, 34,745 belonged to Lutheran or Reformed or Free Churches, and 21,408 belonged to the Roman Catholic Church (in sum, a minimum of 56,153, 78.97 percent, *Mischlinge 1. Grades* belonged to Christian religious communities), while 673 belonged to other religious communities, 3,766 were 'believing-in-God' nonaffiliated, 3,663 declared themselves nonbelievers (*Glaubenslose*), and 511 made no declaration in this category. Of the *Mischlinge 2. Grades*, 24,796 (59.81 percent) belonged to Lutheran or Reformed or Free Churches, and 12,987 belonged to the Roman Catholic Church (in sum, a minimum of 37,783, 91.26 percent, *Mischlinge 2. Grades* belonged to Christian religious communities), while 398 belonged to other religious communities, 1,647 were 'believing-in-God' nonaffiliated, 973 declared themselves as nonbelievers (*Glaubenslose*), and 165 made no declaration in this category.[38] Emigration numbers are not available.

On 20 January 1942, a group of high-level government and *SS* representatives met in a large villa in Berlin-Wannsee to coordinate the deportations of Jews to concentration camps. The conference protocol does not distinguish between German and non-German Jews. The estimate in the protocol is that 360,000 (72.05 percent of the total number of all German and non-German Jews in Germany in 1933, not including the Saar, Austria and Sudetenland) had emigrated from Germany from 30 January 1933 to 31 October 1941, 147,000 (76.8 percent of those counted in the 1934 census) had emigrated from Austria since 15 March 1938, and 30,000 from the Protectorate of Bohemia-Moravia (formerly part of Czechoslovakia) had emigrated since 15 March 1939. The

[36] *Statistik des Bundesstaates Österreich [...] Tabellenheft*, pp. 20–21.
[37] *Statistik des Deutschen Reichs. Band 552*, 4, pp. 6–9.
[38] *Statistik des Deutschen Reichs. Band 552*, 4, pp. 6–9.

protocol estimated that at the end of 1941, there remained in Germany 131,800 (26.38 percent of Jews counted in the 1933 census). The protocol refers to 'Altreich', that is, Germany in the borders of 1937, before the annexation of Austria. The discrepancy of 7,882 Jews (1.57 percent of all those counted in Germany in 1933) may mean that the around 6,000 or more Jews from Berlin, Breslau, Munich, Frankfurt, and Vienna who were deported to Kowno and Riga and shot upon their arrival on 25 and 29 November 1941 were not counted as 'emigrated' in the estimate.[39] In Austria, now referred to as Ostmark, there remained 43,700 Jews (22.83 percent of those counted in the 1934 census) and 74,200 in the Protectorate of Bohemia-Moravia.[40]

The number the protocol implied for 1933 – 360,000 emigrated to 31 October 1941, 131,800 still in the borders of Germany as before the union with Austria, for a total of 491,800[41] – closely corresponds to the 1933 census number for 'religious Jews' (*Glaubensjuden*), including foreigners, although the 1939 census included those whom the 1935 'Nuremberg Laws' designated 'Jews' in addition to 'religious Jews'.[42] This means that the expansion of census categories in which residents were counted as Jews did not substantially increase the numbers of those counted in the category 'Jew'.

The proportion of religious German Jews in the total population of German citizens on balance declined over the decade since 1871, in part

[39] Eugen Kogon, Hermann Langbein, Adalbert Rückerl, et al., eds., *Nationalsozialistische Massentötungen durch Giftgas. Eine Dokumentation*, Frankfurt am Main: S. Fischer Verlag, 1983, pp. 81–212 (killings with gas began in Auschwitz on 3 September 1941); Peter Longerich, *Politik der Vernichtung. Eine Gesamtdarstellung der nationalsozialistischen Judenverfolgung*, Munich, Zurich: Piper, 1998, pp. 434–44, 452–58, 464; Raul Hilberg, *The Destruction of the European Jews*, New York, London: Holmes and Meier, 1985, p. 353.

[40] Besprechungsprotokoll, Berlin, Am Großen Wannsee Nr. 56/58, 20 January 1942, Auswärtiges Amt, Politisches Archiv Inland II g 177 Bll. 165–88 (facsimile in Longerich, *Wannsee-Konferenz*; English in Arad, Gutman, Margaliot, eds., *Documents on the Holocaust*, pp. 249–61 esp. 253/255. It is unclear whether the Jews in the Sudetenland were counted; the law declaring the Sudetenland a part of Germany declared its 'inhabitants of long standing German citizens [*Staatsangehörige*] pending detailed regulation'): 'Gesetz über die Wiedervereinigung der sudetendeutschen Gebiete mit dem Deutschen Reich. Vom 21. November 1938', *RGBl. I 1938*, p. 1641.

[41] Besprechungsprotokoll, Bll. 165–88 (Longerich, *Wannsee-Konferenz*, Protocol pp. 4, 6).

[42] Kieffer, 'Goerdelers Vorschlag', p. 495, estimates that more than 80 percent of German Jews derived their German citizenship from before 1 July 1871 – Goerdeler's category (b). There is no statistical basis for this. But he appears to assume that the number of Jews with German citizenship counted in the 1933 census as 80.2 percent of *all* Jews in Germany included virtually only Jews who would have found themselves in one of Goerdeler's four categories; cf. *Statistik des Deutschen Reichs. Band 451, 5*, p. 13.

through a greater increase in the non-Jewish population, in part through conversions, apostasy, and emigration. A minimum of 16,929 Jews were baptised in a Protestant denomination from 1881 to 1932 (newborn babies who were baptised were usually not registered as baptised Jews).[43] The statisticians believed they had reasons to assume that Jews who left their religious communities after 1900 increasingly remained without religious affiliation, or became Catholics as that group's political influence was growing. The Jewish religious communities lost further numbers through mixed marriages.

The largest numbers of conversions are recorded for the years 1886 to 1925: between 1,219 (1921–1925) and 2,294 (1896–1900). From 1926 to 1930, the number declined to an annual average of 710, and in 1931 and 1932 the annual average was only 334.[44]

Jews from Russia and Southeast Europe, particularly Romania, tended not to be affiliated with established Jewish communities or associations and may have been missed by the census.[45]

Unless a massive exchange of emigrants and immigrants had occurred, the great majority of the 400,935 Jews with German citizenship who were living in Germany in 1933 were descendants of those who had been living in Germany in 1871.

Restrictive German immigration and naturalisation policies exclude a massive population exchange as a possible consideration.[46] During the nineteenth century, there had been a steady stream of immigration into Prussia from Russian Poland, Russia, and Austrian Poland (Galicia). There were peaks from 1842 when Jews in Russian controlled Poland (Congress Poland) – who had been able to avoid service in the Russian Army through a monetary payment – were no longer allowed to avail themselves of this exemption. From 1881 the persecutions of Jews in Russia reenforced migration.[47] But in 1884/1885, 32,000 mostly Polish persons who were Russian citizens were expelled from Prussia, among them about 10,000 Jews.[48] After the Russian Revolution of 1905, the

[43] *Statistik des Deutschen Reichs. Band 451, 5*, p. 8.

[44] *Statistik des Deutschen Reichs. Band 451, 5*, p. 8.

[45] *Statistik des Deutschen Reichs. Band 451, 5*, pp. 8, 13.

[46] See below at pp. 157–8; cf. Dieter Gosewinkel, *Einbürgern und Ausschließen: Die Nationalisierung der Staatsangehörigkeit vom Deutschen Bund bis zur Bundesrepublik Deutschland*, Göttingen: Vandenhoeck und Ruprecht, 2001, pp. 245–46, 353–73.

[47] Helmut Neubach, *Die Ausweisungen von Polen und Juden aus Preussen 1885/86*, Wiesbaden: Otto Harrassowitz, 1967, pp. 5, 10.

[48] Neubach, *Ausweisungen*, p. 129. Oliver Trevisiol, *Die Einbürgerungspraxis im Deutschen Reich 1871–1945*, Göttingen: Vandenhoeck und Ruprecht, 2006, p. 154, says 48,000

Prussian government took the view that Jews of Russian citizenship should be excluded from naturalisation; exceptions were made if they were deemed in the interest of the state with regard to military service or expected large tax payments.[49] After 1900, the '*völkisch* world view', that is, an emphasis upon ethnic purity, increasingly influenced, and stifled, naturalisation procedures. Applications for naturalisation from formerly Jewish candidates who had converted to Christianity were in principle refused. Moreover, the Prussian government attempted to prevail upon the South German states to refuse naturalisation applications from Jews.[50] After 1918, the lost war further radicalised bureaucratic nationalism.[51]

Before and after 1918, Prussia, representing about two-thirds of German territory and population, and most of Germany's industry, attracted the vast majority of all immigrants to Germany. After 1918, most of them came from territories Germany had lost through the Treaty of Versailles. During national and provincial election campaigns in 1924, the Prussian minister of the interior was accused of having naturalised 90,000 'Eastern Jews' in one year alone.[52] In fact, the totals of all naturalisations in Prussia – non-Jews and Jews – were 6,953 in 1921 and included only 757 'Eastern' ethnic non-Germans. No doubt some of these 'Eastern' ethnic non-Germans were Jews, but they were a minute number; 10,895 persons were naturalised in 1922, which included 638 'Eastern' ethnic non-Germans, and 17,847 in 1923, including 309 'Eastern' ethnic non-Germans. The numbers of Jews among those 'Eastern' ethnic non-Germans were insignificant, and declining. The number of 'Eastern Jews' who applied for naturalisation in Prussia in 1925 was 49, or 0.9 percent of all applications. In 1930 the Prussian minister of the interior replied to questions from the National Socialists in the Prussian Chamber of Deputies by stating that

were expelled from Prussia, among them 9,000 Jews, and cites Hans-Ulrich Wehler, *Deutsche Gesellschaftsgeschichte*, vol. 3, Munich: C.H. Beck, 1995, p. 963; Wehler states that 48,000 were expelled in overnight actions in March and July 1885, without citing a specific source; in a collective source reference of 1 ½ pages for 4 ½ pages of text, he includes Neubach without page references, leaving it unclear from where he took his figures.

[49] Trevisiol, *Einbürgerungspraxis*, p. 155, cites Acta Borussica N.F., Protokolle des preußischen Staatsministeriums, Sitzung vom 20.12.1905, MF 905.

[50] Trevisiol, *Einbürgerungspraxis*, p. 156, cites 'Der preußische Minister des Innern an Minister der auswärtigen Angelegenheiten', 15.6.1885, GStA PK I. HA, Rep. 77, Tit. 226 B Nr. 38'.

[51] Trevisiol, *Einbürgerungspraxis*, p. 158.

[52] For this and the following: Trude Maurer, *Ostjuden in Deutschland 1918–1933*, Hamburg: Hans Christians Verlag, 1986, pp. 316–17.

from 1919 to 1929, Prussia had naturalised 107,599 foreigners, of whom 98,864 were ethnic Germans and 7,654 'Eastern' ethnic non-Germans.

However, German citizens who opted for permanent residence in Poland, which means mostly residents of territories annexed by Poland after the armistice of 11 November 1918, became *ipso facto* Polish citizens and lost their German citizenship.[53] In the 16 June 1933 census, the National Socialist authorities sought to exaggerate the numbers of Jewish immigrants. To this end, they counted German Jews who had resided in German territories that had become Polish after 1918 and who had opted for German citizenship under Article 90 of the Versailles Treaty as 'foreigners', to swell the numbers of 'foreign' Jews in Germany. Salomon Adler-Rudel has exposed this deception.[54]

Since the National Socialists were eager not only to exaggerate Jewish immigration into Germany, but also to de-naturalise as many Jews as possible, and to force 'all non-Germans who had immigrated into Germany

[53] *The Treaty of Peace between the Allied and Associated Powers and Germany, The Protocol Annexed Thereto, the Agreement Respecting the Military Occupation of the Territories of the Rhine, and the Treaty between France and Great Britain Respecting Assistance to France in the Event of Unprovoked Aggression by Germany. Signed at Versailles, June 28th, 1919*, London: His Majesty's Stationery Office, 1919, Article 91: 'German nationals habitually resident in territories recognised as forming part of Poland will acquire Polish nationality ipso facto and will lose their German nationality. German nationals, however, or their descendants who became resident in these territories after January 1, 1908, will not acquire Polish nationality without a special authorisation from the Polish State. Within a period of two years after the coming into force of the present Treaty, German nationals over 18 years of age habitually resident in any of the territories recognised as forming part of Poland will be entitled to opt for German nationality.

Poles who are German nationals over 18 years of age and habitually resident in Germany will have a similar right to opt for Polish nationality.

Option by a husband will cover his wife and option by parents will cover their children under 18 years of age.

Persons who have exercised the above right to opt may within the succeeding twelve months transfer their place of residence to the State for which they have opted.

They will be entitled to retain their immovable property in the territory of the other State where they had their place of residence before exercising the right to opt.

They may carry with them their movable property of every description. No export or import duties or charges may be imposed upon them in connection with the removal of such property.

Within the same period Poles who are German nationals and are in a foreign country will be entitled, in the absence of any provisions to the contrary in the foreign law, and if they have not acquired the foreign nationality, to obtain Polish nationality and to lose their German nationality by complying with the requirements laid down by the Polish State'.

[54] Fritz Kieffer, 'Material zum Thema: Die jüdische Immigration und die Einwanderungspolitik Preussens und des Deutschen Reichs von 1870–1933', typescript, Mainz, 1 July 2006, p. 14, cites Adler-Rudel, *Ostjuden in Deutschland 1889–1940*, p. 149.

since 2 August 1914 immediately to leave the *Reich*' (Point 8 in the Party Programme[55]), it must be concluded that they attempted to de-naturalise at least as many Jews as had immigrated since 2 August 1914.

Naturalisations came under the authority of the state (*Land*) governments, but they could not become effective if any state objected; in such cases the States' Council (*Reichsrat*) had to decide whether the reasons for an objection were compelling.[56] The existing guidelines had been agreed upon by the national government and the *Länder* governments in 1921. The guidelines stipulated that only such persons should be naturalised who 'represented a valuable addition to the population in the civic, cultural and economic regard'; the guidelines included a ten-year residency requirement. This ten-year rule had been met by a large number of immigrants who 'had flooded into Germany uncontrolled across the as yet unprotected borders' during and after the First World War; as foreign-stock (*fremdstämmig*) and foreign-culture (*kulturfremd*) foreigners, they represented, in the view of the great majority of *Länder* representatives, a 'great danger for German nationhood [*Volkstum*]'.[57] The restrictive rules and attitudes, as has been shown, kept the numbers of naturalisations of Jews particularly low. They were relatively high, nevertheless, in the first two years of the war, 1914 and 1915, and in the 1920s compared to the time before 1914.[58]

On 5 February 1931, the representatives of the German *Länder* governments in the States' Council agreed on twenty years' residence as a precondition for naturalisation, exceptions notwithstanding. They requested that the national government (*Reichsregierung*) 'as soon as possible contact the *Länder* governments to agree on new guidelines'. They decided to apply the proposed new twenty-year rule to future cases but not to the cases before them on 5 February 1931.[59] In their meetings

[55] Alfred Rosenberg, ed., *Das Parteiprogramm: Wesen, Grundsätze und Ziele der NSDAP*, 21st ed., Munich: Zentralverlag der NSDAP, Franz Eher Nachf., 1941, p. 16.

[56] *RuStAG, RGBl. 1913*, p. 585.

[57] *Niederschriften über die Vollsitzungen des Reichsrats: Jahrgang 1931, Berlin 1931*, Berlin: Carl Heymanns Verlag, Berlin W8, 1931, p. 22.

[58] Kieffer, 'Material zum Thema', pp. 8–11; cf. Maurer, *Ostjuden*, p. 317; Gosewinkel, 'Unerwünschte Elemente', p. 82.

[59] The *Reichsrat* decided on 5 February 1931 to agree upon twenty years' residence as a precondition for naturalisation, and to request that the national government (*Reichsregierung*) 'as soon as possible contact the Länder governments to agree on new guidelines' to replace those of 1921, and to apply the twenty-year rule to future cases. See *Niederschriften über die Vollsitzungen des Reichsrats: Jahrgang 1931, Berlin 1931*, Berlin: Carl Heymanns Verlag, Berlin W8, 1931, pp. 19–29 ('Niederschrift der vierten Sitzung [§§ 38 bis 56]. Geschehen Berlin, den 5. Februar 1931.'); on 26 November 1931

on 12 February and 26 November 1931, however, the *Reichsrat* agreed to apply the twenty-year rule – 'these provisional principles' agreed upon on 5 February 1931– to the cases then before it.[60] The twenty-year rule had thus provisionally become the custom. In effect this meant that there would be virtually no more naturalisations in 1931 of residents who had not been living in Germany continuously since 1911, none in 1932 of such persons resident in Germany since 1912, and so forth. After 30 January 1933, naturalisations of Jews ceased in principle. This did not appreciably affect numbers in Württemberg, the only state for which naturalisation statistics for the 1930s are available, since Jews had little chance of naturalisation in Württemberg even before 1933.[61] The *Reich* Ministry of the Interior declared a general halt to naturalisations on 28 February 1942.[62]

Since immigration and naturalisation policies were severely restrictive, and since residency requirements were ten years, expanded to twenty in 1931,[63] the overlap between emigration and immigration/naturalisation also must be considered negligible. However, the German citizenship law of 1913 enabled immigrants to acquire citizenship. The law stipulated that a foreigner who had actively served at least a year 'like a German' in the army or navy must be naturalised if he met the other requirements (such as a good reputation and the ability to support himself and his dependants). Naturalisation was automatic for foreigners employed as civil servants in the *Reich* or in a federal state.[64]

('Niederschrift der vierunddreißigsten Sitzung', p. 394) the requested consultations between the national and *Länder* governments had not yet taken place, and the *Reichsrat* now agreed 'to treat the cases before it on that day on the basis of those provisional principles'. See the abridged second-hand account in Maurer, *Ostjuden*, p. 322, based on reports in *Jüdische Rundschau* and *Der Israelit*; Trevisiol, *Einbürgerungspraxis*, pp. 68–73; Maurer, *Ostjuden*, pp. 316–17, 322. See also Zechlin, *Die deutsche Politik*, pp. 260–77, on efforts to limit Jewish immigration; Zechlin (p. 260) cites Adler-Rudel, *Ostjuden*, pp. 21, 24, 32–34 (see also 20, 149), for his statement that from the 1880s to 1914, around 90,000 East European Jews had arrived in Germany.

60 'Niederschrift der fünften Sitzung', 12 February 1931, p. 33; 'Niederschrift der vierunddreißigsten Sitzung', 26 November 1931, p. 394.

61 Trevisiol, *Einbürgerungspraxis*, pp. 67–68.

62 Trevisiol, *Einbürgerungspraxis*, pp. 56–57, cites a directive from the *Reich* minister of the interior to the governors in provinces (Reichsminister des Innern an die Reichsstatthalter in den Reichsgauen: Einbürgerungssperre, 28.2.1942), in StAF A96/1 Nr. 2071.

63 *Niederschriften über die Vollsitzungen des Reichsrats. Jahrgang 1931*, pp. 19–29 ('Niederschrift der vierten Sitzung [§§ 38 bis 56]. Geschehen Berlin, den 5. Februar 1931'); on 26 November 1933 ('Niederschrift der vierunddreißigsten Sitzung', p. 394); the requested consultations between the national and *Länder* governments had not yet taken place, and the *Reichsrat* now agreed 'to treat the cases before it on that day on the basis of those provisional principles'.

64 *RGBl. 1913*, §§ 12, 14, pp. 585–86.

The number of German Jews who would not have been protected in Goerdeler's categories (b), (c) and (d) against losing their German citizenship would be small; at the same time, Jewish citizenship would have given this minute number a protection they did not have in Hitler's state. They were mostly Jews who had been naturalised after 1871. There are indicators that allow estimates.

It must be understood that the following calculations are not Goerdeler's. They are a historian's analysis of immigration, naturalisation, and census numbers that are incomplete and fragmentary to begin with. They are numbers, moreover, that Goerdeler could not have had at hand even to the fragmentary extent to which they are now available, nor could he have had the time to research them. Goerdeler's declaration of what he intended with his proposal, namely, 'a new order for the status of the Jews [that] seems required in the entire world; because everywhere there are movements in progress which, without an organic order in place, cannot be halted, and which, without such order, will lead only to injustices, atrocities', is in the first sentence of the passage in his memorandum that proposes the new order.[65] After the categories of 'exemptions', Goerdeler adds: 'In the past years undoubtedly an injustice has been bred through expropriation, destruction etc. of Jewish property and life in Germany, which we cannot answer for before our consciences and before history'.[66] In these statements, the first of which Goerdeler links with the word 'because', and the second of which he bases upon 'our consciences' and 'history' ('history' representing the world community now and in future), Goerdeler made clear and unequivocal declarations of motivation and intent. He declared his intention to protect 'the Jews' in the entire world, that is, all Jews. The categories of 'exceptions' he listed are not designed to exclude any Jews from being protected, but to set a legal framework that he hoped would conform to the existing state citizenship law (*Reichs- und Staatsangehörigkeitsgesetz*) and would be accepted by a post-Hitler administration (that would necessarily include supporters of the National Socialist ideology). The fact that the German citizenship law of 1913 was not revised until after the reunification of Germany in 1990 casts a light upon the complexities involved.

In order to establish a reasonably reliable estimate, in the absence of complete statistics, of those persons who were naturalised after Goerdeler's date of 1 July 1871 and were not in one of his categories (a) to (d) of 'exceptions', one must make what one can of the statistics

[65] Carl Goerdeler, 'Das Ziel', typescript [1941/42], Bundesarchiv N 1113/54, p. 31.
[66] Goerdeler, Das Ziel, p. 33.

that are available. A documentation for Prussia shows that in the years 1849 to 1880, 3,036 Jewish immigrants from the Russian part of Poland, or about one-hundred annually, were naturalised.[67] Practices in Saxony (the state with the largest number of Jewish residents after Prussia) and Bavaria suggest an average annual naturalisation rate in Germany for Jews who came from the Russian part of Poland during the years 1871 to 1880 of one-hundred and fifty. Since there was a good deal of Jewish immigration from Russia itself, from Austrian Galicia and other Eastern European regions, the annual total for Germany may be estimated as four-hundred and fifty for the ten years from 1871 to 1880, for a total of *4,500*.[68] Precise numbers are available for Prussia for some of the years from 1883 to 1886 and 1895 to 1911; from 1894 to 1898 and 1904 to 1919, Prussia also kept detailed secret naturalisation statistics.[69] The Prussian statistics for the years 1883 to 1886 record an annual average of 181 foreign Jews naturalised in Prussia. In 1883 naturalisations of foreign Jews in Prussia were 7.9 percent of all persons naturalised in Prussia. In 1884 they amounted to 10.7 percent. There followed the expulsions of 32,000 foreigners from Prussia in 1885 and 1886 that targeted Poles and included about 10,000 Jews. These Jews had not yet been naturalized, but many of them would have been candidates for naturalisation. In consequence of the expulsions, the rate of naturalisations of Jews fell to 4.7 percent in 1885 and 4.3 percent in 1886. In the 1890s if fell to 1.77 percent in 1896 and 0.68 percent (= 24 persons) in 1897. From 1896 to 1911, the annual average was 88. For the years from 1892 to 1911, the number of naturalised Jews in Germany can be estimated at *1,672*. In 1905 and 1906, the numbers stabilised at 0.94 percent and 1.59 percent, respectively, of all naturalisations in Prussia. In 1910 Prussia naturalised 104 foreign Jews. The rate was down to 0.72 percent in 1911, and it did not exceed 1.07 percent for the remaining years before the outbreak of the First World War.[70]

[67] Gosewinkel, '"Unerwünschte Elemente"', pp. 78–79.

[68] Kieffer, 'Material zum Thema', p. 9, cites Gosewinkel, '"Unerwünschte Elemente"', pp. 76–7, and Jack Wertheimer, *Unwelcome Strangers: East European Jews in Imperial Germany*, New York, Oxford: Oxford University Press, 1987, p. 58.

[69] Gosewinkel, *Einbürgern und Ausschliessen*, p. 245.

[70] 'Der Erwerb und Verlust der Reichs- und Staatsangehörigkeit im preussischen Staate während des Jahres 1883', *Zeitschrift des Königlich Preussischen Statistischen Bureaus* 24 (1884) (Berlin: Verlag des Königlichen Statistischen Bureaus, 1884, pp. 56–78): ninety-four persons of the Jewish faith from other federal states (pp. 58–59) and 173 foreigners of the Jewish faith (pp. 62–63). The total number of persons naturalised as German citizens (*Reichs- und Staatsangehörige*) in Prussia during 1872–1883 (p. 74) was 34,997, the average per annum was 2,916; Gosewinkel, *Einbürgern und Ausschliessen*, pp. 245–46;

A method of measuring naturalisations in Germany overall is to consider proportions of populations. Prussia's population during the years 1871 to 1913 was on average 61.2 percent of the total German population. If naturalisations of Jews are estimated to have occurred in the same proportions to the populations in the other German states as in Prussia, then the national annual average came to 297 for the years 1883 to 1886. During most of the years from 1881 to 1895, Prussia kept detailed naturalisation statistics. In the last decade of the century, Prussia imposed a veto right in the national upper house (*Bundesrat*) and successfully limited naturalisations of Jews in the other states. Applying the annual average of 297 for all of Germany to the years 1881 to 1895, the result for these fourteen years is *4,158*.[71] Allowing for the percentage changes, an annual average of 257 is assumed for 1881–1914, resulting in 5,830 naturalisations of Jews in those years.[72] It can be estimated that during the years 1914 to 1918, a total of *3,120* Jews were naturalised in Germany, many of them due to service in the armed forces.[73]

There are no statistics of naturalisations of Jews for all of Germany during the years 1919 to 1933.[74] But there is a way to arrive at an approximate number. The law of 14 July 1933 enabled the government to de-naturalise 'undesirable' persons who had been naturalised from 9 November 1918 to 30 January 1933. It was designed by the National Socialists to de-naturalise as many Jews as possible.[75] German authorities in the 1980s compiled a list of de-naturalisations for the years 1933 to 1945, based on the publications during those years of de-naturalisations in the official gazette (*Reichsanzeiger*); it came to 19,291 de-naturalised persons. It is incomplete but may be said to contain well above 90 percent of all de-naturalisations in the years 1933 to 1945.[76] The official gazette (*Reichsanzeiger*) did not indicate nationalities or religious affiliations. The de-naturalisation law of 14 July 1933 explicitly targeted

Kieffer, 'Material zum Thema: Die jüdische Immigration und die Einwanderungspolitik Preussens und des Deutschen Reichs von 1870–1933', typescript, 1 July 2006, p. 10.

[71] Kieffer, 'Material zum Thema', p. 10.

[72] Kieffer, 'Material zum Thema', pp. 8–11, citing also Wertheimer, *Unwelcome Strangers*, p. 57.

[73] Kieffer, 'Material zum Thema', p. 12.

[74] Gosewinkel, '"Unerwünschte Elemente"', pp. 80–81; Kieffer, 'Material zum Thema', pp. 7–8.

[75] 'Gesetz über den Widerruf von Einbürgerungen und die Aberkennung der deutschen Staatsangehörigkeit. Vom 14. Juli 1933' and 'Verordnung zur Durchführung des Gesetzes über den Widerruf von Einbürgerungen und die Aberkennung der deutschen Staatsangehörigkeit. Vom 26. Juli 1933', *RGBl. I 1933*, pp. 480, 538–39.

[76] Bundesverwaltungsamt to the author 6 March 2009.

"Eastern Jews" (*Ostjuden*), and otherwise only criminals and persons who damaged the common weal (e.g., writers, artists, university professors, political opponents),[77] an estimate of two-thirds of the compilation of 19,291 – that is, *12,860* persons will serve as an approximation.[78]

The estimated total naturalisations from 1871 to 1933 then come to *26,310*. This number is 6.56 percent of the 400,935 German Jews counted in the 16 June 1933 census. An estimated 26,310 persons had not been state citizens (*Staatsangehörige*) on the date that Goerdeler set, 1 July 1871, nor were they descended from persons who had been state citizens (*Staatsangehörige*) at that date.

The Nuremberg Race Laws and their implementation decrees established definitions for *Mischlinge*, or 'full Jews', 'half Jews', 'quarter Jews'. These were included in the 17 May 1939 census. The results of this census were published only in 1944. Goerdeler did not address the question of whether the *Mischlinge* would qualify for Jewish citizenship. In any case, an estimated number of *Mischlinge* who would not have been included in one of Goerdeler's four categories will have to be added to the number arrived at above, 26,310. If the same percentage of 6.56 percent as for 'full Jews' is applied to the 112,582 *Mischlinge* who were counted in the 16 June 1933 census,[79] then 7,386 persons would have to be added to the 26,310 arrived at above. There is no record of how many *Mischlinge* had emigrated since the 16 June 1933 census and were not counted in 1939; but since *Mischlinge* were less endangered than 'full Jews', a smaller proportion of them must be considered to have emigrated. But only about 10 percent of them must be estimated as not having had a Christian religious

[77] 'Verordnung zur Durchführung des Gesetzes über den Widerruf von Einbürgerungen und die Aberkennung der deutschen Staatsangehörigkeit. Vom 26. Juli 1933', *RGBl. I 1933*, pp. 538–539.

[78] Kieffer, 'Material zum Thema', p. 16, used the erroneous number of 6,943, whom Lehmann in Michael Hepp, ed., *Die Ausbürgerung deutscher Staatsangehöriger 1933–45*, p. XIII (see note 4 above), had listed as having received notices of de-naturalisations; assuming that most of them were men, and adding wives and children, Kieffer concluded that an estimate of two and a half to three times the number of notices represented as approximately as possible the number of those de-naturalised, amounting to *17,358*, and that this number came close to the number of those who had been naturalised in the period. But see Trude Maurer, *Ostjuden*, p. 317: 12,500 'Eastern Jews' (*Ostjuden*) were naturalised in Prussia from 1919 to 1931.

[79] *Statistik des Deutschen Reichs. Band 552,4. Volks-, Berufs- und Betriebszählung vom 17. Mai 1939. Volkszählung. Die Bevölkerung des Deutschen Reichs nach den Ergebnissen der Volkszählung 1939. Heft 4. Die Juden und jüdischen Mischlinge im Deutschen Reich.* Bearbeitet im Statistischen Reichsamt. Berlin 1944, Berlin: Verlag für Sozialpolitik, Wirtschaft und Statistik, Paul Schmidt, pp. 4, 7–8.

affiliation,[80] so that the number of 7,386 *Mischlinge* is reduced to 738 persons. The calculated total of those not included in Goerdeler's categories (a) to (d) therefore stands at 27,048 or 5.27 percent of 512,935.

These calculations, based upon estimates and approximations, can result only in another approximation. This result is that at least 485,888 or 94.73 percent of 'full Jews' and *Mischlinge* who were German citizens (*Staatsangehörige*) fell into Goerdeler's categories (a) to (d). And at least 374,625 or 6.56 percent of the 400,935 'full Jews' who were counted as German citizens in the 16 June 1933 census at the same time fell into Goerdeler's categories (a) to (d).

The analysis of the numbers demonstrates that Goerdeler's plan, if implemented, would have secured German citizenship not for a negligible minority, as historians misreading Goerdeler's plan and his works and actions overall have been asserting,[81] but on the contrary, for the overwhelming majority of German Jews.

[80] Kieffer, 'Material zum Thema', pp. 3–4, cites James F. Tent, *In the Shadow of the Holocaust: Nazi Persecution of Jewish-Christian Germans*, Lawrence, Kansas: University Press of Kansas, 2003, p. 29.

[81] Cf. Dipper, Widerstand, pp. 364–65.

Appendix

Statistics of German and non-German Jews in Germany and Austria, 1871–1933

	1871[1]	1880	1885	1890	1900	1910	1925	1933
G	41,058,641[2]	44,556,402[3]	46,855,704[4]	49,428,470	56,464,109[5]	64,925,993	62,410,619	65,218,461
DStA	40,852,037[6]	44,958,205[7]	46,482,912[8]	48,995,199[9]	55,587,642	63,664,341	61,453,523	64,461,701
I	512,158		563,172[10]	567,884	586,833	615,021	564,379	499,682[11]
	561,612							563,743[12]
RA	206,755[13]	275,856[14]	372,792	433,271[15]	778,698[16]	1,259,873	921,900[17]	756,760[18]
RAI						76,387	107,747	98,747[19]
P							259,804	148,092[20]
PI								56,480
A-H		117,997	156,762	201,542	390,914	667,062		
A							128,859	81,226[21]
AI								4,647[22]
CI								4,275[22]
R		15,097	26,402[23]	17,107	46,971	137,697	47,173	12,873[24]
NI								19,960

	1939	1941[25]
G	79,375,281	
DStA	78,355,594	
RA	1,019,892	
P	148,687[26]	
I		
J	330,539[27]	131,800[28]
		43,700[29]
		74,200[30]
R	4,535	

Abbreviations:

G = *Gesamtbevölkerung*/total population
DStA = *Bevölkerung mit deutscher Staatsangehörigkeit* /population of German citizens
RA = *Reichsausländer* /foreigners
RAI = *Reichsausländer*/foreigners who are religious Jews
P = Polish nationals; before the foundation of the Polish state in 1919, the numbers of Polish inhabitants can only be estimated as part of the Austro-Hungarians and Russians
PI = Polish religious Jews
A-H = citizens of Austria-Hungary
A = Austrians
AI = Austrian Jews
CI = Czech Jews
R = Russians
NI = Jews without citizenship ('stateless')
I = *Israeliten*/Israelites/religious Jews (*Glaubensjuden*)
J = Jews according to the Nuremberg racial laws, including religious Jews, baptised Jews, and Jews with other or without religious affiliation according to the 1939 census

Note: Adjustments and corrections in later volumes of *Statistik des Deutschen Reichs* show slight variations of some numbers.

Sources:

[1] *Vierteljahreshefte zur Statistik des Deutschen Reichs für das Jahr 1873. Zweites Heft, erste Abtheilung*. Herausgegeben vom Kaiserlichen Statistischen Amt. [Erster Jahrgang.] *Band II. Heft II. Abtheil. 1 der Statistik des Deutschen Reichs*. Berlin, 1873 [*sic*; the title page of the main volume II has the publication year 1874]. Verlag des Königlich Statistischen Bureaus. (Dr. Engel.), pp. 122, 144.

Statistik des Deutschen Reichs. Herausgegeben vom Kaiserlichen Statistischen Amt. *Band LVII. (In 2 Theilen ausgegeben.) Die Volkszählung im Deutschen Reich am 1. Dezember 1880*. Berlin, 1883. Verlag von Puttkammer and Mühlbrecht, Buchhandlung für Staats- und Rechtswissenschaft, [darin Erläuterungen S. I-LXXXIV, Tabellarische Uebersichten über die Ergebnisse der Volkszählung pp. 1–251] pp. 5, 248–50.

Statistik des Deutschen Reichs. Herausgegeben vom Kaiserlichen Statistischen Amt. *Neue Folge. Band 32*. Berlin, 1888. Verlag von Puttkammer and Mühlbrecht, Buchhandlung für Staats- und Rechtswissenschaft, p. 95, Tabellarische Uebersichten, p. 7. *Die Volkszählung im Deutschen Reich am 1. Dezember 1885*. Herausgegeben vom Kaiserlichen Statistischen Amt. *Statistik des Deutschen Reichs. Neue Folge. Band 32*. Berlin, 1888. Verlag von Puttkammer and Mühlbrecht, Buchhandlung für Staats- und Rechtswissenschaft. [2 Teile:] 'Einleitung', pp. 2–96; 'Tabellarische Uebersichten', pp. 1–245.

Statistik des Deutschen Reichs. Herausgegeben vom Kaiserlichen Statistischen Amt. Neue Folge. Band 68. Berlin, 1894. Verlag von Puttkammer and Mühlbrecht, Buchhandlung für Staats- und Rechtswissenschaft. [second title page:] *Die Volkszählung am 1. Dezember 1890 im Deutschen Reich. Tabellen mit Erläuterungen und graphischen Darstellungen*. Herausgegeben vom Kaiserlichen Statistischen Amt. Statistik des Deutschen Reichs. *Neue Folge. Band 68*. Berlin, 1894. Verlag von Puttkammer and Mühlbrecht, Buchhandlung für Staats- und Rechtswissenschaft, Tabellenanhang, pp. 5, 198–99.

Statistik des Deutschen Reichs, Band 150. Die Volkszählung am 1. Dezember 1900 im Deutschen Reich. Bearbeitet im Kaiserlichen Statistischen Amt. Erster Teil. Berlin, Verlag von Puttkammer and Mühlbrecht Buchhandlung für Staats- und Rechtswissenschaft, 1903, pp. 42, 104–5, 134;

Statistik des Deutschen Reichs, Band 240. Die Volkszählung im Deutschen Reiche am 1. Dezember 1910. Bearbeitet im Kaiserlichen Statistischen Amte. Berlin, Verlag von Puttkammer and Mühlbrecht, Buchhandlung für Staats- und Rechtswissenschaft, 1915, pp. 27, 134–53, 204, 210 [total numbers of German nationals include those in the colonies=Schutzgebiete].

Statistik des Deutschen Reichs, Band 401,I. Volks-, Berufs- und Betriebszählung vom 16. Juni 1925. Volkszählung. Die Bevölkerung des Deutschen Reichs nach den Ergebnissen der Volkszählung 1925. Teil I: Einführung in die Volkszählung 1925. Tabellenwerk. Teil II: Textliche Darstellung der Ergebnisse. Bearbeitet im Statistischen Reichsamt. Berlin 1930, Verlag von Reimar Hobbing in Berlin SW 61, pp. 353, 356–357, 383, 386.

Statistik des Deutschen Reichs, Band 451,3. Volks-, Berufs- und Betriebszählung vom 16. Juni 1933. Volkszählung. Die Bevölkerung des Deutschen Reichs nach den Ergebnissen der Volkszählung 1933. Heft 3. Die Bevölkerung des Deutschen Reichs nach der Religionszugehörigkeit. Bearbeitet im Statistischen Reichsamt. Berlin 1936. Verlag für Sozialpolitik, Wirtschaft und Statistik G.m.b.H., Berlin SW 68, pp. 5, 36 [reprint Otto Zeller Verlag Osnabrück 1978].

Statistik des Deutschen Reichs, Band 451,4. Volks-, Berufs- und Betriebszählung vom 16. Juni 1933. Volkszählung. Die Bevölkerung des Deutschen Reichs nach den Ergebnissen der Volkszählung 1933. Heft 4. Die Ausländer im Deutschen Reich. Die Bevölkerung einiger Gebiete des Deutschen Reichs nach der Muttersprache. Bearbeitet im Statistischen Reichsamt. Berlin 1936. Verlag für Sozialpolitik, Wirtschaft und Statistik, Paul Schmidt, Berlin SW 68, pp. 5–9.

Statistik des Deutschen Reichs, Band 451,5. Volks-, Berufs- und Betriebszählung vom 16. Juni 1933. Volkszählung. Die Bevölkerung des Deutschen Reichs nach den Ergebnissen der Volkszählung 1933. Heft 5. Die Glaubensjuden im Deutschen Reich. Bearbeitet im Statistischen Reichsamt. Berlin 1936. Verlag für Sozialpolitik, Wirtschaft und Statistik, Paul Schmidt, Berlin SW 68, p. 7, gives lower figures for the total populations and the Jewish populations from 1816 to 1933 than did the previously cited statistics.

Statistik des Deutschen Reichs. Band 470. Die Hauptergebnisse der Volks-, Berufs- und Betriebszählung im Deutschen Reich (einschl. Saarland) auf Grund der Zählung vom 16. Juni 1933 und der Ergänzungszählung im Saarland vom 25. Juni 1935. Bearbeitet im Statistischen Reichsamt. Berlin 1937. Verlag für Sozialpolitik, Wirtschaft und Statistik, Paul Schmidt, Berlin SW 68 (Nachdruck der Ausgabe Berlin 1937, Otto Zeller Verlag, Osnabrück 1979).

Statistik des Deutschen Reichs. Band 552, 1–5. Volks-, Berufs- und Betriebszählung vom 17. Mai 1939. Volkszählung. Die Bevölkerung des Deutschen Reichs nach den Ergebnissen der Volkszählung 1939. Bearbeitet im Statistischen Reichsamt. Berlin1941–1944. Verlag für Sozialpolitik, Wirtschaft und Statistik, Paul Schmidt, Berlin SW 68.

Statistik des Deutschen Reichs. Band 552,1. Volks-, Berufs- und Betriebszählung vom 17. Mai 1939. Volkszählung. Die Bevölkerung des Deutschen Reichs nach den Ergebnissen der Volkszählung 1939. Heft 1. Stand, Entwicklung und Siedlungsweise der Bevölkerung des Deutschen Reichs. Tabellenteil. Bearbeitet im Statistischen Reichsamt. Berlin1943. Verlag für Sozialpolitik, Wirtschaft und Statistik, Paul Schmidt, Berlin SW 68, p. 18.

Statistik des Deutschen Reichs. Band 552,3. Volks-, Berufs- und Betriebszählung vom 17. Mai 1939. Volkszählung. Die Bevölkerung des Deutschen Reichs nach den Ergebnissen der Volkszählung 1939. Heft 3. Die Bevölkerung des Deutschen Reichs nach der Religionszugehörigkeit. Tabellenteil. Bearbeitet im Statistischen Reichsamt. Berlin 1942. Verlag für Sozialpolitik, Wirtschaft und Statistik, Paul Schmidt, Berlin SW 68 [not reprint, original, but bound together with Heft 1 and 2 =reprints], pp. 8–14 lists religious groups /affiliations without Jews, without foreigners.

Statistik des Deutschen Reichs. Band 552,4. Volks-, Berufs- und Betriebszählung vom 17. Mai 1939. Volkszählung. Die Bevölkerung des Deutschen Reichs nach den Ergebnissen der Volkszählung 1939. Heft 4. Die Juden und jüdischen Mischlinge im Deutschen Reich. Bearbeitet im Statistischen Reichsamt. Berlin 1944. Verlag für Sozialpolitik, Wirtschaft und Statistik, Paul Schmidt, Berlin SW 68, pp. 4, 7–8.

Statistik des Deutschen Reichs. Band 552,5. Volks-, Berufs- und Betriebszählung vom 17. Mai 1939. Volkszählung. Die Bevölkerung des Deutschen Reichs nach den Ergebnissen der Volkszählung 1939. Heft 5. Die Ausländer im Deutschen Reich. Tabellenteil. Bearbeitet im Statistischen Reichsamt. Berlin 1943. Verlag für Sozialpolitik, Wirtschaft und Statistik, Paul Schmidt, Berlin SW 68, [original, not reprint], pp. 6/7.

Bella Schlesinger, *Führer durch die jüdische Gemeindeverwaltung und Wohlfahrtspflege in Deutschland 1932–33*, Berlin: Zentralwohlfahrtsstelle der deutschen Juden, 1932, pp. 13, 262, 320, 330, 343, 371, 376, 408, 410, 414, 417, 419, 421.

Besprechungsprotokoll, Berlin, Am Großen Wannsee Nr. 56/58, 20 Jan. 1942, Auswärtiges Amt, Politisches Archiv Inland II g 177 Bll. 165–88 (facsimile in Peter Longerich, *Die Wannsee-Konferenz vom 20. Januar 1942: Planung und Beginn des Genozids an den europäischen Juden*, [Berlin]: Edition Hentrich, 1998, pp. 67 et sequ.); English in Yitzhak

Arad, Israel Gutman, Abraham Margaliot, *Documents on the Holocaust*, 8th ed., Lea Ben Dor, trans. London and Jerusalem: University of Nebraska Press and Yad Vashem, 1999, p. 253. It is unclear where the Jews in the Sudetenland were counted; they became German citizens on 21 November 1938 through 'Gesetz über die Wiedervereinigung der sudetendeutschen Gebiete mit dem Deutschen Reich. Vom 21. November 1938', *RGBl. I 1938*, p. 1641.

[2] *Statistik* for 1890, p. 5, has the total as 41,058,792.

[3] From *Statistik* for 1880, p. 5, without Luxemburg; a later edition (for 1890) gives 45,234,061 for 1880.

[4] *Statistik des Deutschen Reichs* vol. 150, p. 105, has 46,844,42.

[5] *Statistik* for 1900, p. 105, has 56,367,178.

[6] From *Statistik* for 1890; not in *Statistik* vol. for 1871.

[7] From *Statistik* for 1890; not in *Statistik* vol. for 1880.

[8] From *Statistik* for 1890; not in *Statistik* vol. for 1885.

[9] From *Statistik* for 1890.

[10] *Statistik* vol. 32 for 1885 does not include religious affiliation of foreigners.

[11] *Statistik des Deutschen Reichs* 451,5 p. 13: Of the 499,682 religious Jews counted in Germany on 16 June 1933 (without Saarland), 400,935 were German citizens, and 98,747 were foreign citizens or without citizenship. *Statistik des Deutschen Reichs. Band 470. Die Hauptergebnisse der Volks-, Berufs- und Betriebszählung im Deutschen Reich (einschl. Saarland) auf Grund der Zählung vom 16. Juni 1933 und der Ergänzungszählung im Saarland vom 25. Juni 1935*. Bearbeitet im Statistischen Reichsamt. Berlin 1937. Verlag für Sozialpolitik, Wirtschaft und Statistik, Paul Schmidt, Berlin SW 68 (reprint of ed. Berlin 1937, Otto Zeller Verlag, Osnabrück 1979), p. 5, has 502,799 as the total; p. 7 lists 403,432 with German citizenship and 99,367 foreigners of the Jewish religion (*Glaubensjuden*).

[12] Statistic from Bella Schlesinger, *Führer durch die jüdische Gemeindeverwaltung und Wohlfahrtspflege in Deutschland 1932–33*, Berlin: Zentralwohlfahrtsstelle der deutschen Juden, 1932, pp. 13, 262, 320, 330, 343, 371, 376, 408, 410, 414, 417, 419, 421, 427, 429.

[13] From *Statistik* for 1890; not in *Statistik* vol. for 1871.

[14] From *Statistik* for 1890; not in *Statistik* vol. for 1880; *Statistik des Deutschen Reichs* vol. 150, p. 134, has 276,057. *Statistik* vol. LVII does not include religious affiliation of foreigners.

[15] *Statistik des Deutschen Reichs* vol. 150, p. 134, has 433,254.

[16] *Statistik* 150 does not list foreigners' religions or religiously affiliated persons by nationality.

[17] *Statistik des Deutschen Reichs, Band 451,4*, p. 9, lists 957,096 foreigners. Neither are foreigners' religions included, nor are religiously affiliated persons listed by nationality.

[18] *Statistik* 470, p. 10, has 764,079.

[19] *Statistik* 470, p. 7, has 99,367 foreigners who were religious Jews (*Glaubensjuden*). There are statistics on married and unmarried state, on married Jewish women (total 109,749) and the same category with children born in their current marriage – most interesting for predicting the future of Jewry in Germany.

[20] *Statistik* 470, p. 10, has 148,787.

[21] *Statistik* 470, p. 10.

[22] *Statistik* 451, 4, p. 9.

[23] Foreigners from Russia and Finland are combined in one number.

[24] *Statistik* 470, p. 10.

[25] These numbers are given in the Wannsee Conference Protocol.

[26] *Statistik* 552,5, p. 6, has this number as from 'Ehem. Polen'.

[27] This census counted religious Jews (*Glaubensjuden*) and those who according to the Nuremberg racial laws were considered Jews, such as baptised Jews and *Mischlinge* who were descended from one, two, or three Jewish grandparents.

[28] In the *Altreich*, meaning presumably Germany in the borders of 1937.

[29] In Austria (*Ostmark*).

[30] In Czechia (*Protektorat Böhmen-Mähren*).

8

Conclusion

There was in Germany no sustained, concerted, or widespread opposition to the regime's anti-Jewish policies. There was, however, the consistent, pertinacious, and courageous opposition of Carl Goerdeler.

Ulrich von Hassell characterised Carl Goerdeler as naive and sanguine. In fact, Goerdeler was at least as well 'connected' as Hassell. On 30 June, the day of the massacre of *SA* leaders, the commander of No. 11 Infantry Regiment in Leipzig, Colonel Erich Friderici,[1] had received an order to keep all troops in their barracks; he appealed to Goerdeler to determine whether the garrison was being used for political ends (something military men generally abhorred), Goerdeler rushed to Berlin to see the war minister, Field Marshal von Blomberg, who received him on that day at 3 P.M.[2] Goerdeler had seen Hitler on several occasions and succeeded in convincing the *Führer* to support his, Goerdeler's, view on certain economic issues, and once after such a conference in March 1935, Hitler invited him to lunch with him.[3] This 'naive' man drafted a plan, an approximation to which became reality three years after his death with the foundation of the state of Israel.

It has been shown in the preceding chapters how Goerdeler progressed from what he himself called 'a narrow kind of nationalism' (*Nationalismus enger Art*)[4] at home, to frequent contact with the world, as mayor of Leipzig, the city famous for close to a thousand years for the Leipzig

[1] *Rangliste des Deutschen Reichsheeres. Nach dem Stande vom 1. Mai 1932*, ed. Reichwehrministerium (Heeres-Personalamt), Berlin: E.S. Mittler and Sohn, [1932].

[2] Gillmann and Mommsen, *Politische Schriften*, pp. 1211–12.

[3] Gillmann and Mommsen, *Politische Schriften*, pp. 1209–10.

[4] Ritter, *Goerdeler*, p. 30; Gillmann and Mommsen, *Politische Schriften*, p. 1225.

Trade Fair; to prominence as a conservative politician and candidate for *Reich* chancellor, and as *Reich* prices commissioner; to a national reputation as an administrator and politician, inspired by religion and humanism, concerned above all with bettering the human condition. It has been seen how the persecution of the Jews from 1933 forward became an issue in which he attempted to change government policy and how he, in the months before the November 1938 pogrom, reached a point of desperation when he committed treason in his attempts to influence German policy through unauthorised secret contacts with the British government. The international context in which Goerdeler found his concerns placed was outlined in Chapter 3, and Goerdeler's place in the growing conspiracy against Hitler, his role as chancellor-in-waiting, in Chapter 4. The central document of this study, Goerdeler's memorandum 'The Aim', was analysed in Chapters 6 and 7.

It has been pointed out that German law required, in legal matters, commercial transactions, and all transactions among members of society, a search for an author's or originator's 'true will', the author's intention as opposed to a purely literal interpretation.[5] It is an unalterable obligation upon the historian. Capitalising on technical errors, or narrowly interpreting a text, and thereby ignoring its author's overarching goals and intentions, misrepresents Goerdeler's purpose: the protection of all Jews, German Jews in particular.

Goerdeler believed in the truth, and he believed in the power of true statements when he confronted Hitler's government in the 1930s, as in 1936 when he advised reducing armaments, before he became an anti-Hitler conspirator in 1938. He was never politic and diplomatic. His uppermost concerns were truth, the rule of law, and the rights 'which God gave to all humans'.[6] The farthest thing from his mind was what the world today calls political correctness.

Goerdeler's memorandum 'The Aim' (*Das Ziel*) was written at a turning point in Hitler's war and at the time of the ultimate radicalisation of Hitler's anti-Jewish policies into a campaign to kill all Jewish men, women, and children. Goerdeler knew this was happening, and he often referred to it. In a typescript headed 'In prison Christmas 1944', he wrote of 'the brutal, even bestial murder of 1 million Jews'.[7] If it was 'naive' to

[5] Bürgerliches Gesetzbuch: '§ 133 Auslegung einer Willenserklärung.
Bei der Auslegung einer Willenserklärung ist der wirkliche Wille zu erforschen und nicht an dem buchstäblichen Sinne des Ausdrucks zu haften', *Reichs-Gesetzblatt. 1896*, p. 217.

[6] Gillmann and Mommsen, *Politische Schriften*, pp. 1184–85.

[7] 'Im Gefängnis Weihnachten 1944', p. 2, Bundesarchiv Koblenz N 1113 Band 26; not in Gillmann and Mommsen, *Politische Schriften*.

hope and to try to devise a means to save the millions who had not yet been murdered, it was nevertheless a noble effort.

The idea that a Jewish state might be founded in Canada or in South America was unrealistic. States do not voluntarily cede territory. Still, Goerdeler proposed the idea with more sincerity than did many of the statesmen who in the 1930s had mentioned such regions as the Cameroons, all former German colonies, Angola, South America, British and French Guiana, Kenya, Tanganyika, Northern Rhodesia, Madagascar, Australia, Santo Domingo, Jamaica, Guatemala, Peru, and Mindanao as possible territories for Jewish settlement.[8] Goerdeler knew that for the time being, Palestine was not a realistic option because of the Mandate's restrictions upon immigration, the dangerous tensions between Arabs and Jews, and Palestine's limited capacity for receiving millions of settlers.

Goerdeler knew a good deal about the political obstacles, the public mood, and the dominant attitudes in countries such as Great Britain, France, and America. Perhaps he did not realise that a consent of the United States to large-scale Jewish settlements in South America would 'import' European troubles into the American sphere of influence and involve America in European conflicts, undermining the Monroe Doctrine.[9] He was not ignorant, however, of the problems of financing, the labour market, and unemployment. He probably had no notion of how strong and deep the opposition to a settlement solution ran. As the Assistant Secretary of State George S. Messersmith had put it, Congress would never increase but, given the chance, only lower American immigration quotas.[10] When in February 1939 Senator Robert F. Wagner (Democrat) and Representative Edith Nourse Rogers (Republican) introduced identical bills to admit 20,000 'refugee' children from Germany beyond the quota, the Senate Immigration Committee agreed only to admit them *within* the quota, knowing this was a meaningless gesture since the quota was already exceeded, and the House Immigration Committee declined to report out any version of the bill, which died.[11] Similar proposals in England fared no better.[12]

Goerdeler's concepts were part of a global discussion that included statesmen at the highest level and Jewish communities and

[8] Cf. McDonald, *Refugees*, pp. 64, 84, 119, 148, 154, 172, 181, 207–8, 309; see pp. 71–3 above.

[9] McDonald, *Refugees*, p. 155.

[10] McDonald, *Refugees*, pp. 161–62.

[11] McDonald, *Refugees*, pp. 161–62.

[12] Sherman, pp. 171–72, 180.

organisations. Goerdeler discussed them with figures ranging from British Foreign Office emissaries to Rabbi Leo Baeck.[13] He raised questions of worldwide importance. He certainly bore no responsibility for the failure of governments to lead more energetically, for the hostility of public opinion, or for the lack of unity among the Jewish leaders. The tragedy is that a solution existed, but six million were murdered before it could be implemented.

In the last months of his life, awaiting his execution, Goerdeler wrote an accounting of his public life, an appeal to Germans, and last letters to family members and friends. In September 1944, in 'Thoughts of One Condemned to Death about the German Future', he repeated his proposal, again in a section on 'foreign-policy aims', to found a sovereign Jewish state, in 'Palestine or South America', by international agreement. All Jews in the world, wherever they lived, were to become citizens of this state and in many cases lose the citizenship of their host countries. He had nothing to say about the German Jews, most of whom he knew had been murdered; three years earlier most of them could have been saved.[14] He appears embittered, having been sentenced to death, as he saw it, after all his honest efforts to save his fatherland from ruin. For a moment now, he assigned to the Jews a 'great guilt' for having 'pushed into our public life' without restraint, reflecting gentile hostility toward the Jews' refusal to surrender their ethnic identity and separateness, while insisting on equality in all other respects.[15] He had no intention of shifting responsibility from the German authorities – and the population at large – to the Jews. He placed his emphasis upon the citizens' obligations, rights, and duties. The true, generous, and just Goerdeler then takes the stage again, still not giving up hope, still concerned to seek a method to protect the surviving Jews in the world. He concluded by asserting for Jews the rights 'which God gave to all humans'.[16]

[13] In a letter of 4 January 1955 to Baurat Albrecht Fischer, an executive of the Robert Bosch Company, Leo Baeck wrote: 'When after decades our time shall have attained its proportions, he [Carl Goerdeler] and the men who joined themselves with him shall stand as the great ones in their [land?] and that for which they staked their lives will be recognized in its full dramatic greatness. For Germany, much depends on this being recognized with full gratitude'. Fischer Papers in Bosch Archive and Bundesarchiv Koblenz N 1113/35.

[14] Bundesarchiv Koblenz, N 1113 Band 26, pp. 32, 37; Gillmann and Mommsen, *Politische Schriften*, pp. 1179, 1184.

[15] Bundesarchiv Koblenz, N 1113 Band 26, pp. 37–38; Gillmann and Mommsen, *Politische Schriften*, pp. 1185; Walter Wagner, *Der Volksgerichtshof im nationalsozialistischen Staat*, Stuttgart: Deutsche Verlags-Anstalt, 1974 [actually 1975], pp. 715, 727.

[16] Gillmann and Mommsen, *Politische Schriften*, pp. 1184–85.

No less a personage than Max Warburg, senior partner in the M.M. Warburg Bank in Hamburg, a patriotic German Jew who had helped the German war effort in the First World War and in 1933 saw that as many Jews as possible must emigrate from Germany to save themselves, had in November 1933 expressed a view similar to Goerdeler's, namely, that 'the Jews as a whole' needed 'so to reorient their lives as to fit more harmoniously into the life about them'. Warburg thought it necessary for Jewish committees everywhere deliberately to redirect the education of their children 'so that in the course of time their professional, industrial, and agricultural occupations might be so varied as to avoid giving the sort of excuse which had been so ruthlessly capitalized by the Nazis'. He opposed Weizmann's thesis about racial Judaism and Jewish political nationality, believing that only on the religious and cultural basis could Jews avoid recurrent and more terrible tragedies.[17]

In an account of his professional work since 1933, without a heading, written in prison in January 1945, four months after his 'Thoughts of One Condemned to Death', Goerdeler exhorted his readers to abandon race hatred: God 'does not know races and nations, he knows only humans'. He recommended to his readers earnestly to consider the history of the Jewish nation that showed how that nation continuously had 'struggled with God for knowledge about its being', continuously had been seeking God – to consider a history, recorded in the Old Testament, that also showed 'where a nation got to that no longer honoured God's commandments'.

Twice he addressed the Jews, once to ask them to understand that they had made mistakes 'in pushing to the fore just when it would have been better to practice modesty and wise restraint'. He continued by saying that their aspiration for their 'own state in which you all have citizenship' was just and must be fulfilled:

> I have for years included this solution in my plans and advise all nations to bring it about at once and in generous manner, then in this question, too, calm will take hold in the hearts! Only there are the dreadful crimes with which Jews, men, women and children were exterminated! Look in your history: "Vengeance is mine", says the Lord. Woe to the human who takes it for *him*self! And God's judgement is prevailing even now. When you will read this, Germany has lost 6 to 10 million human beings, 4 to 500 billion marks in debts, sees the greatest part of its cities in rubble, half its household goods destroyed, with perhaps 200 billion worth of assets left, meaning it is bankrupt. The most fearful punishment

[17] McDonald, *Advocate*, pp. 180–82.

that ever struck a nation, under which now the just and the unjust are suffering, exactly as among you Jews.

He returned to the theme a few pages on, accusing Hitler: 'His hands are soaked in the blood of innocent murdered and starved-to-death Jews, Poles, Russians *and Germans*, in the blood of millions of soldiers of all nations who lie on his conscience'. Once more, he offered counsel, recognition of crimes committed, and reassurance: He implored statesmen and nations 'to accept as atonement the sacrifices of our women and children, the sacrifice of hundreds of thousands of Germans whose patriotism has been abused, the destruction of their cultural heritage and their homes, and to renounce revenge and retribution'; and:

You Jews, do not stoke the fire. If anyone respects you and your history, the only one that makes the struggle with God and his commandments its centre, it is I. You deserve an independent state in which every Jew has citizenship rights. However, your far-sighted men have warned you decades ago to practice restraint concerning the internal tensions of other nations. Now accept the hand of reconciliation and make the hour a truly great one. It will be attested to that in Germany I did for your protection all that was possible; the outrage in my heart over the barbarity with which Hitler persecuted and annihilated you has driven me to my actions equally as the pain over the abuse of my nation.[18]

On 27 January 1945, Goerdeler wrote an appeal to all humans and emphasised the crimes against the Jews[19]: He asserted that he had always endeavoured to serve humanity and since 1933 to avert the calamity from Germany that the person of Hitler brought upon it. Hitler was possessed by demonic beliefs 'about nation, race, his calling and power', and he had acted as Satan in this world. Goerdeler did not make a list of his efforts and interventions on behalf of the Jews, but he recounted the two occasions when he had taken a stand in public: when he had driven *SA* hooligans from Jewish shops in Leipzig on 1 April 1933, and when he resigned as mayor of Leipzig to protest the removal of the Mendelssohn statue in Leipzig. He also mentioned how the foreign governments did nothing, although at the time they could have saved the Jews in Europe, without, of course, trying to shift blame from the German side. He declared:

[18] Gillmann and Mommsen, *Politische Schriften*, pp. 1222–29. James G. McDonald had given similar advice to the Administrative Committee of the American Jewish Congress on 12 May 1933, warning of rising American antisemitism and against stimulating it; McDonald, *Advocate*, p. 68.

[19] Gillmann and Mommsen, *Politische Schriften*, pp. 1235–48.

Never has the world seen equally merciless ruthlessness and inhumanity. Hundreds of thousands of Jews have been slaughtered by him [Hitler]; some shot, others poisoned or gassed, others again starved to death. Men before the eyes of their wives, women before the eyes of their husbands, children before the eyes of the parents, parents before the despairing gaze of their own children, yet all before the countenance of God! The ones had to bury the others! German men, German young men are forced to carry out these orgies of murder!

Hundreds of thousands, at Christmas Goerdeler had mentioned 'the brutal, even bestial murder of 1 million Jews'[20] – even Goerdeler did not know the true extent of the tragedy.

He ended his last will and testament on 31 January 1945, two days before his execution, saying that he knew 'that God sits in judgement for the horrific exterminations of the Jews, for murder, expulsion, robbery and other crimes committed against other nations'.[21]

Reviewing Goerdeler's activities since 1933, one realises how little of his numerous efforts he cited in his last writings after having been sentenced to death on 8 September 1944. He could have mentioned his memoranda of the summer of 1934, when he made clear to Hitler's government his general rejection of racial policies, and of January 1938, when he suggested that the German government take

the occasion of the development of the Jewish Question in Eastern Europe to suggest a positive solution of the Jewish Problem among all involved and interested states – Palestine is not sufficient – then every reservation connected with this issue, also in the United States, would be removed because then the greatest interest of all [states] in a positive solution would have to reveal itself.[22]

[20] 'Im Gefängnis Weihnachten 1944', p. 2, Bundesarchiv Koblenz N 1113 Band 26; not in Gillmann and Mommsen, *Politische Schriften*.

[21] Typescript titled 'Anlage', Bundesarchiv Koblenz N 1113 Band 26, pp. 18–19, 26; Gillmann and Mommsen, *Politische Schriften*, p. 1222, print from a manuscript in Goerdeler's hand, 'in private possession' (p. 1202), headed 'Rechenschaftsbericht', but this does not appear to have been Goerdeler's heading; Gillmann and Mommsen, *Politische Schriften*, p. 1235, end their rendition '1½' pages before the end of the manuscript, without explanation; the typescript in Bundesarchiv Koblenz N 1113 Band 26, pp. 33–34, does contain the omitted final paragraphs that list Goerdeler's contacts on his trip to Brussels and London in June 1937, which included Ambassador Joachim von Ribbentrop, Foreign Secretary Lord Halifax, Lord Riverdale, Anthony Eden, A.P. Young, Richard Stopford, Sir Archibald Sinclair, M.P., Reinhold Schairer, and Norman Montagu (governor of the Bank of England); Deuteronomy 32.35; Romans 12.19; further quotations are from the Goerdeler papers cited and from Gillmann and Mommsen, *Politische Schriften*, pp. 1222, 1228, 1236, 1239–40, 1251–52.

[22] 1934: The editors of Goerdeler's principal political works date 'August/September 1934'; Gillmann and Mommsen, *Politische Schriften*, p. 342. Theodore S. Hamerow, *On the Road*, p. 128, apparently following Ritter, *Goerdeler*, 2nd ed., 1956, pp. 72, 75

He also could have mentioned that he acted against an unlawful anti-Jewish boycott attempt in his municipal administration when he signed a list, on 11 April 1935, of 'non-Aryan' physicians who were *not* excluded by law from practice under public health-insurance plans and of those who were legally excluded, and that he circulated the list in the Leipzig municipal administration, to counter the National Socialists' attempt to boycott *all* Jewish physicians.[23] Three months before the November pogrom, A.P. Young, who had visited Goerdeler on 6 and 7 August 1938 on behalf of the British government's chief diplomatic adviser Sir Robert Vansittart, reported upon his visit[24]: 'In discussing the persecution of the Jews X [Goerdeler] said he thought we should be more forceful in expressing our disgust of the Nazi methods. He even went so far as to suggest that we might tactfully indicate that if such practices continued it would make it exceedingly difficult for us to negotiate those "life problems"

(Hamerow cites the 1954 1st ed., p. 64; Gillmann and Mommsen also cite the 1st ed., p. 68), describes the memorandum as addressed to Hitler, which is what Ritter must have read on a copy at his disposal since he quotes in quotation marks 'An den Reichskanzler', but Ritter cites no evidence; Gillmann and Mommsen, p. 342, consider unconfirmed that Goerdeler had addressed the memorandum to Hitler, since they could not find any copy with this heading or notation.

Typescript carbon copy headed 'U.S.A.', dated '2. January 1938', without signature, fifty-five pages, here p. 39; Gillmann and Mommsen, *Politische Schriften*, pp. 547–48, 578–79, say that their copy was in private possession, presumably now in Bundesarchiv in Koblenz; they do not say whether their copy is an original or a carbon copy or other copy, whether it has a heading, whether the signature they show, 'Goerdeler', was in Goerdeler´s hand or typed so that a manuscript signature could be placed above it; yet they also cite a copy in the files of the Reichskanzlei, Bundesarchiv Berlin R 43F/3503 Bll. 35–75, that they do not further describe. Jewish Organisations in the 1930s discussed the question of settlements in Madagascar; this island does not appear in Goerdeler's report; cf. Magnus Brechtken, *"Madagaskar für die Juden": Antisemitische Idee und politische Praxis 1885–1945*, Munich: R. Oldenbourg Verlag, 1997, pp. 116–19; Gillmann and Mommsen, *Politische Schriften*, pp. 368, 578–79: '*Meines Erachtens ist die ganze Boykottbewegung zu Ende in dem Augenblick, in dem Deutschland praktisch zu erkennen gibt, dass ihm am* Grundsatz *gelegen ist, daß aber der* einzelne *Jude im Rahmen des Gesetzes nicht mit außerordentlichen Mitteln um jede Existenzmöglichkeit gebracht werden soll.* Wenn *aber Deutschland die Entwicklung der Judenfrage in Osteuropa zum Anlass nimmt, eine positive Lösung des Judenproblems – Palästina reicht nicht aus – unter allen beteiligten und interessierten Staaten anzuregen, so würde sofort jede Hemmung, die mit dieser Frage in Verbindung steht, auch in den Vereinigten Staaten beseitigt sein, da sich dann das grösste Interesse aller an einer positiven Lösung offenbaren müsste*'. While Jewish organisations in the 1930s considered Madagascar as at least a possible supplemental receiving area for Jewish settlers, the island does not appear in Goerdeler's proposals..

23 Stadtarchiv Leipzig, Kap. 1 Nr. 122; see p. 43 above.

24 For the following see A.P. Young, *The 'X' Documents*, ed. Sidney Aster, London: Andre Deutsch, 1974, pp. 45–49, 59, 139, 154–62, 177; Hoffmann, *German Resistance to Hitler*, pp. 281–82; Hoffmann, 'German Resistance, the Jews', pp. 73–88.

which awaited solution'.[25] In meetings with Reinhold Schairer who this time stood in for Young on 6 and 7 November 1938, three days before the pogrom, Goerdeler spoke of 'the barbaric, sadistic, and cruel persecution of 10,000 Polish Jews in Germany'.[26] In December 1938 and January 1939, he spoke to Young about the 'cruel and senseless persecution of the Jews' and demanded that 'as soon as the planned persecution of the Churches begins, or the new persecution of the Jews is started, it is absolutely essential to break diplomatic relations'.[27] Hitler wanted to conquer the world, and, 'to achieve this purpose he has decided to destroy Jews – Christianity – Capitalism'.[28] This, in Goerdeler's view, was the order of Hitler's priorities. On 16 March 1939, Goerdeler met with A.P. Young in London and listed three 'milestones' Hitler had already passed on the path to his own destruction: '1. *The Pogrom against the Jews on November 9 and 10*. Hitler personally ordered this pogrom'. The other two milestones were, according to Goerdeler, the dismissal of Dr Schacht as minister of economics, and the brutal aggression against Czechoslovakia.[29] Goerdeler had committed, on behalf of German and non-German Jews, 'treason against the country' (*Landesverrat*) as defined in German law. This crime carried the death penalty.[30]

[25] Young, *The 'X' Documents*, p. 59.
[26] Young, *The 'X' Documents*, p. 139.
[27] The expelled Jews were allowed to bring with them only 10 Reichsmarks and had to leave behind their other assets and property; *The Times* 3 November 1938, p. 13.
[28] Young, *The 'X' Documents*, pp. 160–61.
[29] Young, *The 'X' Documents*, pp. 176–77.
[30] 'Gesetz zur Änderung von Vorschriften des Strafrechts und des Strafverfahrens. Vom 24. April 1934', *RGBl. I 1934*, pp. 341–48 (death penalty for high treason against the *Reich* president, *Reich* chancellor, or 'Constitution', and for relations with a foreign government for such a purpose) included the establishment of the 'People's Court' (*Volksgerichtshof*) for deciding cases of high treason and treason against the country and the stipulation that no appeals were allowed against decisions of the 'People's Court'; 'Gesetz gegen heimtückische Angriffe auf Staat und Partei und zum Schutz der Parteiuniformen. Vom 20. Dezember 1934', *RGBl. I 1934*, pp. 1269–71; *Strafgesetzbuch mit Nebengesetzen und Erläuterungen: Vierunddreißigste Auflage*, ed. Eduard Kohlrausch, Berlin: Walter de Gruyter, 1938, §§ 88–93a, pp. 210–26 (§ 89: '*Wer es unternimmt, ein Staatsgeheimnis zu verraten, wird mit dem Tode bestraft*'. P. 210, § 88: 'Staatsgeheimnisse = Tatsachen oder Nachrichten darüber, 'deren Geheimhaltung vor einer ausländischen Regierung für das Wohl des Reichs, insbesondere im Interesse der Landesverteidigung, erforderlich ist'. 'Verrat im Sinne der Vorschriften dieses Abschnitts begeht, wer mit dem Vorsatz, das Wohl des Reichs zu gefährden, das Staatsgeheimnis an einen anderen gelangen lässt, insbesondere an eine ausländische Regierung oder an jemand, der für eine ausländische Regierung tätig ist, oder öffentlich mitteilt. Since the 'People's Court' was empowered to arbitrarily use whatever 'evidence' it pleased, the defence of intent, difficult in the best circumstances, was ineffective, as the trials of the conspirators amply demonstrated.

In 1941, Goerdeler prepared a comprehensive plan for Germany's political, constitutional, judicial, and social renewal after Hitler's removal. He included in this plan a proposal to establish by international agreement, 'through the powers' concerted action', a Jewish state, and to confer upon all Jews the citizenship of this state. At the same time, he wanted the German Jews to retain or regain their German citizenship.

The analysis of Goerdeler's plan reveals that the categories of Jews covered by Goerdeler's 'exception' for German Jews included as nearly as possible all German Jews, not a miniscule minority, as critics assert without the benefit of any numerical analysis. Virtually all German Jews would have retained or regained their German citizenship with all attendant rights if Goerdeler's plan had been implemented.

Goerdeler was a municipal administrator, a civil servant at the national level, (still after 1937 despite his resignation) in close contact with active civil servants and at least one serving minister (the Prussian minister of finance, Johannes Popitz), and he was an economics expert whom the government called upon for advice. He was familiar with demographic statistics. Controversies and debates about immigration and naturalisation in the 1920s and early 1930s had been carried on in public. Goerdeler knew enough about the intentions and methods of the National Socialists to hedge against them in categories (c) and (d) in his memorandum.

By his own account, he had been driven to his actions 'by the barbarity with which Hitler persecuted and annihilated' the Jews.

Critics have argued that Goerdeler did not propose to repeal such laws as the 'Law concerning the Revocation of Naturalisations and Withdrawal of Citizenship' or the Nuremberg Race Laws.[31] Goerdeler was under great pressure, it will be recalled, when he wrote 'The Aim', and it shows the signs of haste. The critics disregard this. They ignore the fact that new law (Goerdeler's plan) displaces old law if the new law contradicts the old law. Old law then were all of the anti-Jewish laws and decrees. The critics ignore Goerdeler's statement of motive: 'I did for your protection all that was possible; the outrage in my heart over the barbarity with which Hitler persecuted and annihilated you has driven me to

[31] Mommsen, *Alternative*, S. 388–91. 'Reichsbürgergesetz. Vom 15. September 1935', *RGBl. I 1935*, p. 1146; 'Gesetz zum Schutze des deutschen Blutes und der deutschen Ehre. Vom 15. September 1935', *RGBl. I 1935*, pp. 1146–47; 'Gesetz über den Widerruf von Einbürgerungen und die Aberkennung der deutschen Staatsangehörigkeit. Vom 14. Juli 1933', and 'Verordnung zur Durchführung des Gesetzes über den Widerruf von Einbürgerungen und die Aberkennung der deutschen Staatsangehörigkeit vom 26. Juli 1933', *RGBl. I 1933*, pp. 480, 538–39.

my actions'.[32] They ignore Goerdeler's active efforts to enlist the British government in his attempts to change German anti-Jewish policy.[33]

Furthermore, they either disregard Goerdeler's categorical definition of those of whom he declared, in his antiquated jurist's turn of phrase, that they 'are' German citizens, or, if they do refer to this definition, they assert that it applied only to a miniscule minority of German Jews. The issue of numbers has been addressed in the last chapter.

Prison writings are problematic, even though Goerdeler anticipated this concern and insisted the following in his appeal, dated 27 January 1945: 'The enclosed appeal to all humans does not emanate from a prison-cell psychosis'.[34] Goerdeler tormented and reproached himself for having given too little time to his family and for having failed in 1932 to join the unspeakable Franz von Papen's cabinet; he accused himself of errors in his conspiratorial activities, and he held to the belief that he might still bring the war to a more tolerable conclusion if only he could personally speak with Hitler, or if he were sent to the Allies as an intermediary.[35] Goerdeler knew that Himmler was toying with the idea of succeeding Hitler and of seeking a separate peace with the Western Allies.[36] When Goerdeler was asked to write down his thoughts about Germany's reconstruction after the war, he hoped to make a serious contribution.[37]

Goerdeler's reference to Germany's status in the world and to foreign-policy considerations in favour of changing the treatment of the Jewish population has also drawn criticism.[38] The critics, again, ignore the fact that Goerdeler stated the following as his first motive: 'In the past years undoubtedly an injustice has been bred through expropriation, destruction etc. of Jewish property and life in Germany, which we cannot answer for before our consciences and before history'. In face of this statement, some critics, at least one of whom is on the editorial board of a learned periodical, had the temerity to accuse Goerdeler of not having 'mentioned with one syllable the beginning holocaust', ignoring the clear words just quoted, not to mention the numerous condemnations of the mass murder of the Jews in Goerdeler's subsequent writings.[39]

[32] Gillmann and Mommsen, *Politische Schriften*, pp. 1222–29.
[33] See pp. 52, 76–82 above.
[34] Gillmann and Mommsen, *Politische Schriften*, p. 1236.
[35] Ritter, *Goerdeler*, pp. 416–45, esp. 431–45; Gillmann and Mommsen, *Politische Schriften*, pp. 1251; cf. Gillmann and Mommsen, pp. 1194–95.
[36] Ritter, *Goerdeler*, pp. 427–30.
[37] Ritter, *Goerdeler*, pp. 424–26.
[38] Mommsen, *Alternative*, S. 390.
[39] Hans Woller, Institut für Zeitgeschichte, Munich, letter to the author on 29 June 2009.

Historians have misread, misquoted, and misrepresented what Goerdeler wrote. With the exception of Hans Mommsen, none took any notice of the circumstances in which Goerdeler composed his proposals. Historians whose views have been prevalent in the public dialogue have asserted that Goerdeler 'wanted to withdraw German citizenship from the German Jews albeit excepting those who were most assimilated'; or, 'Goerdeler proposed to deprive all Jews automatically of their German citizenship, except for those who could prove their assimilative efforts through front-line duty during World War I, naturalization before 1871, or baptism'; or, that Goerdeler 'wanted to treat all Jews living in Germany as registered aliens and to deprive them of citizenship, the right to vote and access to public office'; or, that Goerdeler wanted to 'place most German Jews in the category of resident aliens'.[40] The evidence proves, as the

[40] Gillmann and Mommsen, *Politische Schriften*, p. 863. Sabine Gillmann and Hans Mommsen, the editors of a selection of Goerdeler's political writings, did not address the issue of numbers. Dipper in his poorly researched 1983 article convicts Goerdeler of antisemitism on the basis of the following statement: 'It is a commonplace that the Jewish nation belongs to another race'. Dipper, 'Widerstand', p. 365; Dipper, 'Resistance', pp. 51–93, here pp. 66–67, 71–73 (p. 72, commenting on Goerdeler's proposals regarding the Jews in the entire world: 'The discriminating nature of these immediate measures could be explained by Goerdeler's long-term goal – a result of the "commonplace" that the "Jewish people belong to a different race" – to establish a Jewish state "under livable conditions in parts of Canada or South America" through international cooperation. As soon as this was achieved, Goerdeler proposed to deprive all Jews automatically of their German citizenship, except for those who could prove their assimilative efforts through front-line duty during World War I, naturalization before 1871, or baptism. Baptized Christians, "descendants of a mixed marriage" contracted before the Nazi takeover, would also be recognized. A parallel to the Nuremberg Laws suggests itself for obvious reasons'; Mommsen, 'Widerstand gegen Hitler und die nationalsozialistische Judenverfolgung', in Mommsen, *Alternative*, pp. 388–91; Mommsen, *Alternatives*, pp. 258–62, here – p. 259 – Mommsen writes that Goerdeler 'wanted to treat all Jews living in Germany as registered aliens and to deprive them of citizenship, the right to vote and access to public office'; Hamerow, p. 296, makes the same sweeping statement that Goerdeler wanted to 'place most German Jews in the category of resident aliens'; Kieffer, 'Goerdelers Vorschlag', p. 480n44 cites Heinemann and Krüger-Charlé, 'Arbeit am Mythos', pp. 475–501, esp. p. 490n62.

See Gillmann and Mommsen, *Politische Schriften*, p. 886. Hamerow, 'On the Road', p. 296, and Hamerow, *Attentäter*, p. 319, writes as though Goerdeler had intended that *in consequence of* the 'truism' that the Jews belonged to a different race, most German Jews should be placed 'in the category of resident aliens'. Goerdeler also wrote 'it is stupid and presumptuous to speak of Germans as a master race. It is foolish to demand respect for one's national honour and independence and deny it to others. The nation that will naturally take over the leadership of Europe is one that respects smaller nations and tries to guide their destiny with wisdom and skill, not with brute force'. Walter Lipgens, *Documents on the History of European Integration*, vol. 1, New York: Walter de Gruyter, 1985, p. 399; Gillmann and Mommsen, *Politische Schriften*, p. 889.

present study has demonstrated, that the vast majority of German Jews would have qualified for categories (a) and (b) and would *not* have been deprived of their German citizenship but indeed would have retained or regained it. The present study has demonstrated Goerdeler's consistent and dedicated humanity and concern for Jews, to protect them, to find a humane solution to the 'Jewish Question'.

In the Prologue to the present study, it was pointed out that the fact that some Germans risked and lost their lives for their opposition to National Socialism is an embarrassment to many German historians. An additional 'stone of offense, and a rock of stumbling' is the fact that many of those who risked and sacrificed their lives to try to overthrow Hitler were motivated – partially or primarily – by the persecution of the Jews. A prominent historian sees a 'fundamental anti-Semitic sentiment' (*antisemitische Grundstimmung*) in the German Resistance to Hitler and to National Socialism.[41] He includes Goerdeler and asserts that Goerdeler 'wanted to treat all Jews living in Germany as registered aliens and to deprive them of citizenship, the right to vote and access to public office'.[42] It was not difficult to disprove this incorrect assertion by a careful reading of what Goerdeler wrote and placing it in the context of his actions relating to Jewish matters in the 1930s and early 1940s.

Other historians have not been more diligent. The author of a dissertation asserted that Goerdeler had 'internalized nationalist thinking which was a root of academic antisemitism', and that nationalist thinking 'formed a nationalist mentality that was antisemitically coloured. It [the nationalism] was Christian-socialist, anti-manchesterly, social-reformist, antisemitic, anti-socialist, imperialist and partially *völkisch*'.[43] Such, in that scholar's view, was Goerdeler's mentality. She also misrepresents Goerdeler as having refused to join the Papen cabinet in August 1932 because it did not include any National Socialists, whereas in fact Goerdeler had explained to President von Hindenburg that he had no

[41] Mommsen, 'Widerstand', in *Alternative*, pp. 388–91; Mommsen, *Alternatives*, pp. 258–62, esp. 259.

[42] Mommsen, 'Widerstand', in *Alternative*, pp. 388–91; Mommsen, *Alternatives*, pp. 258–62, esp. 259.

[43] '*Er war christlich-sozial, antimanchesterlich, sozialreformerisch, antisemitisch, antisozialistisch, imperialistisch und zum Teil völkisch eingestellt*'. Ines Reich, *Carl Friedrich Goerdeler: Ein Oberbürgermeister gegen den NS-Staat*, Cologne, Weimar, Vienna: Böhlau Verlag, 1997, p. 156; this dissertation was prepared under the supervision of DDR historian Kurt Finker in Potsdam; Gerald Wiemer, 'Ines Reich, Carl Friedrich Goerdeler: Ein Oberbürgermeister gegen den NS-Staat', review in *Neues Archiv für Sächsische Geschichte* 69 (1998): 349.

confidence in Papen.[44] In her statements, although they were published eight years after the collapse of the East German regime in which they had been 'politically correct', one detects an ideological bias.

The difficult question is why so many historians, including those who repeat the statements of their prominent colleagues about Goerdeler's position toward the Jews and in particular toward the German Jews, do not recognise that their positions are untenable in face of the evidence. Is Hannah Arendt's phrase the answer, 'where all are guilty, no one is'?[45] No nation has tormented itself as have the Germans with the guilt for the crimes of Hitler and National Socialism. It is an extreme form of a guilt complex to accept or postulate that all Germans were antisemites and therefore co-responsible for the mass murder of the Jews.

The contemporary dominant historiographic school brands as 'apologists' those who do not accept their general line of argumentation. In January 2004, Joachim Fest received a prize in honour of Eugen Bolz, state president of Württemberg 1928–1933, a resister associated with Robert Bosch and Goerdeler, and hanged for this on 23 January 1945.[46] In his speech on receiving the prize, Fest spoke of the middle-class groups to which Eugen Bolz had belonged; he concluded that 'the dominant denunciatory caprice toward the Resistance has as good as obliterated these middle-class groups' in the public regard.[47] In their search for Goerdeler's antisemitic attitude and mentality that so many historians and publicists take for granted, they also mostly ignore Goerdeler's active efforts to protect Jews – be they physicians who were permitted by law to treat patients (1935),[48] be they German Jews at large who were persecuted by the Hitler government (1938), or be they Polish or stateless Jews when in the first days of November 1938, before the pogrom, he deplored the failure of 'the democracies', the press, the church, and the (British) Parliament to react to 'the barbaric, sadistic and cruel persecution of 10,000 Polish Jews in Germany'[49] – they ignore the fact that after the pogrom, on 4 December 1938, Goerdeler again deplored 'the cruel and senseless persecution of the Jews', and 'the way in which the Nazi leaders enriched themselves by stealing Jewish property'; they ignore many other

[44] See pp. 27–28 above.

[45] Hannah Arendt, *Responsibility and Judgment*, New York: Schocken Books, 2003, p. 21.

[46] Wagner, *Der Volksgerichtshof*, pp. 744–45.

[47] Joachim Fest, 'Das verschmähte Vermächtnis: Rede zur Verleihung des Eugen Bolz-Preises am 24.1.04', typescript, from J. Fest 18 June 2003.

[48] Young, *The 'X' Documents*, pp. 45–49, 59.

[49] Young, *The 'X' Documents*, pp. 154–62.

clear statements in which Goerdeler deplores the treatment of Jews.[50] They ignore Goerdeler's clear and unequivocal declaration of intent in two sentences in his 1941/42 memorandum 'The Aim':

> A new order for the status of the Jews seems required in the entire world; because everywhere there are movements in progress which, without an organic order in place, cannot be halted, and which, without such order, will lead only to injustices, atrocities and if to nothing else to an unsatisfactory disorder.[51]
>
> In the past years undoubtedly an injustice has been bred through expropriation, destruction etc. of Jewish property and life in Germany, which we cannot answer for before our consciences and before history.[52]

These are not the words, and Goerdeler's actions were not the actions, of an antisemite. They are the words of one who did all in his power to protect the Jews, and who gave his life by being hanged in the execution shed of Plötzensee Prison on 2 February 1945.

[50] Young, *The 'X' Documents*, pp. 154–62.
[51] Carl Goerdeler, Das Ziel, typescript [1941/42], Bundesarchiv N 1113/54, p.28; Gillmann and Mommsen, *Politische Schriften*, p. 873.
[52] Carl Goerdeler, Das Ziel, typescript [1941/42], Bundesarchiv N 1113/54, p.30; Gillmann and Mommsen, *Politische Schriften*, p. 874.

Index

Note: Carl Goerdeler, Hitler, Jews, war and names and terms in the Prologue have no independent entries in the index. Names and terms in the notes are not included unless they direct the reader to substantive information other than source references.